فهرس

Index

Jeddah Roundabouts
Circling the City

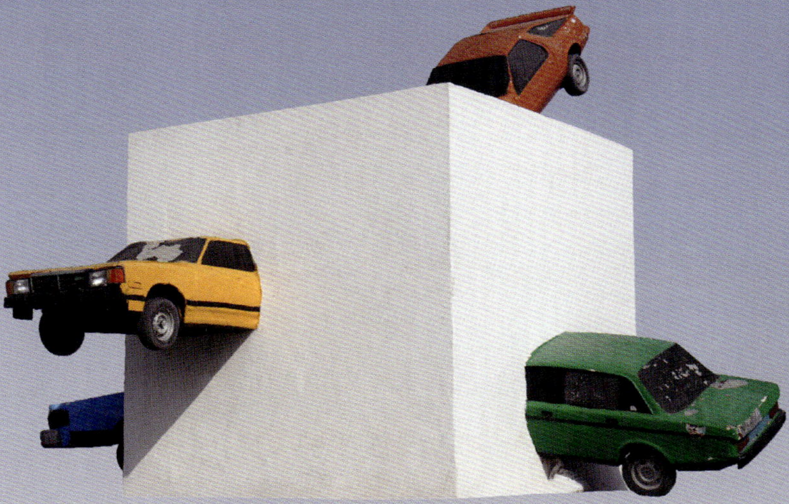

في العُمرانِ الدائر
جدّة ودواراتها

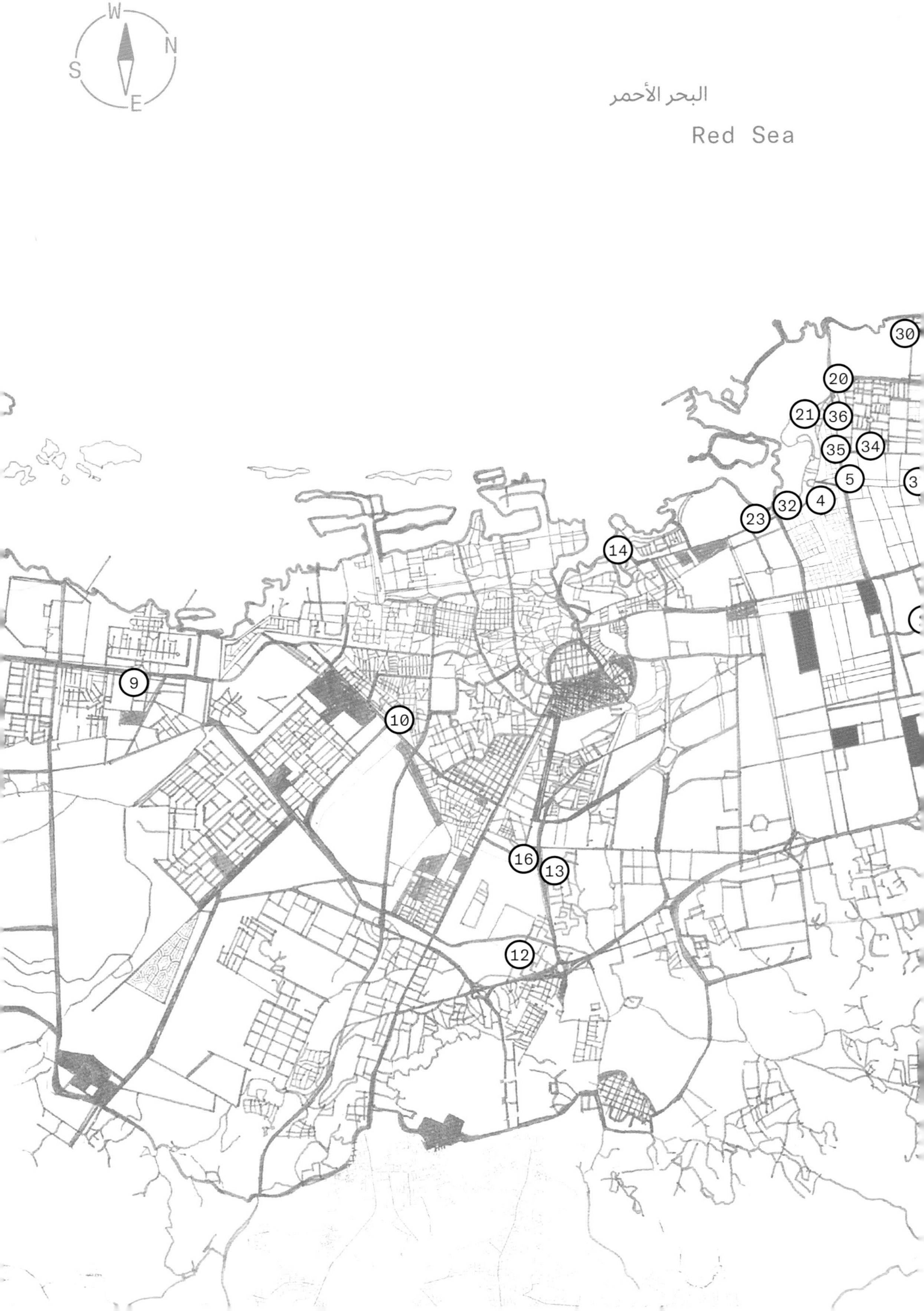
W
N
S
E
البحر الأحمر
Red Sea
30
20
21
36
35
34
5
4
32
23
14
9
10
16
13
12

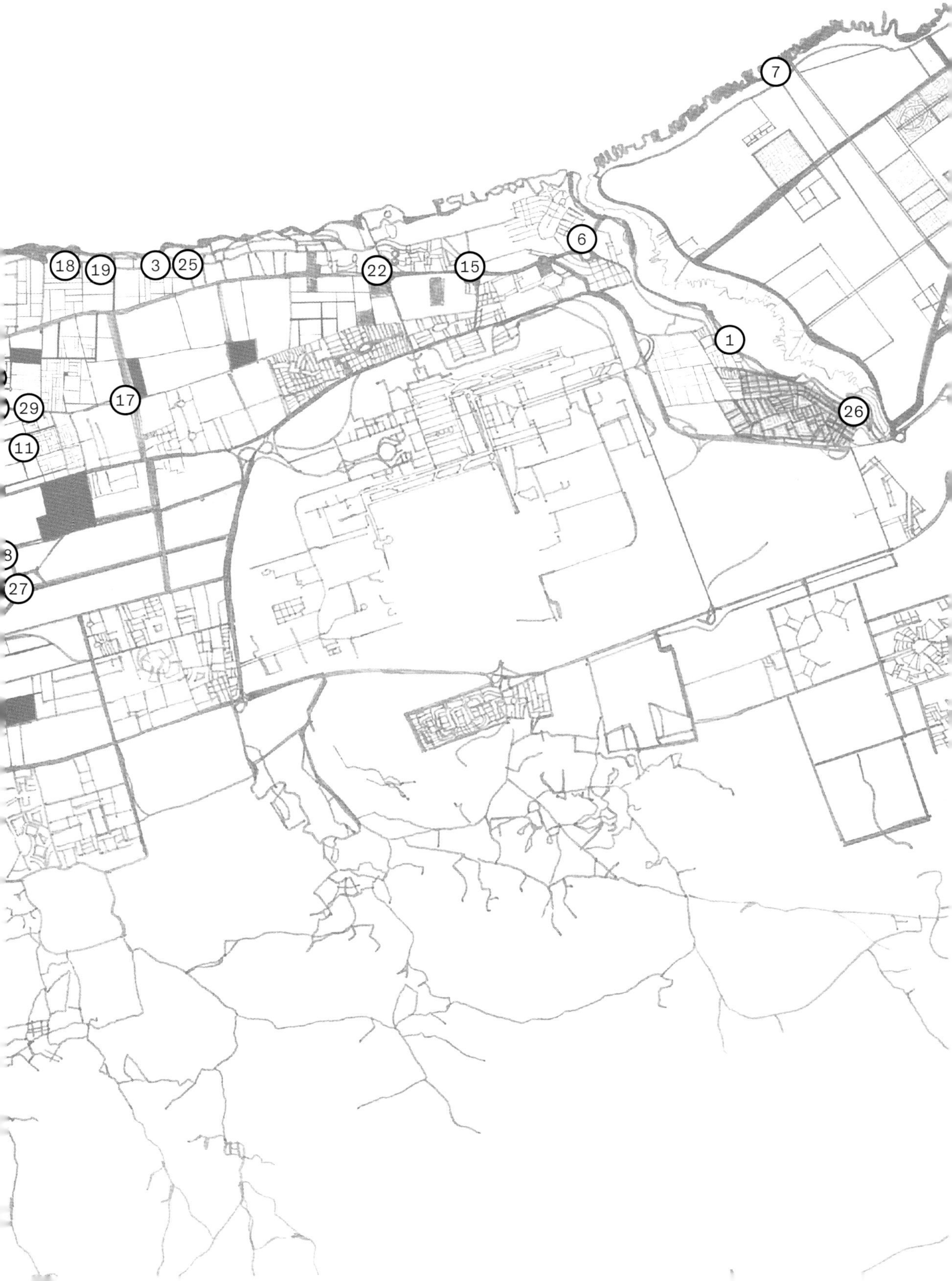

7
6
18
19
3
25
22
15
1
26
17
29
11
27

تقديم

Foreword

إيمان النعيم
وسارة حمامي

البرامج العامة، المكتبة والبحث
فن جميل

Eiman Elnaiem
Sara Hammami

Art Jameel Public Programmes
Library & Research

In 2024, a week-long sound research lab titled 'Echoes of Shells: Sounds of the Red Sea' in Jeddah brought together artists, researchers, and musicians to reflect on new ways of documenting local visual and sonic cultures. The programme explored alternative methods of research and storytelling that move beyond traditional written forms, asking how practices, histories, and ephemeral experiences might be recorded differently. Jeddah, long shaped by its role as a harbour city and crossroads between regions, naturally became both the setting and the metaphor for these conversations. Often described as a place where East and West meet, the city reflects a constant movement of people, sounds, and ideas. Within this dynamic landscape, a shared sense of connection emerges, shaped as much by difference and distance as by proximity.

Throughout the process, we found ourselves returning to conversations at work, during car rides home, and whilst travelling, about how sound is carried, called, and reshaped over time by people, objects, public spaces, and languages. We began to wonder how these transmissions inform identity, gendered narratives, and artistic experimentations, particularly in ways that are often overlooked or untold. From these exchanges, we looked to explore and reflect on the ties between fluid, non-academic frameworks and practices such as somatic play, storytelling, dance research, and poetry. Rather than remaining in separate realms, it became increasingly important to bring these approaches together through meaningful and participatory encounters, acts of observing, documenting, recording, and gathering. As all of these interactions took place in physical realms, it quickly appeared that borders within these spaces created central receptacles for interaction, as producers and enablers of social fabric. Ideas around the importance of urbanism, in Jeddah and beyond, expanded towards philosophical and aesthetic considerations: how does urbanism, in the public as well as in the private sphere,

استضافت مدينة جدّة في عام ٢٠٢٤ مختبرًا بحثيًّا للصوت امتدّ أسبوعًا كاملاً بعنوان «عرّاف الصوت: حكايات غنائية من البحر الأحمر»، جمع فنّانين وباحثين وموسيقيين للتأمّل في سُبلٍ جديدة لتوثيق الثقافات البصرية والسمعية المحليّة. سعى البرنامج إلى استكشاف طرائق بديلة للبحث والسرد تتجاوز الأشكال الكتابية المألوفة، متسائلاً: كيف يمكن تسجيل الممارسات والتواريخ والتجارب الزائلة على نحوٍ مختلف؟ وكانت جدّة التي تشكّلت هويتها عبر تاريخها مدينةً للميناء ومفترقًا بين الأقاليم مسرحًا طبيعيًّا ومجازًا حيًّا لهذه الحوارات. كثيرًا ما تُوصَف هذه المدينة بأنها موضع التقاء الشرق والغرب، إذ تعكس حركةً متواصلة للبشر والأصوات والأفكار وفي مشهدها المتحوّل هذا تنشأ روحٌ مشتركة من العلاقات المرتبطة تتحدى المسافات والاختلافات.

خلال مسار البرنامج، كنّا كثيرًا ما نتوقّف عند نقاشاتٍ عفويّة نشأت في أثناء تنقّلاتنا إلى موقع البرنامج، أو في رحلات العودة بالسيارة، أو حتى خلال ساعات العمل. تمحورت هذه الأحاديث حول الكيفية التي يُحمَل بها الصوت ويُستدعى ويُعاد تشكيله عبر الزمن، بفعل الناس والأشياء والفضاءات العامة واللغات. ومن هذه النقاشات انبثق تساؤلٌ عن الكيفية التي تسهم بها تلك الكيفيات في صياغة الهوية والسرديات المرتبطة بالنوع الاجتماعي والتجارب الفنية، ولا سيّما أن كثيرًا من هذه السرديات يُهمَل أو يظلّ غير مرويّ. من خلال هذه الحوارات سعينا إلى استكشاف الروابط بين الأطر المرنة غير الأكاديمية وممارساتٍ متعدّدة، مثل اللعب الجسدي، والسرد الشفهي، وبحوث الرقص، والشعر. ولم يكن ممكنًا إبقاء هذه المقاربات في عوالم منفصلة؛ إذ بات جمعها ضمن لقاءاتٍ ذات معنى تشاركيّ ضرورةً ملحّة، وهذا الذي حاولنا تحقيقه في لقاءاتٍ تقوم على الملاحظة والتوثيق والتسجيل والجمع والحوار.

بدا سريعًا -ومع وقوع هذه التفاعلات في فضاءاتٍ مادية- أن الحدود داخل تلك الفضاءات تتحول إلى أوعيةٍ مركزية للتفاعل، وإلى منابع لتشكيل النسيج الاجتماعي. ومن هنا اتسعت الأفكار حول أهمية العمران الحضري

contribute to narrating stories that can be experienced, remembered, shared, and carried forward? What shape can this narrative take in a city that is principally experienced through the practice of driving?

Fascinated by the roundabouts that punctuate and hallmark the coastal city, photographer Hatun Al-Harthi, Olivier Duport, and Alan Marzo of FLEE Project chose to further engage with the questions that emerged during these past encounters, approaching these monumental artworks as case studies. A moving story that would culminate in this photobook tracing Jeddah's roundabouts, roads, and urban imprints. Within its folds, the publication starts with a historical essay by architect Turki Gazzaz tracing the genealogy of the roundabouts – their commissioning, planning, and edification by the former mayor of Jeddah, Mohammed Said Farsi, and reflecting upon the subjective feelings that these monuments instigate among their main users: the motorists. It then moves into a more intimate register as researcher and writer Nouf al Harthi gathers the voices of male and female taxi drivers, migrant workers, and long-time residents who ponder Jeddah's architectural landmarks, while photographer Hatun Al-Harthi documents many of the city's monuments. The two artists gather these testimonies to create a tactile portrait of the city. The roundabouts are no longer exclusively an urban fact, but become the source of an almost psychoanalytical journey, in which they reflect the soul of the city's inhabitants. In this sense, the book places dialogue and listening as critical cultural practices, coexisting with the fleeting rhythms of everyday life and the poetics of space.

Looking back, Art Jameel's role in this project came from a sense of familiarity with the subject of sculptural roundabouts; tracing back to 2011, when the organisation, together with the municipality of Jeddah, began a large-scale restoration project,

بالتعاون مع أمانة جدّة مشروعًا واسعًا لترميم الأعمال الفنية، شمل نقل أكثر من عشرين تمثالاً إلى كورنيش جدّة لتشكيل أكبر متحف مفتوح في الهواء الطلق. وكما يحمل البحر الأحمر الأصوات ويستدعيها ويعيدها كذلك تفعل الدوّارات. فقد ظل حضورها وسكونها قائمين فيما كانت المدينة تتسع وتتحول سريعًا. ولكل دوار شخصيته الخاصة، المرحة، والمعقّدة، والمهيبة، وتروي حكاياته في هدوء عبر الشكل والخيال.

هكذا ينفتح هذا الكتاب الفوتوغرافي متخذًا من دوّارات جدّة وبنيتها التحتية موضعًا للذاكرة وإعادة التأويل والتأمل في صدى يوازي المسار الفكري الذي انطلق منه مختبر البحث الصوتي. من خلال هذا المشروع تتجسّد المدينة في خطوطٍ وأشكال وإيماءات، وفي مسحةٍ من الحنين تكتسب معناها بشكل رسمي وغير رسمي في ذات الوقت. ويغدو اللعب والتجريب -وهما من المحاور الرئيسة التي بُني عليها البرنامج- أكثر من مجرد أدوات لاستكشاف الهجرة والطقوس والذاكرة الجمعية، ويظهران امتدادًا لمساراتٍ متنامية من التساؤل تقوم على التعاون وتبادل الأفكار والإنصات المتبادل.

ويستحضر هذا الكتاب شعورًا يشبه ذلك الذي رافقنا حين بدأنا هذه الرحلة قبل عامٍ ونصف تقريبًا، وكأننا نعود إلى اكتمال دائرةٍ لا تنغلق. دائرةٌ مستمرة تُغذّيها علاقاتٌ نشأت وأخرى لا تزال تتشكّل وثالثةٌ لم تأتِ بعد. وكما الدوّارات نفسها فضاءات للعودة وإعادة التوجّه حيث تلتقي الذاكرة بالإمكانية، يغدو الدوران نفسه سبيلاً لرؤيةٍ متجددة في قلب المدينة والذكرى.

نود أن نتقدم بخالص الشكر إلى هتون ونوف وأوليفييه وآلان، وإلى العديد من المبدعين الذين منحت أصواتهم هذا الكتاب الفوتوغرافي معناه وطبقاته وعمقه وبنيته الجماعية. إن هذه التجربة -وما سيتبعها من تجارب- تجسّد قصة جدّة المتحوّلة وإرثها الثقافي، وتحتفي بها وتوسّع آفاقها. قصةٌ تلتقط بوهجٍ خاص ذكريات المدينة وسبل عيش أهلها ومسار تطوّرها العمراني.

which included relocating more than 20 statues to Jeddah's Corniche to form the largest open-air museum. In the same way the Red Sea carried, called, and returned, so did the roundabouts. Their presence and stillness endured as the city expanded and rapidly transformed. Each circle held its own character, playful, intricate, monumental, quietly narrating stories through form and imagination. The photobook unfolds, using Jeddah's roundabouts and infrastructure as a site of remembrance, reinterpretation, self and reflection, mirroring a similar thought process to the sound research lab. Through the project, the city reifies in lines, shapes, gestures, and a sense of nostalgia that gains meaning both formally and informally. Play and experimentation - both guiding themes for building the programme - become much more than tools for exploring migration, rituals, and collective memory, but an extension of evolving threads of inquiry grounded in collaboration, open exchange, and vulnerability.

The publication evokes a similar feeling to when we first embarked on this journey over a year and a half ago, becoming somewhat of a full circle moment, though not a closed one. Rather, it is perpetual and sustained by relationships formed, forming, and yet to come. Much like the roundabouts themselves, spaces of return and reorientation, where memory and possibility meet, and where the act of circling becomes a way of seeing anew. We want to extend our sincere thanks to Hatun, Nouf, Olivier, Alan, and the many creatives whose voices define and layer meaning, depth, and structure to the collectiveness of this photobook. The experience in itself, and the many more to come, embody, embrace, and expand on Jeddah's evolving story, legacy, and culture that magically capture memories, livelihoods, and the city's urban development.

في جدّة لتلامس اعتباراتٍ فلسفية وجمالية: كيف يسهم العمران، في الفضاء العام كما في الخاص، في رواية قصصٍ يمكن اختبارها وتذكّرها وتداولها وحملها إلى المستقبل؟ وما الصورة التي يمكن أن تتخذها هذه السردية في مدينة تُعاش في المقام الأول من خلال تجربة القيادة؟

استهوت الدوّارات التي تتناثر في المدينة الساحلية وتُشكّل معالمها اهتمام المصوّرة هتون الحارثي، ومعها أوليفييه دوبور وآلان مارزو من مشروع فلي، فاختاروا التعمّق في الأسئلة التي نشأت خلال اللقاءات مع المدينة، متخذين من الأعمال النحتية الضخمة في دوّاراتها دراساتٍ للحالة. ومن هنا بدأت حكاية متحرّكة تُتوَّج بهذا الكتاب الفوتوغرافي الذي يتتبّع دوّارات جدّة وطرقاتها وبصماتها العمرانية.

يفتتح الكتاب بمقالة تاريخية للمعماري تركي قزاز يتتبّع فيها نشأة فكرة المنحوتات في وسط الدوّارات من تكليفها وتخطيطها إلى تشييدها في عهد أمين جدّة الأسبق محمد سعيد فارسي، مع تأمّلٍ في المشاعر التي تثيرها هذه المعالم لدى مستخدميها الرئيسيين: سائقي المركبات. ثم ينتقل النص إلى نبرةٍ أكثر حميمية، إذ تجمع الباحثة والكاتبة نوف الحارثي أصوات سائقي سيارات الأجرة من الرجال والنساء، والعمّال المهاجرين، وسكان المدينة القدامى وهم يتأملون معالم جدّة المعمارية، في حين توثّق المصوّرة هتون الحارثي عددًا كبيرًا من نصب المدينة. ومن خلال هذه الشهادات تصوغ الفنّانتان صورة حسّية ملموسة للمدينة؛ حيث يصبح التأمل في الدوّارات منطلقًا لرحلةٍ تكاد تكون ذات طابعٍ سيكولوجي تحليلي تعكس روح سكان المدينة لا مجرد عناصرها المعمارية، ولذلك يضع الكتاب الحوار والإنصات في منزلة ممارساتٍ ثقافية أساسية تتجاور مع إيقاعات الحياة اليومية العابرة وشعرية المكان.

وإذا عدنا بالذاكرة فإن دور فن جميل في هذا المشروع ينبع من صلةٍ سابقة بموضوع الدوّارات النحتية؛ إذ تعود جذوره إلى عام ٢٠١١ حين أطلقت المؤسسة

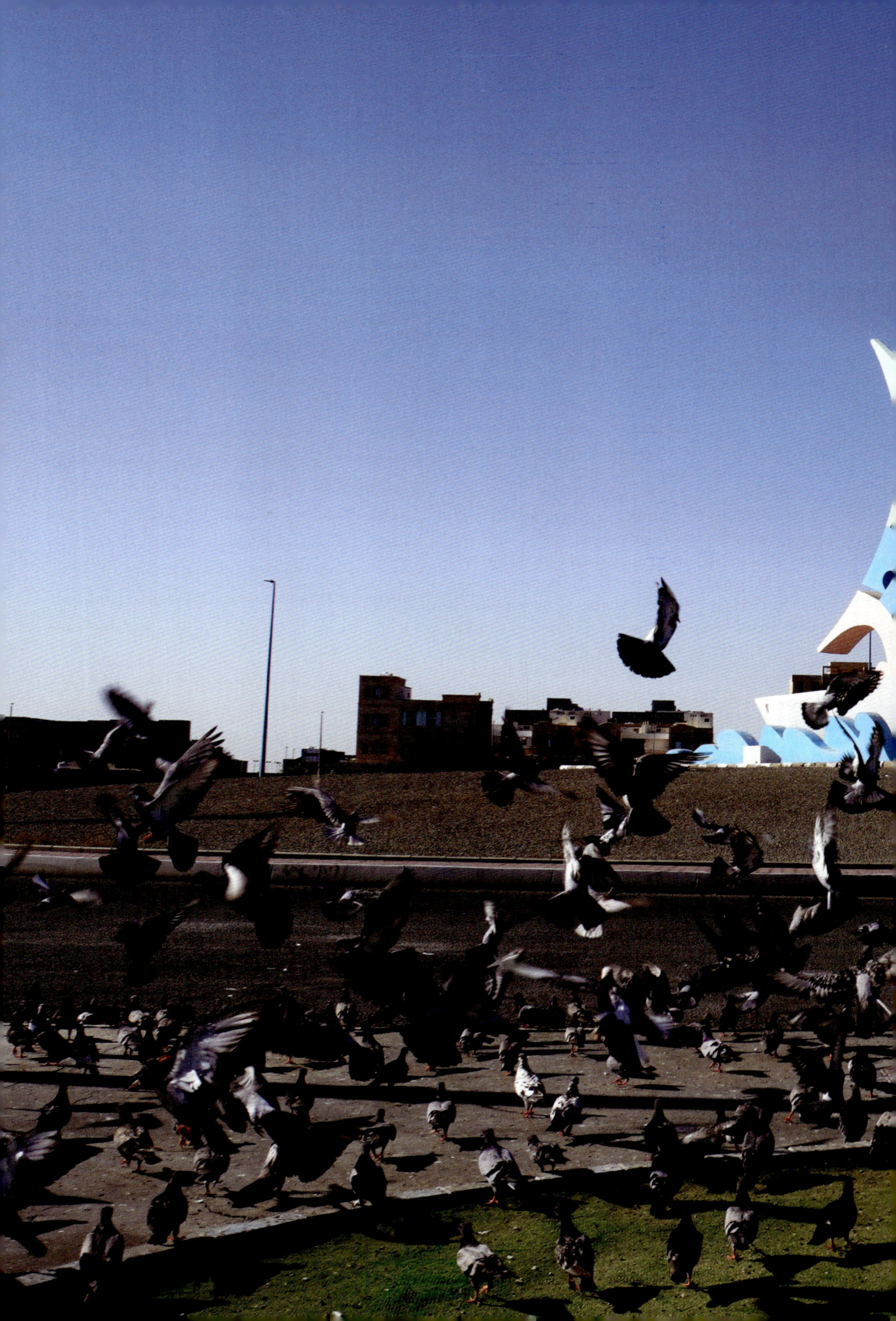

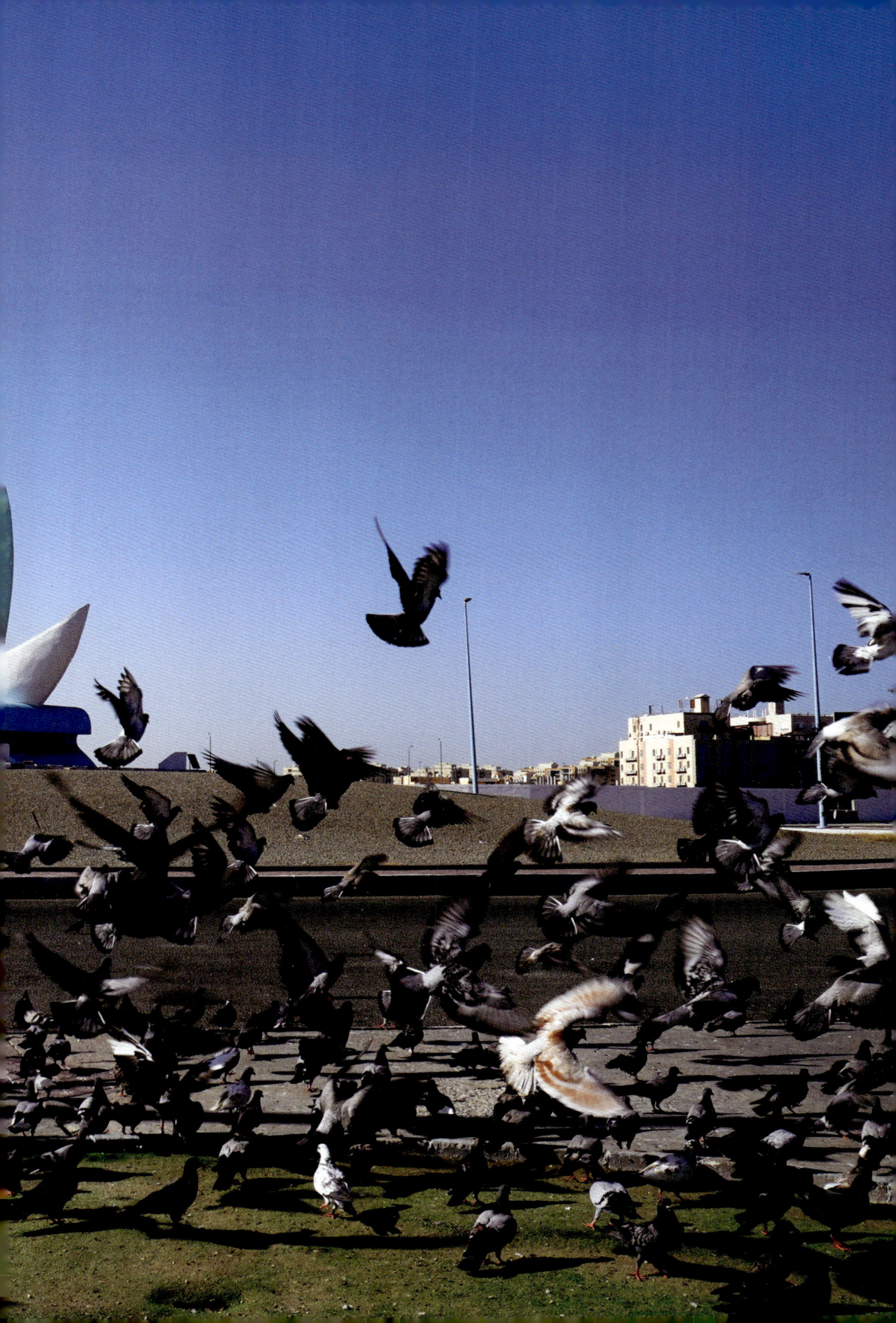

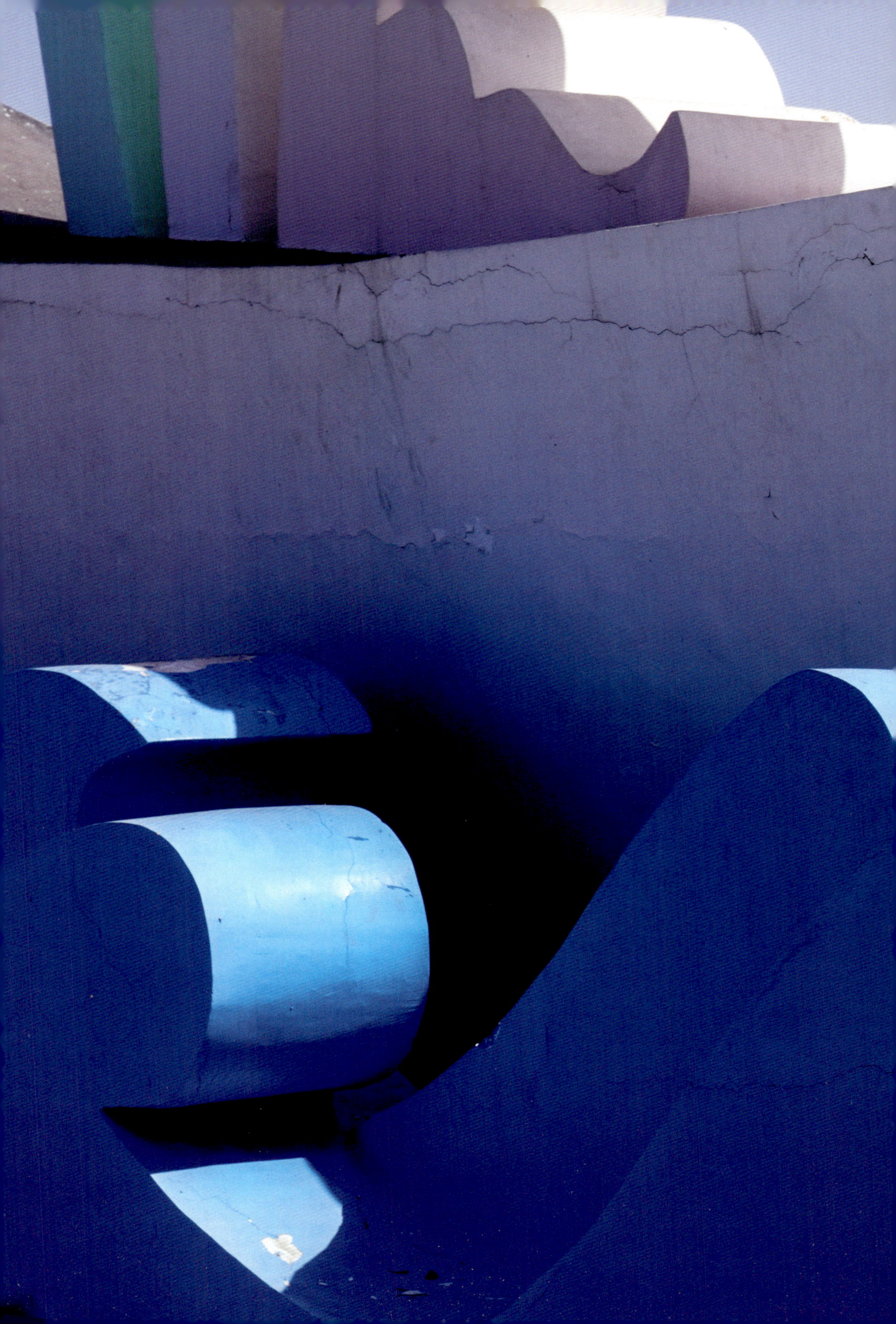

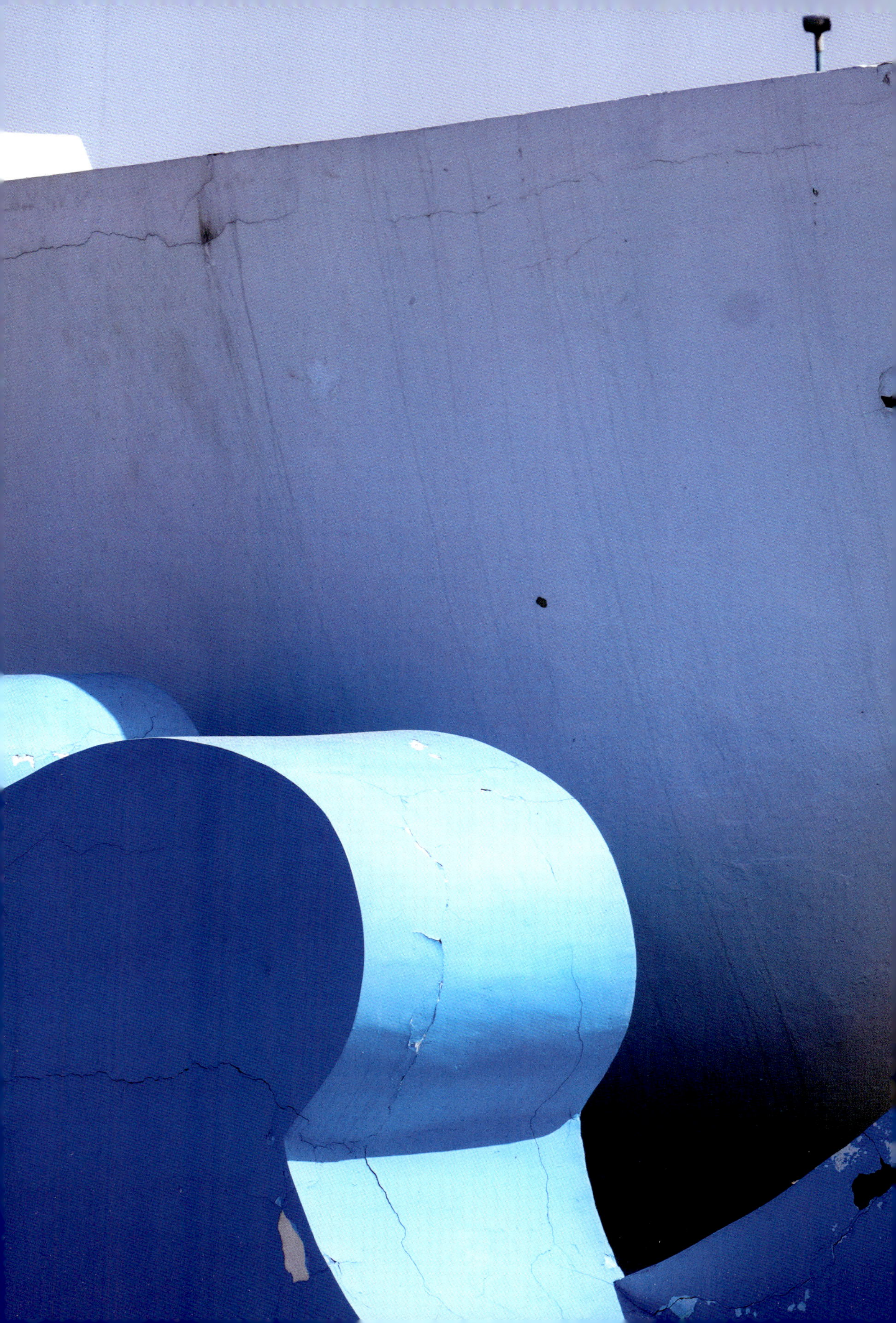

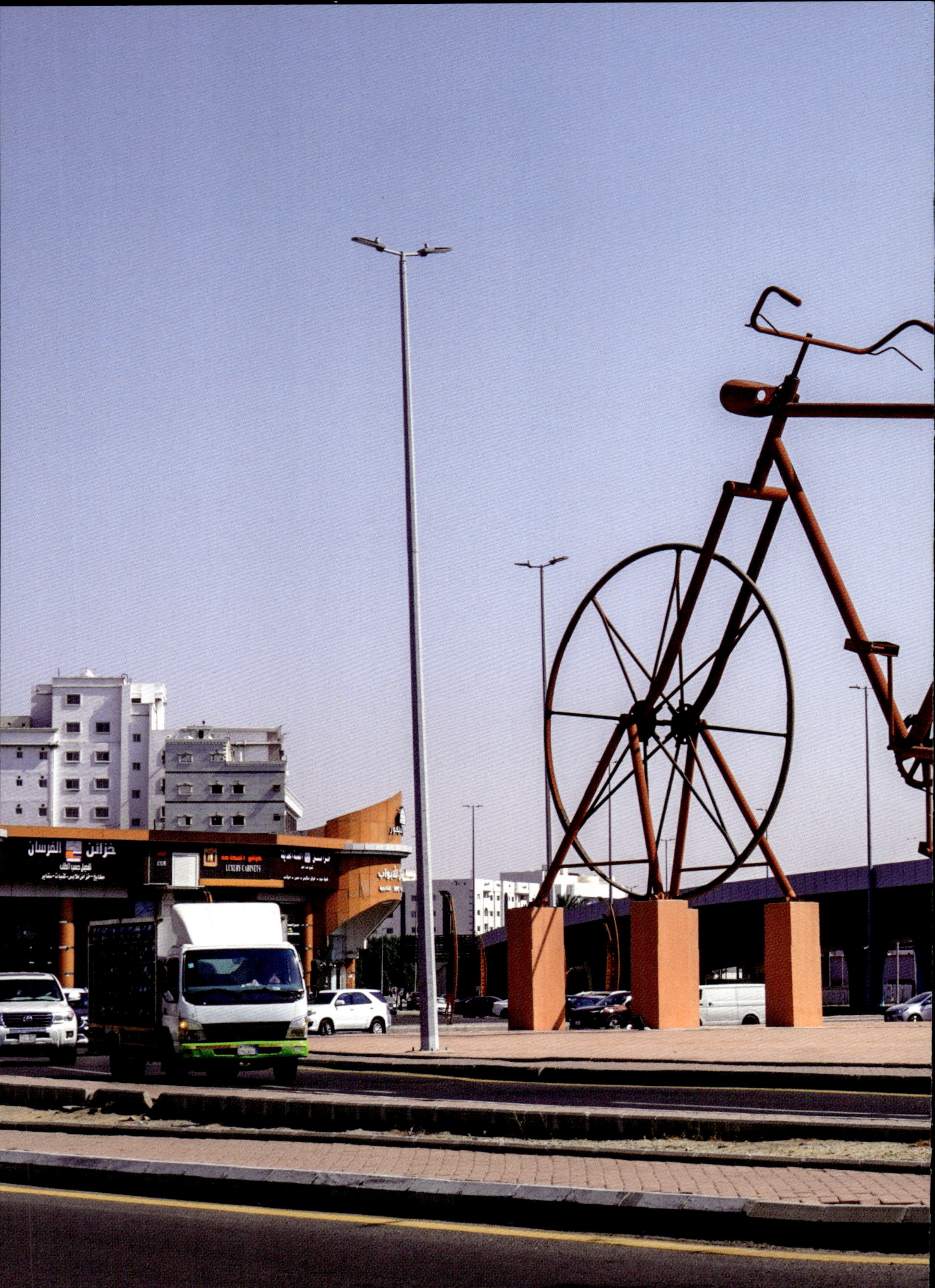
خزائن الفرسان
LUXURY CABINETS

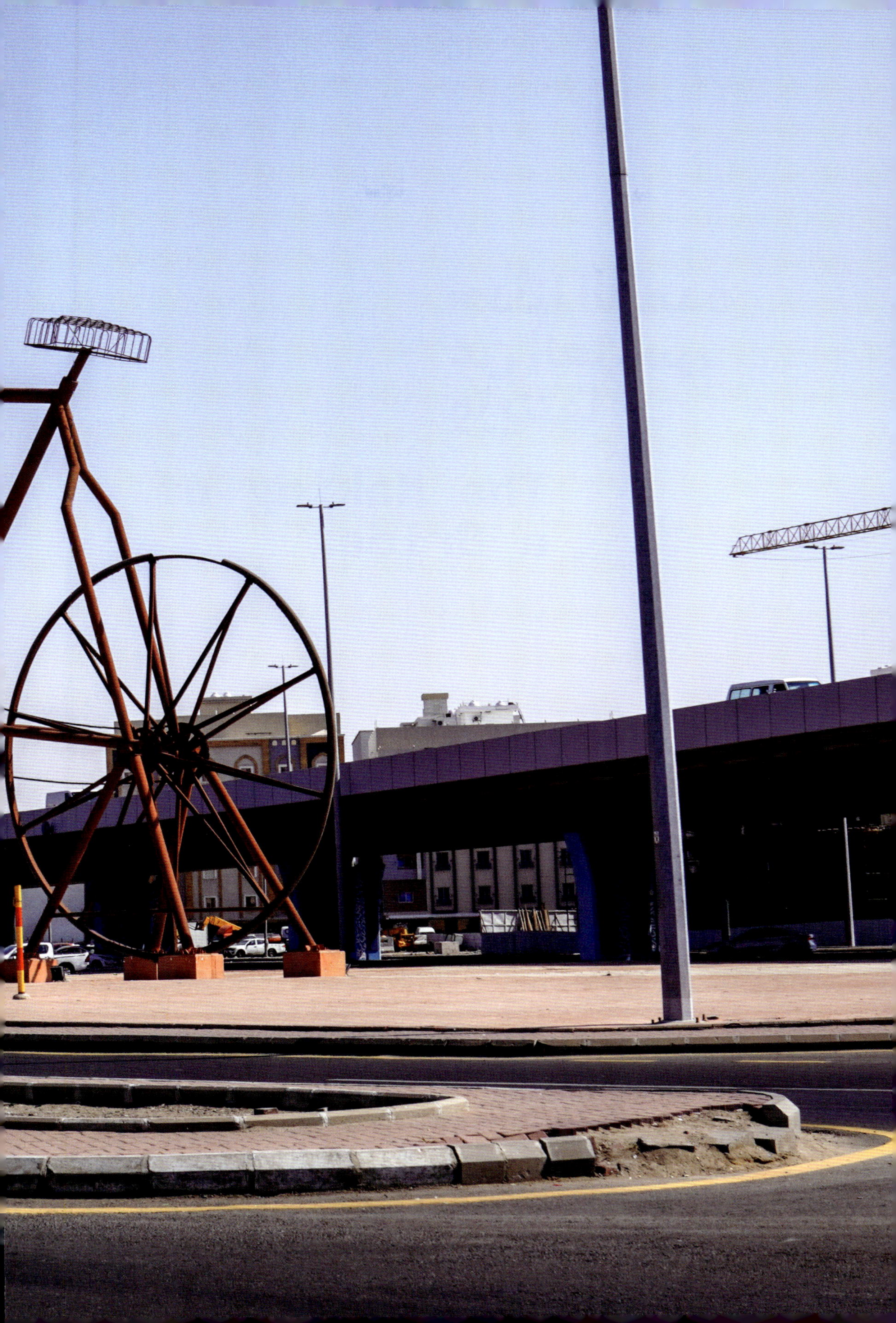

حدثنا العمدة
عن العروس
وزينتها

The Making of
a Bride

تركي قزاز
Turki Gazzaz

A fifteen-meter-high bicycle rumoured to have been modelled on the scale of Adam, or a replica of a lighthouse often confused with a baby bottle or a traditional English milk bottle. A car floating on a flying carpet to symbolise the confluence of modernisation and local tradition, or a series of birds by Joan Miró. The sculptures scattered across the roundabouts and public spaces of the coastal city of Jeddah are not only a defining feature of a rapidly modernising urban landscape, but an act of love, care, and civic responsibility that has endured over generations and established a personal relationship between the city and its inhabitants.

During the 1970s and 1980s, Mohammed Said Farsi launched what would become one of his most enduring legacies as mayor: the "Jeddah Beautification Project". Serving as Mayor of Jeddah during this period, Farsi oversaw a large-scale urban renewal initiative that fundamentally reshaped the city's public realm. Educated in civic planning in Alexandria in the 1950s, he was deeply influenced by the city's Mediterranean cosmopolitanism and its integration of art into everyday urban life. Under his leadership, the urban initiative delivered more than 600 large-scale, site-specific commissions alongside extensive landscaping, pedestrian infrastructure, street art, and environmental rehabilitation. Together, these interventions realigned Jeddah's relationship to its Red Sea coastline and articulated a new layer of urban identity: not only as a historic port and gateway for pilgrimage, but also as a culturally ambitious and visually distinctive city celebrated as the "Bride of the Red Sea."

Jeddah's relationship to the sea has long been defined by its strategic position along a perilous coral reef that provided a natural fortification against maritime threats. For over a thousand years, the city has turned its back on the waterfront and aligned its focus towards the northern and eastern land routes towards the holy cities of Makkah and Madinah. However, as the city experienced rapid expansion

دراجة هوائية شاهقة يبلغ ارتفاعها خمسة عشر مترًا، يُشاع أنّ تصميمها جاء على مقياس آدم؛ أو نسخة من منارةٍ يلتبس أمرها على العابرين، فتتراءى تارة زجاجة رضاعة للأطفال، وتارة أخرى قارورةَ الحليب الإنجليزية التقليدية. وسيارة تعوم فوق بساطٍ طائر تُجسد التقاء مسارات التحديث بالتقاليد المحلية، أو سربٌ من الطيور صاغه الفنان خوان ميرو في هيئةٍ حُلمية.

غدت هذه المنحوتات المتناثرة في الدوّارات والفضاءات العامة في المدينة الساحلية جدة، علامةً فارقة في مشهدٍ حضري يتسارع تحوّله، وحملت في الوقت نفسه معنى الاعتناء بالمكان والوفاء له. وعبر الأجيال نمت هذه الأعمال أفعال محبّة مدنية، وتكوّنت بينها وبين سكان المدينة ألفة حميمة تعيد تشكيل صورة المدينة في الذاكرة اليومية ومنحتها حضورًا متجددًا في الوجدان.

خلال سبعينيات وثمانينيات القرن العشرين أطلق محمد سعيد فارسي ما سيغدو لا حقًا أحد أكثر إرثه رسوخًا أثناء تولّيه منصب أمين جدة: مشروع تجميل جدة. أشرف فارسي في تلك السنوات على مبادرةٍ واسعة لإعادة تجديد المدينة أعادت تشكيل المجال العام في عمقه وبنيته. تلقّى تعليمه في التخطيط المدني في الإسكندرية خلال خمسينيات القرن العشرين، وتشرّب من روحها المتوسطية الكوزموبوليتانية ومن حضور الفن في تفاصيل الحياة اليومية. تحت قيادته ظهرت أكثر من ستمائة تكليفٍ فني ضخم صُمّم لمواقع محددة في أنحاء المدينة، ترافق مع تنسيقٍ واسع للحدائق، وبنيةٍ تحتيةٍ للمشاة، وفنونٍ في

in the twentieth century, along with the introduction of air travel, its maritime role as the gateway to the holy sites quickly began to acquire a somewhat symbolic role. When Mohammed Said Farsi became mayor of Jeddah, he was well aware of his hometown's growing significance as the country's major commercial and business hub, its intrinsic role in global maritime trade, and its evolving identity as a result. Orchestrated through the 1973 masterplan led by Sir Robert Matthew and Stirrat Johnson-Marshall (RMJM), Farsi commissioned a network of boulevards, roundabouts, and the now-iconic corniche waterfronts that continue to define the public image of Jeddah today. RMJM, the Edinburgh-based architectural and urban planning agency, had overseen the preparation of the city's first modern masterplan in the 1960s, establishing a comprehensive framework to guide Jeddah's rapid urban expansion, infrastructure development, and zoning as it evolved from a historic port into a modern metropolis.

Farsi's tenure coincided with the oil boom that followed the 1973 oil embargo, positioning him to govern a major city in a nation emerging as a rising power on the global stage. Influenced by his time in the "cultural capital" of Egypt, Alexandria, he sought to reposition Jeddah, and Saudi Arabia in general, as a leading voice in the region. At the time, the city gained strategic socio-economic and cultural leverage because of its geopolitical significance for the Islamic world on the one hand, and its relationship to Western networks of capital on the other. The mayor's approach to Jeddah's urban development aligned well with its political outlook at the time. He initiated this ambitious urban initiative to embody a nuanced balance between traditional values and a progressive

تزامنت فترة تولّي محمد سعيد فارسي أمانة جدة مع الطفرة النفطية عام 1973، وهذا سياق منح موقع إدارة المدينة الكبرى داخل الدولة يرتفع مكانةً على المسرح العالمي. تستعيد ذاكرته سنوات الإقامة في الإسكندرية التي عُرفت طويلاً العاصمة الثقافية لمصر، فيبرز طموح لإعادة تمركز جدة والمملكة العربية السعودية صوتًا مؤثرًا في المنطقة. وفي تلك المرحلة اكتسبت المدينة وزنًا اجتماعيًا واقتصاديًا وثقافيًا متناميًا، بفعل موقعها الجيوسياسي بالنسبة للعالم الإسلامي، وبفضل علاقاتها المتزايدة بشبكات رأس المال الغربية.

انطلقت مبادرة الفن العام جزءًا من رؤية حضرية تبحث عن توازنٍ دقيق بين قيم التراث وروح التطور الحديث. وبالتعاون مع المعماري الإسباني خوليو لافوينتي توسع المشروع الفني ليواكب تسارع تطوير البنية التحتية في المدينة. امتد التواصل إلى فنانين عالميين مثل ألكسندر كالدر، وشمل فنانين محليين صاعدين آنذاك مثل هشام بنجابي، إضافة إلى أسماء من العالمين العربي والإسلامي مثل شفيق مظلوم العامل في مكتب التخطيط ببلدية جدة. منح حضور كالدر البرنامج بعدًا عالميًا، ويؤدي بن في تخطيط أبوظبي الحديثة، حيث قدّم رؤية تخطيطية تجمع بين البنية التحتية الحديثة والهوية الثقافية والمناخ والاستمرارية الاجتماعية. وتتردد أصداء هذه المبادئ بوضوح في الرؤية العمرانية المتشكّلة في جدة.

ينتمي فارسي إلى عائلة تجارية بارزة في المدينة، وهو سياق يضفي على حضوره المدني بُعدًا عمليًا واضحًا. ويظهر مشروع تجميل جدة في هذا الإطار مبادرةً شخصية تسعى إلى الإسهام في تحسين البلد الأم والموطن الأصلي.

spirit of modern development through public art. Together with the Spanish architect Julio Lafuente, he pursued this ambitious public art initiative to counterbalance the rapid development of the city's infrastructure. They reached out to internationally recognised Western artists such as Alexander Calder, alongside emerging local figures like Hisham Benjabi, while also collaborating with established practitioners from across the Arab and Muslim world, including Palestinian-born Shafiq Mazloum, active within Jeddah Municipality's planning office. Calder, renowned for his monumental public sculptures, brought global visibility to the programme, while Benjabi played a formative role in shaping Jeddah's local art scene. Farsi's general vision aimed to highlight the role Islamic scholarship has played in the development of modern science and contemporary culture. His strategic curatorial framework and artist selection aimed to empower voices from the so-called 'global south'. Sculptures ranging in size from a modest human scale to towering structures conceived for the automobile experience were developed to decorate this newly recognised 'Bride'.

Overall, these sculptures function not only as artworks but as urban markers embedded within the city's spatial logic. They embody a traditional sensibility toward civic development, operating as enduring works of *fatto urbano* in the sense articulated by Aldo Rossi, for whom urban artefacts persist over time beyond their original function as carriers of collective memory. Through their distinctive forms and strategic placement, the sculptures also act as mnemonic devices that help organise an "image of the city," aligning with the Lynchian logic developed, in which landmarks play a central role in shaping how urban environments are perceived, navigated, and remembered. The shift from

الشوارع، وبرامجٍ لإعادة التأهيل البيئي. اجتمعت هذه التدخلات في إعادة ترتيب علاقة جدة بساحل البحر الأحمر، وفي صياغة طبقةٍ جديدة من هوية المدينة. ميناءٌ تاريخي وبوابةٌ للحج إلى مكة المكرمة والمدينة المنورة، ومدينةٌ ذات طموحٍ ثقافي وبصمةٍ بصرية مميزة تُحتفى باسم عروس البحر الأحمر.

ترتبط علاقة جدة بالبحر بتاريخ طويل يمتد من موقعها الاستراتيجي بمحاذاة شعاب مرجانية خطرة أدّت دور التحصين الطبيعي في مواجهة التهديدات البحرية. وعلى امتداد أكثر من ألف عام اتجه تركيز المدينة نحو الطرق البرية في الشمال والشرق المؤدية إلى المدينتين المقدستين. ومع التوسع السريع الذي عرفته المدينة في القرن العشرين وظهور السفر الجوي اكتسبت وظيفتها البحرية المرتبطة بالحرمين طابعًا رمزيًا متزايدًا. عندما تولّي فارسي منصب الأمين ظهرت جدة مركزًا تجاريًا رئيسيًا في البلاد ومحطة مؤثرة في حركة التجارة البحرية العالمية، وبدأت ملامح هوية حضرية جديدة في التشكّل.

تبلور هذا التحول عبر المخطط الهيكلي لعام 1973 الذي قاده روبرت ماثيو وستيررات جونسون مارشال من مكتب RMJM. حيث أُقرت شبكة من الجادات العريضة والدوّارات والواجهات البحرية للكورنيش التي تصوغ اليوم الصورة العامة للمدينة. وكان المكتب المعماري في أدنبرة مشرفًا في ستينيات القرن العشرين على إعداد أول مخطط حديث شامل للمدينة، واضعًا إطارًا متكاملاً يقود توسعها العمراني السريع وتطوير بنيتها التحتية وتنظيم استخدامات الأراضي مع انتقالها من ميناء تاريخي إلى حاضرة معاصرة.

a small-scale pedestrian experience of a city to the optimism of the progressive outlook of the efficiency afforded by the automobile registers well with the duality of modernity-tradition that Farsi seems to have been exploring.

In terms of civic agency, Farsi operated in an interesting time marked by a parallel shift in urban governance. In 1965, urban affairs became relegated to a central authority: the newly established Ministry of Municipal Affairs. Drawing on his experience working with Egyptian urban planner Abdulrahman Makhlouf in the Planning Bureau during the 1950s, he was personally involved in shaping the trajectory of Jeddah's urban development. Makhlouf, later renowned for his role in guiding the modern planning of Abu Dhabi, championed an approach that balanced modern infrastructure with cultural identity, climate, and social continuity, principles that would resonate strongly in Jeddah's evolving urban vision. In addition, he was part of a prominent merchant family, probably familiar with civic affairs, thus imbuing a sense of agency in his overall attitude. Viewed in this context, his "Beautification Project" may be understood as a personal endeavour to participate in the improvement of his hometown. Loosely defined, the project framework aimed to embellish the city's new boulevards, key intersections, and most importantly, its central attraction: the new 'corniche' waterfront. Exploring themes such as the Islamic Golden Age and sustainable reuse of scrap materials, the sculptures he commissioned varied in scale, origin, and conceptual framework.

Many of the large-scale works were placed around vehicular roundabouts and were meant to be experienced exclusively by car. Lafuente's Globe and Hisham Benjabi's engineering roundabout still form key

واتجه إطار المشروع إلى تزيين الجادات الجديدة والتقاطعات الكبرى، ومنح الواجهة البحرية للكورنيش موقع القلب في هذه الرؤية. وتناولت المنحوتات موضوعات متعددة، من العصر الذهبي الإسلامي إلى إعادة الاستخدام المستدام للمواد المعدنية، وتنوّعت في أحجامها وأصولها وأطرها المفاهيمية.

وتستقرّ العديد من الأعمال الضخمة في الدوّارات المرورية بحيث تُرى ضمن تجربة الحركة بالسيارة. ويظلّ مجسّم الكرة الأرضية للافوينتي ودوّار الهندسة لهشام بنجابي علامتين واضحتين في المشهد الحضري تحددان اتجاهات الحركة الكبرى. كما تظهر أعمال أصغر حجمًا لفنانين مثل هنري مور وعارف الريّس على امتداد الكورنيش، ترافق تجربة المشي بمحاذاة البحر.

تستعيد منحوتة الكنداسة التي صمّمها لافوينتي بدايات دخول المدينة في مسار التحديث عبر إعادة توظيف مكثّف المياه العثماني من القرن التاسع عشر، بينما يحتفي عمل نافورة التحلية للفنان مصطفى سنبل بنظيره المعاصر. وقد وظّفت هذه الأعمال مواد الخردة لتقديم روايات عن جابي دورًا مؤثرًا في تشكيل المشهد الفني المحلي في المدينة. تحمل رؤية فارسي اهتمامًا بإبراز الدور الذي أدّته المعرفة الإسلامية في مسار العلوم الحديثة والثقافة المعاصرة. ويقوم في اختياره للفنانين إطارٌ قيَمي يفتح المجال لأصوات آتية من الجنوب العالمي. وتتنوّع المنحوتات بين أعمالٍ بمقياسٍ إنساني متواضع وهياكل شاهقة صُمّمت لتُرى من داخل السيارة، فتزيّن العروس التي تتكشف صورتها الجديدة في الفضاء الحضري.

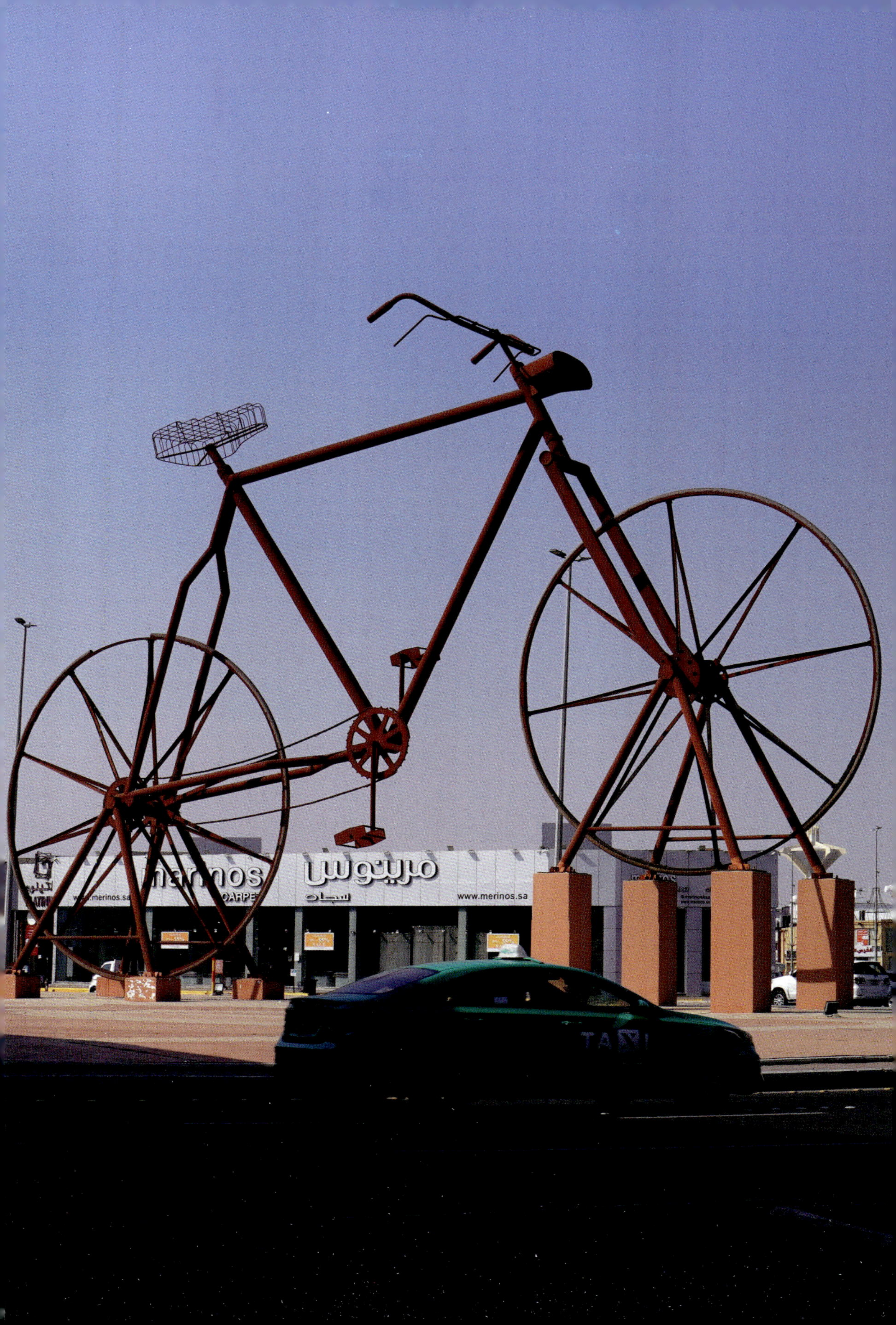
مرينوس
سجاد
www.merinos.sa

markers across the urban landscape that define major directions. Other smaller-scale sculptures, like those of British sculptor Henry Moore and Lebanese artist Aref Al Rayess, were commissioned as objects designed for a pedestrian experience along the waterfront. The *Kindasa* sculptures of Lafuente recall the city's early forays into modernisation by repurposing the 19th century Ottoman condenser, while Mustafa Senbel's Tahlia Fountain celebrates its contemporary counterpart. Both roundabouts deploy scrap materials to provide the city's inhabitants with narratives about their history while championing an environmental consciousness about sustainability. The Moving Atom on Tahlia Street was widely regarded as the region's first mechanically kinetic structure, representing a significant technological achievement within the context of Jeddah's emergence as a cultural capital.

The mayor envisioned the city as an open-air museum, acting somehow as the gallerist, curator, and collector. Indeed, the sculptures littered across the city are the result of his personal engagement with leading artists from the region as well as from the west and beyond. He leveraged his social circles to commission a plethora of both acquired and site-specific artworks that may be read simultaneously as a public and personal collection. Beyond policy and planning, the "Beautification project" was deeply personal. In an essay published by his son Hani in the nineties, he recounts how several major public works were inspired by small desktop ornaments collected during his travels, which later evolved into primary urban markers across the city. To check up on public works or to try out newly asphalted roads, he would randomly pick up his nephew, Zaki Farsi, a fellow architect and planner, to take long drives around the city.

وتحرك داخله صاحبَ معرض وقيّمًا وجامعًا في آنٍ واحد. وانتشرت المنحوتات في أنحاء المدينة ثمرةً لتفاعله الشخصي مع فنانين بارزين من المنطقة ومن الغرب ومن أماكن أخرى؛ إذ سخّر شبكاته الاجتماعية لتكليف مجموعة واسعة من الأعمال، سواء المقتناة منها أو المصمَّمة خصيصًا للموقع، فتبدو هذه المجموعة أرشيفًا فنيًا يجمع بين البعدين العام والشخصي.

ويحمل مشروع التجميل بُعدًا شخصيًا يتجاوز نطاق التخطيط والسياسات. يروي ابنه هاني فارسي في مقال نُشر في تسعينيات القرن العشرين أن عددًا من الأعمال العامة الكبرى استُلهم من قطع زخرفية صغيرة كان والده يجمعها خلال أسفاره، ثم تحوّلت لاحقًا إلى معالم حضرية رئيسية. وكان يصطحب أحيانًا ابن أخيه المعماري والمخطط زكي فارسي في جولات طويلة بالسيارة داخل المدينة لمتابعة المشاريع العامة أو لاختبار الطرق التي جرى سفلتتها حديثًا.

وتتقدم صورة فارسي بوصفه الأب الرمزي للمدينة، ويسهم حضوره في تشكيل التصورات المعاصرة عن جدة. وقد دعم تمويل العديد من المنحوتات عبر مبادرات فردية ومؤسسية، وواصل رعاية الفضاء العام بروح المسؤولية المدنية. تظهر هذه الأعمال اليوم جزءًا طبيعيًا من المشهد الحضري للمدينة؛ حيث تنتشر على امتداد الكورنيش وفي الدوّارات وفي حدائقها، وتنسج حضورها الهادئ في إيقاع الحياة اليومية، وتسهم في صياغة هوية «عروس البحر الأحمر» وفي الكيفية التي تكشف بها المدينة عن نفسها للعالم، وتتشكّل بها صورة العروس.

Acting as a kind of patriarch of his city and playing an important role in shaping contemporary perceptions of Jeddah, Farsi would often vouch for individual and corporate funding for many sculptures, maintaining a sense of continued civic responsibility towards the city. The sculptures he fought for have become a casual feature of Jeddah's urban landscape. Perhaps many of its citizens do not necessarily grasp the intellectual depth of his curatorial framework; however, most cannot help but appreciate the place-making these sculptures have established. Whether along the corniche, at a busy roundabout, or in the quiet clearing of a park, these works have gently woven themselves into the city's rhythms, shaping the identity of the Bride of the Red Sea and the subtle, ever-renewed ways in which she reveals herself to the world.

تعمل هذه المنحوتات أعمالاً فنيةً وعلاماتٍ حضرية في آنٍ واحد، وتندمج في المنطق المكاني للمدينة. وتحمل حسًّا تقليديًا تجاه التطوير المدني، وتظهر شواهدَ دائمةً على مفهوم «fatto urbano» الذي صاغه ألدو روسي، حيث تستمر العناصر الحضرية عبر الزمن حاملةً الذاكرة الجمعية. وتسهم أشكالها المميّزة ومواقعها المختارة بعناية في تشكيل «صورة المدينة» وفق المنطق الذي طوّره كيفن لينش، إذ تحتل المعالم موقعًا مركزيًا في إدراك الفضاء الحضري والتنقّل داخله وتذكّره. ويغدو الانتقال من تجربة مدينة تُعاش على مقياس المشاة إلى تفاؤلٍ حداثي يرتبط بكفاءة الحركة بالسيارة صورةً واضحة لجدلية الحداثة والتقاليد في رؤية فارسي.

تحرّك فارسي في سياق الفاعلية المدنية خلال مرحلة شهدت تحولات في بنية الحكم الحضري. ففي عام 1965 انتقلت الشؤون الحضرية إلى سلطة مركزية جديدة هي وزارة الشؤون البلدية والقروية. واستند فارسي إلى خبرته المبكرة في العمل مع المخطّط المصري عبد الرحمن مخلوف داخل مكتب التخطيط في خمسينيات القرن العشرين، وشارك مباشرة في توجيه مسار التطور العمراني في جدة. وقد اكتسب مخلوف لاحقًا شهرة واسعة من خلال دوره تاريخ المدينة لسكانها، وتعزيز وعيٍ بيئي يتصل بفكرة الاستدامة. ويحظى مجسّم الذرة المتحركة في شارع التحلية بسمعة واسعة أحد أوائل الهياكل الحركية الميكانيكية في المنطقة، ويبرز إنجازًا تقنيًا في سياق صعود جدة مركزًا ثقافيًا.

تخيّل فارسي المدينة متحفًا مفتوحًا في الهواء الطلق،

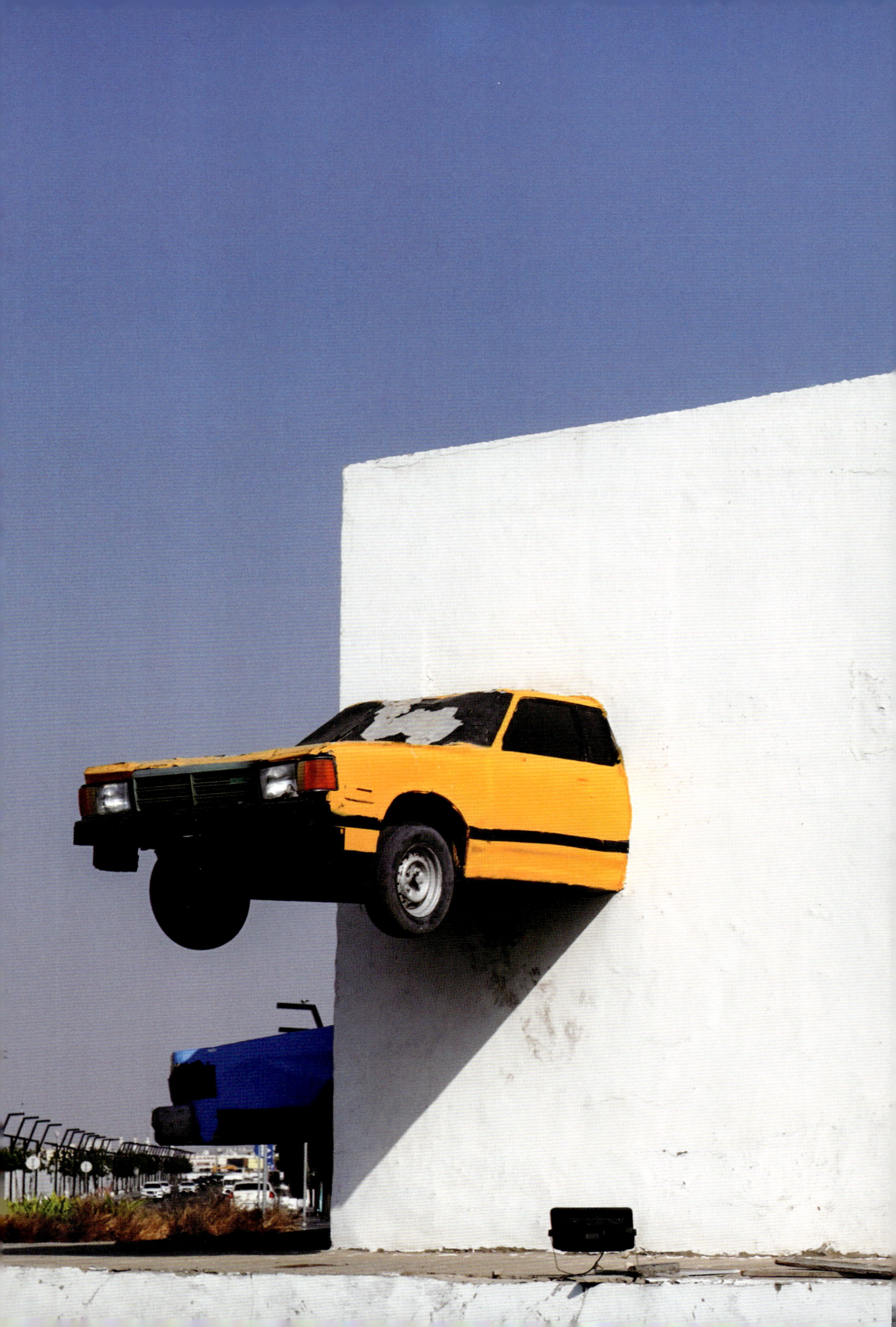

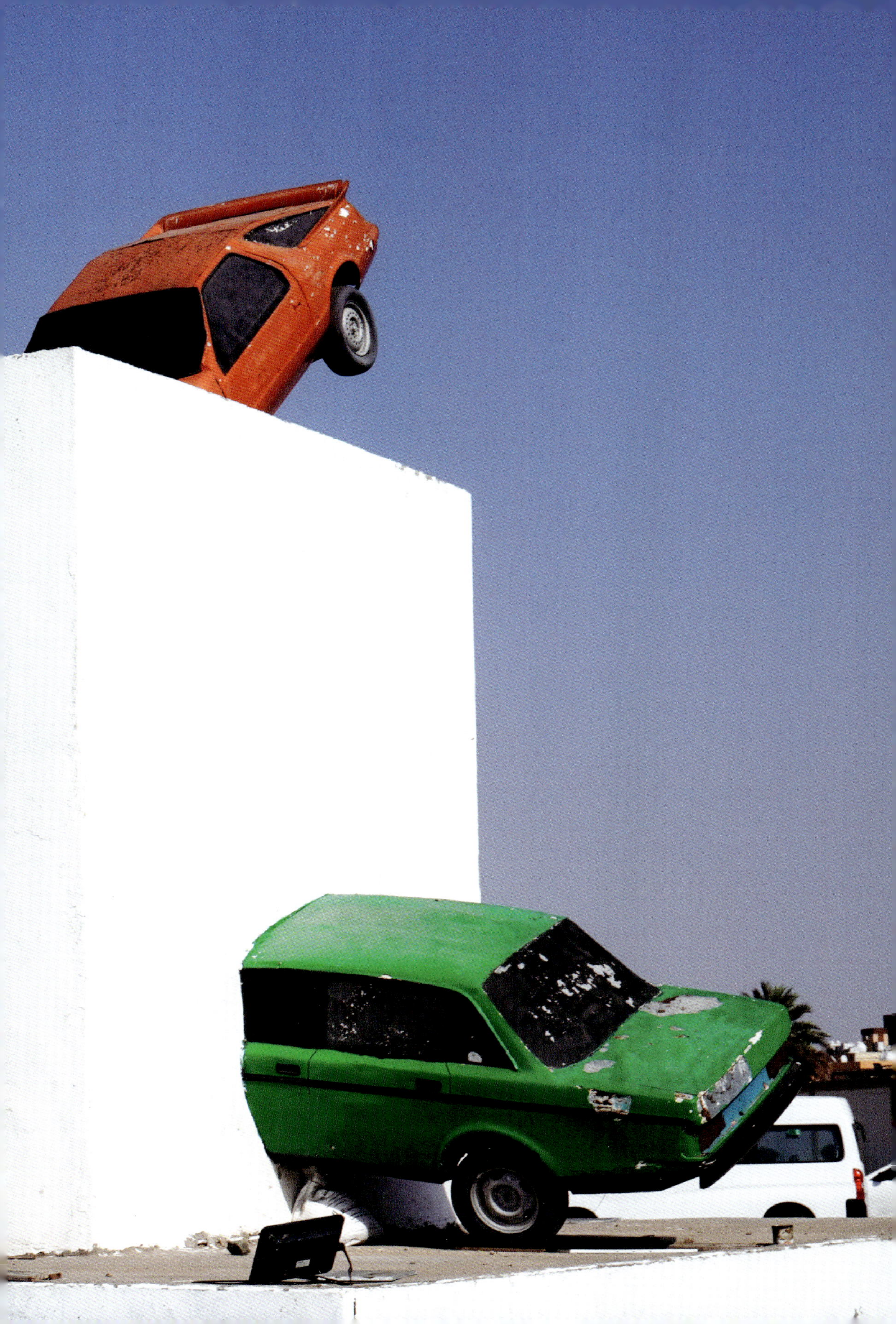

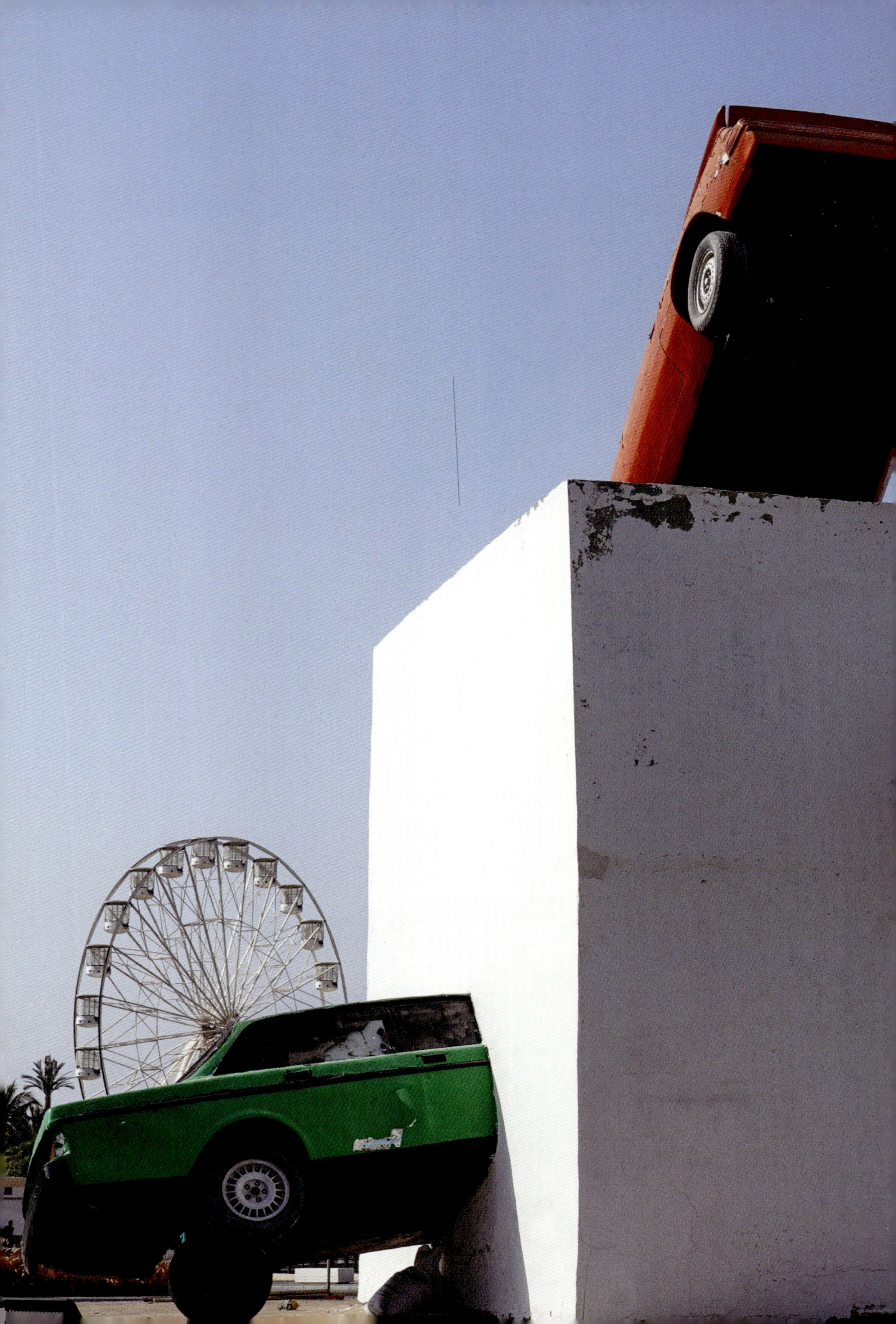

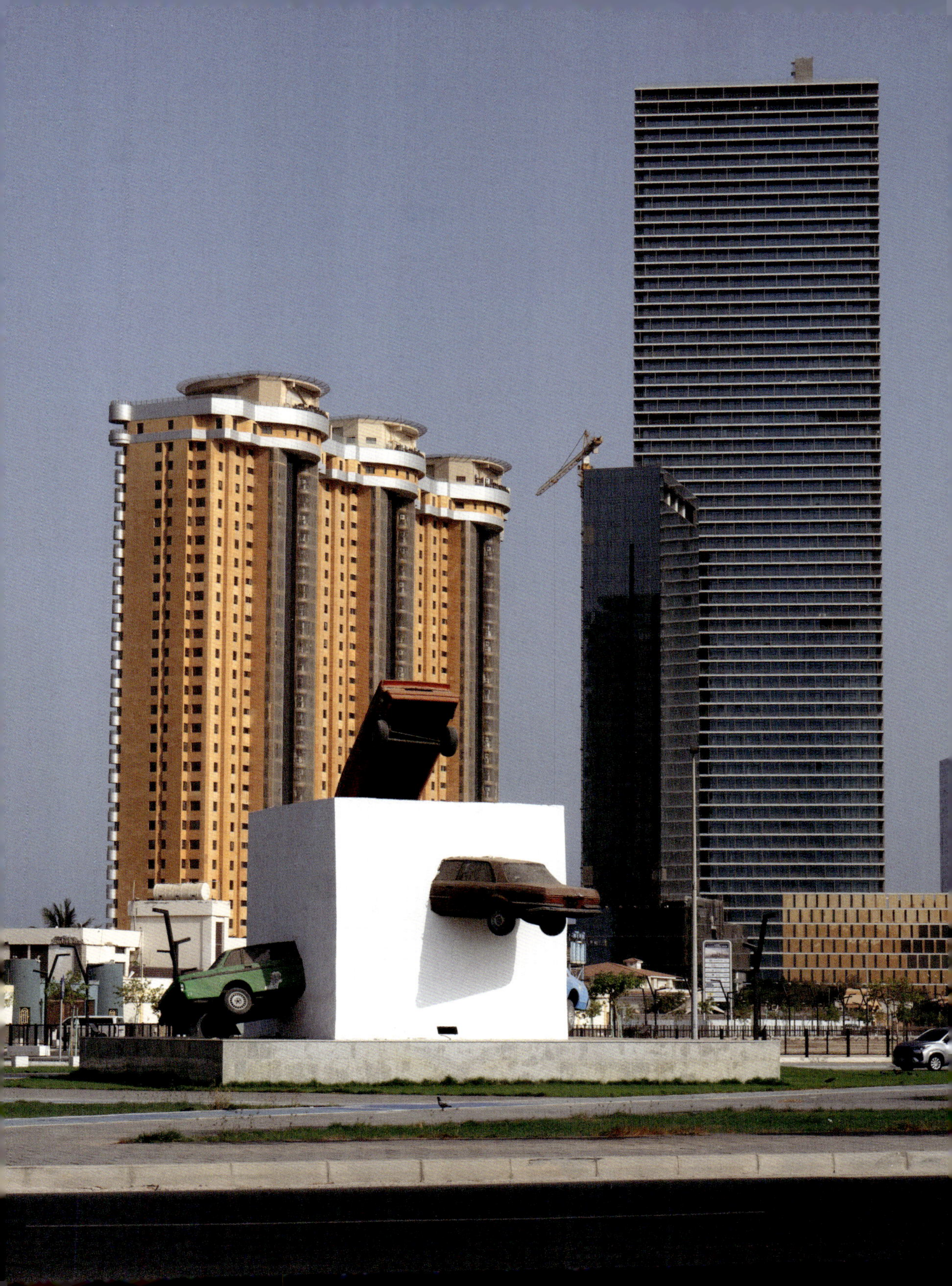

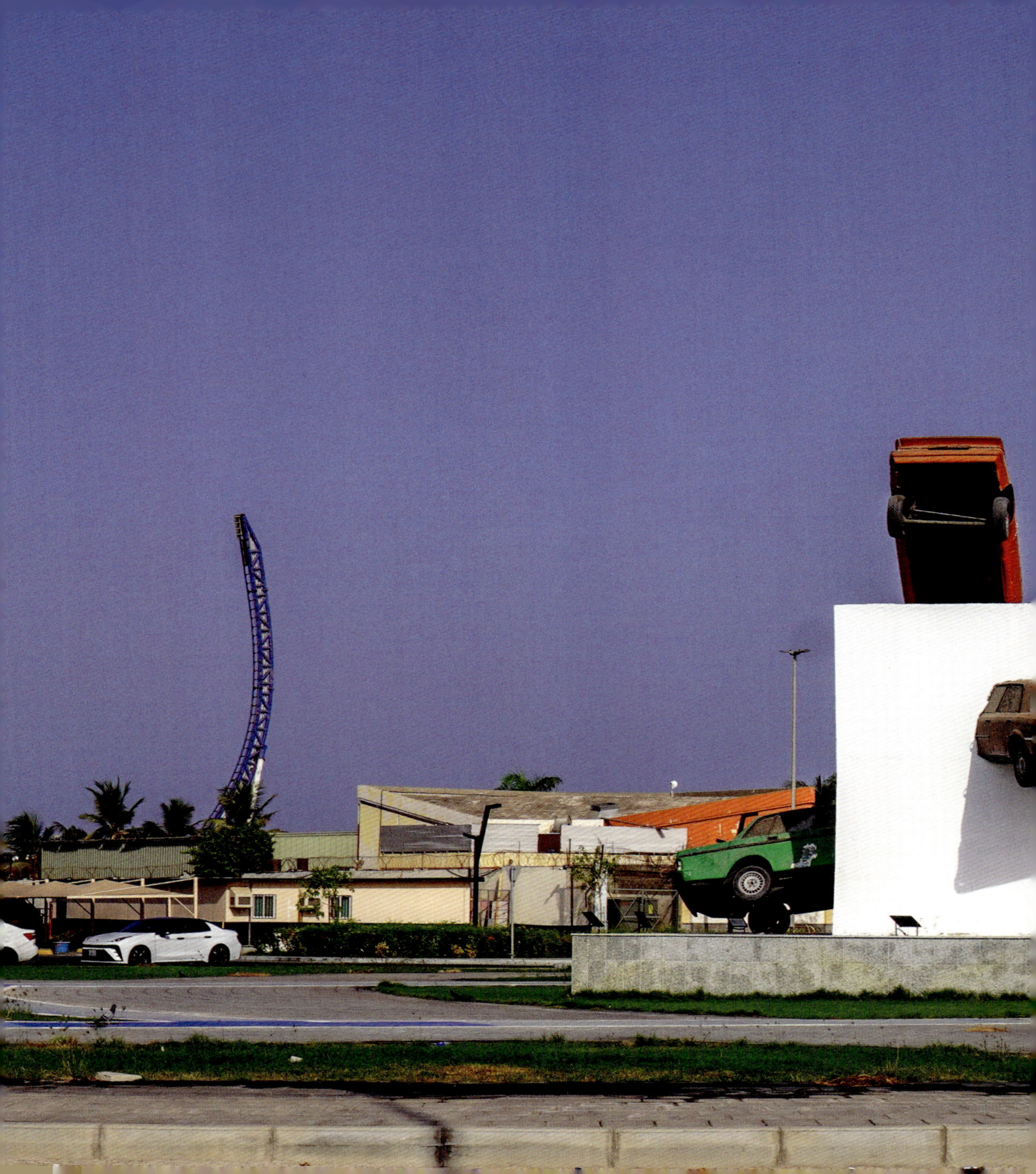

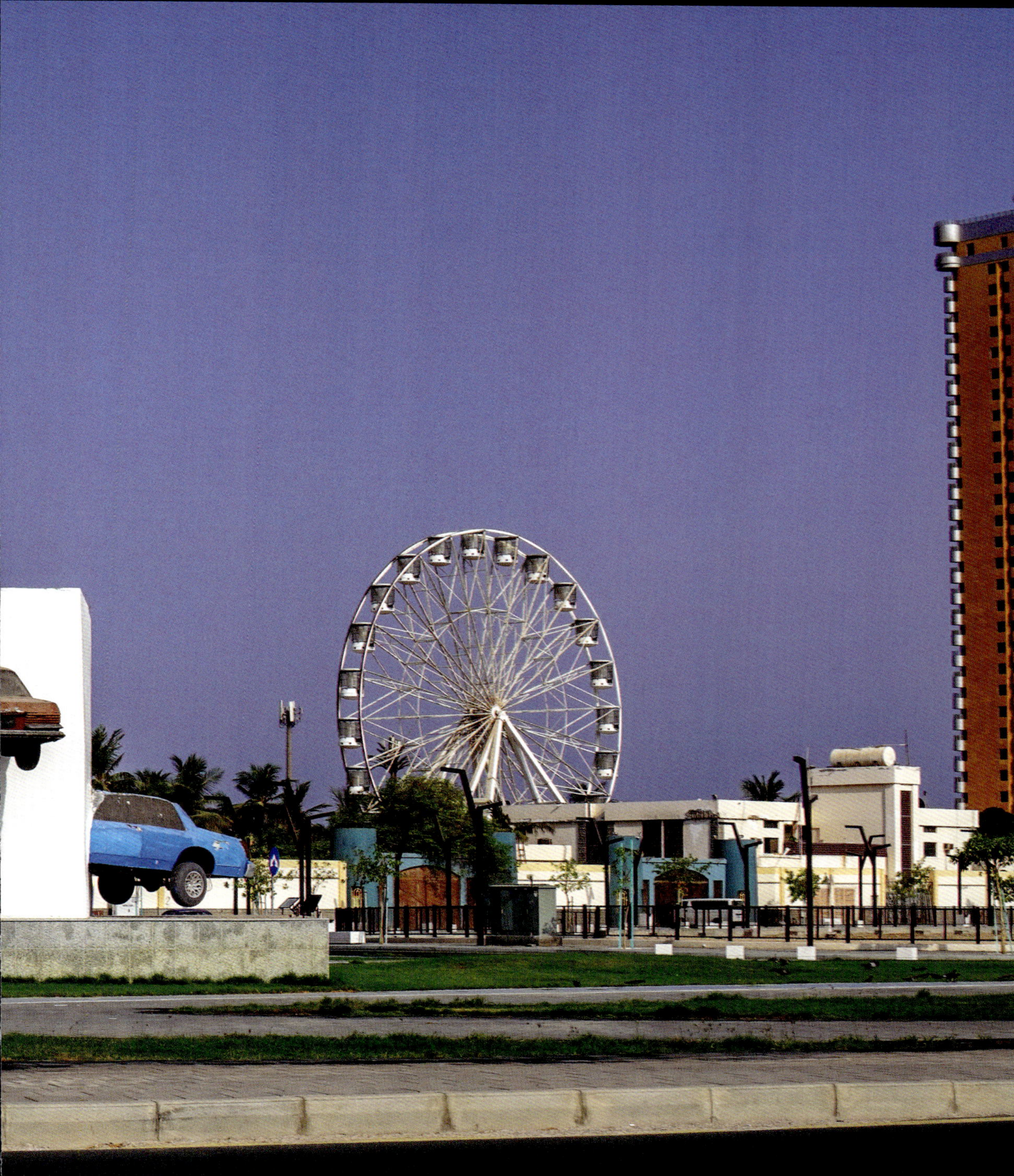

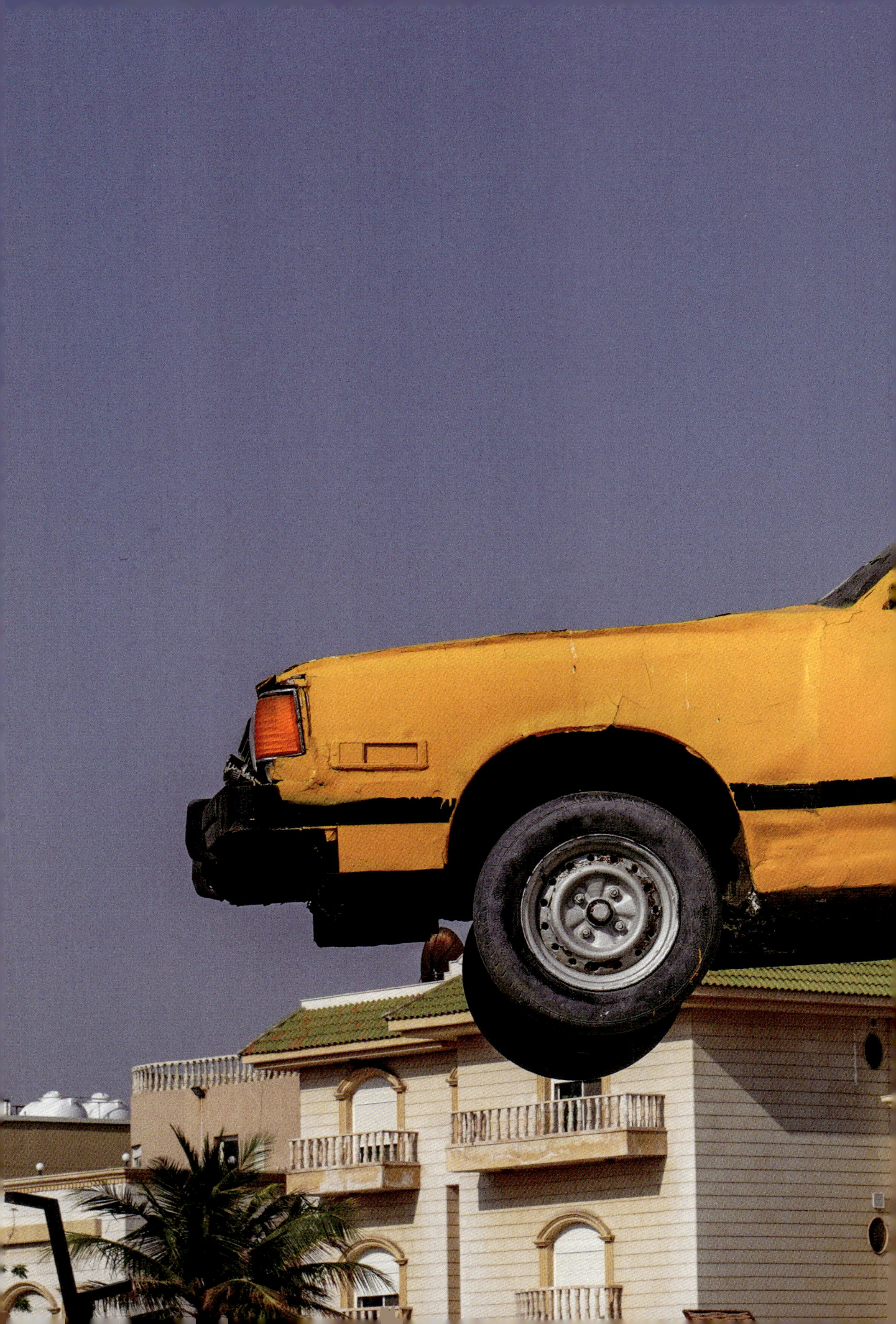

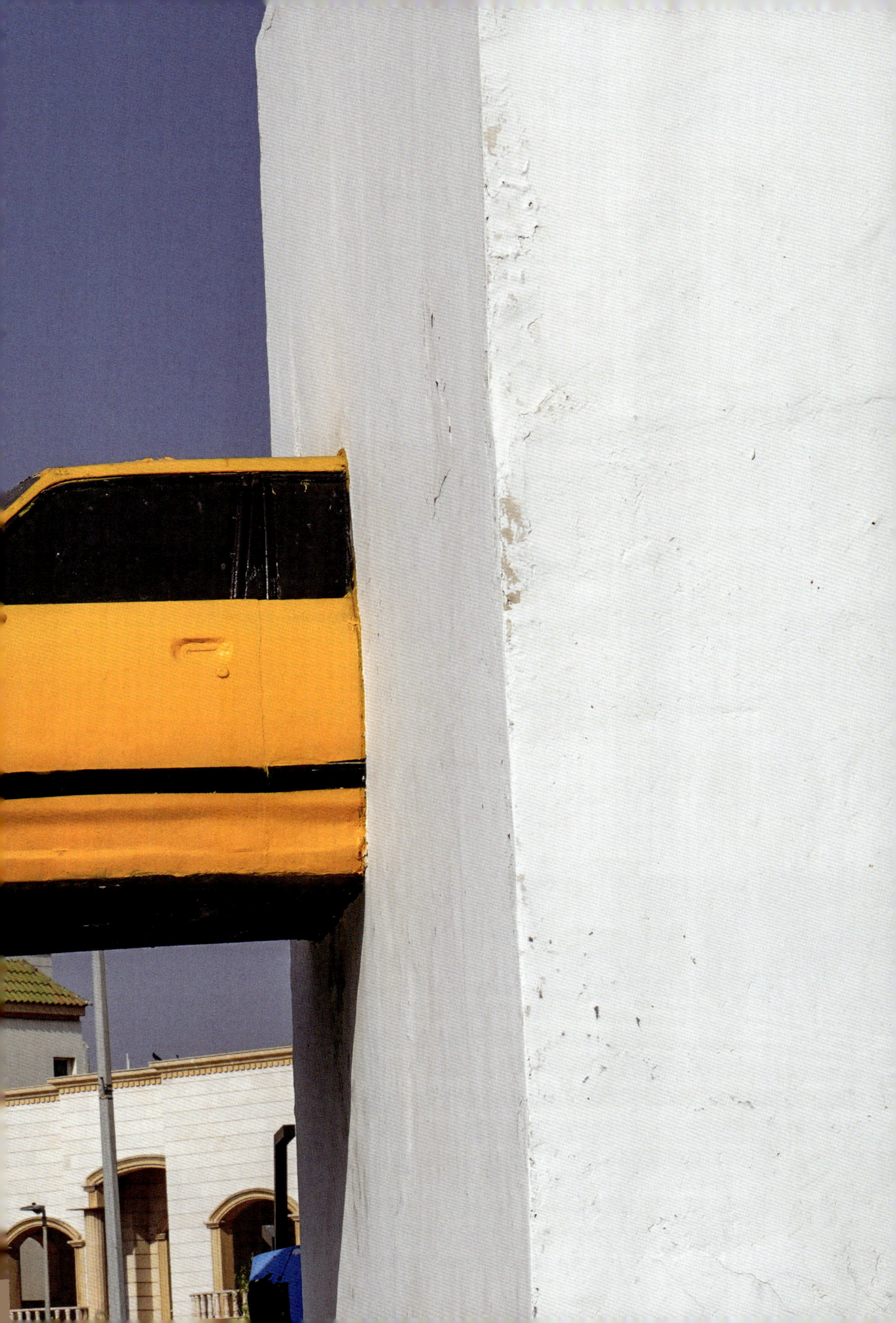

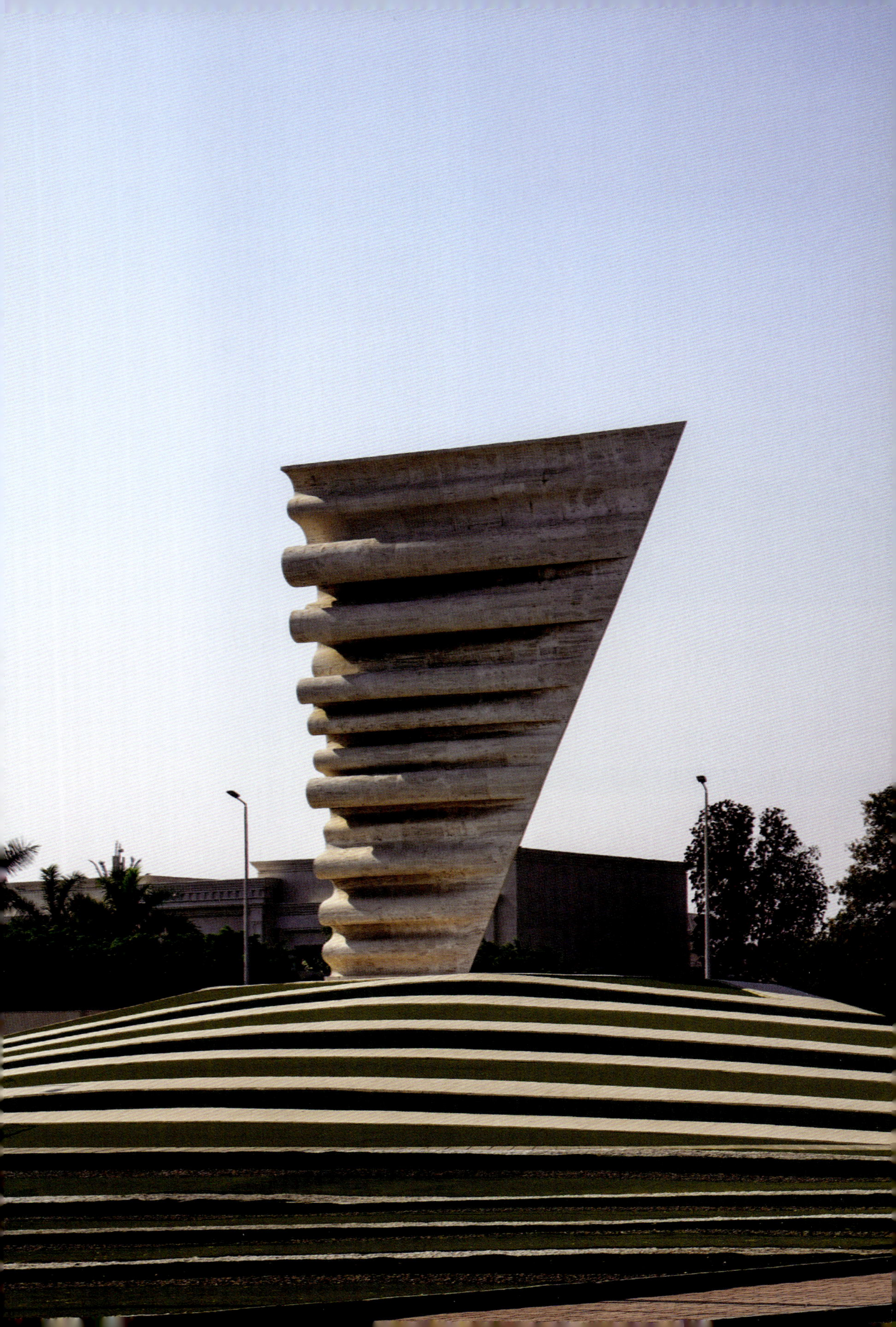

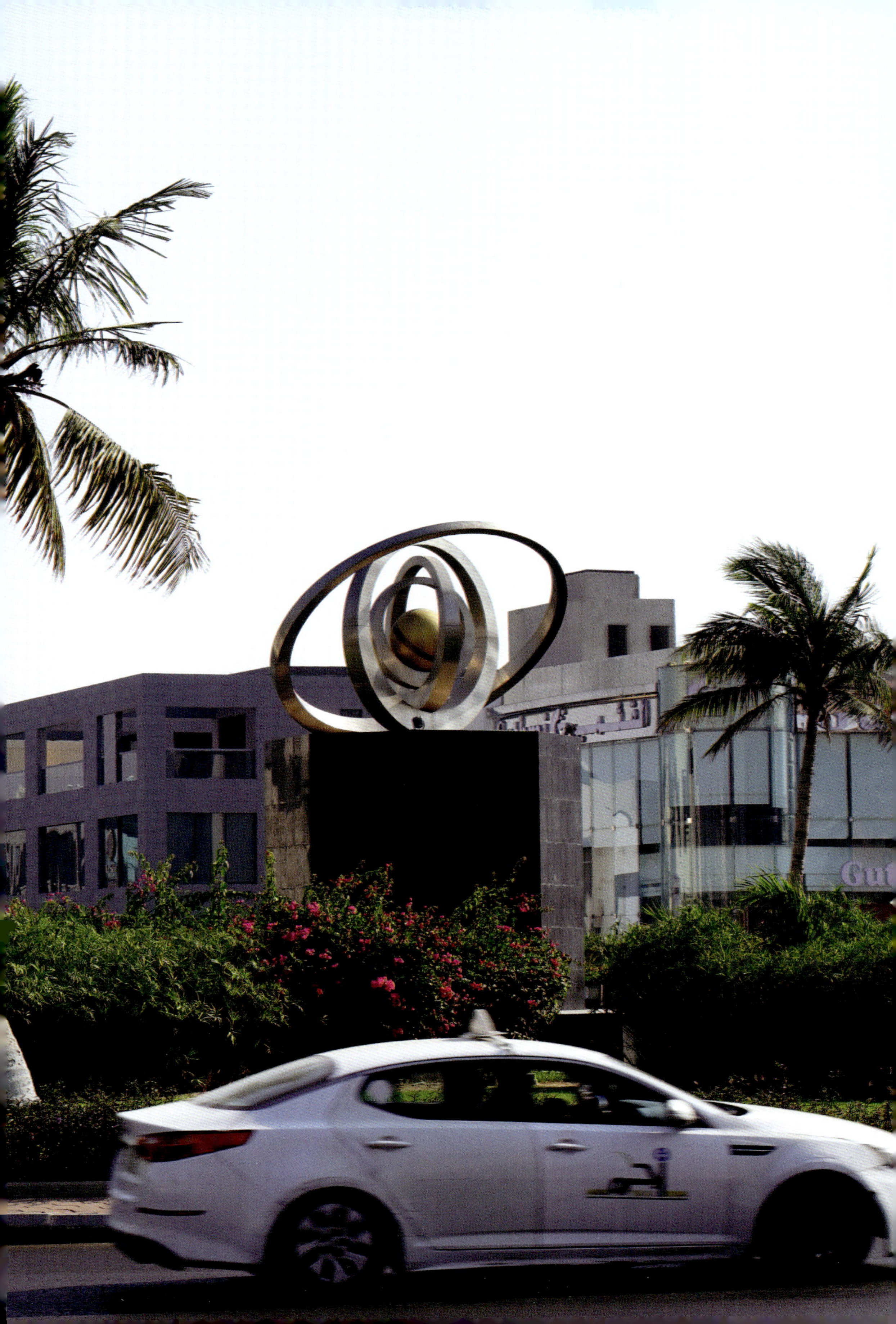

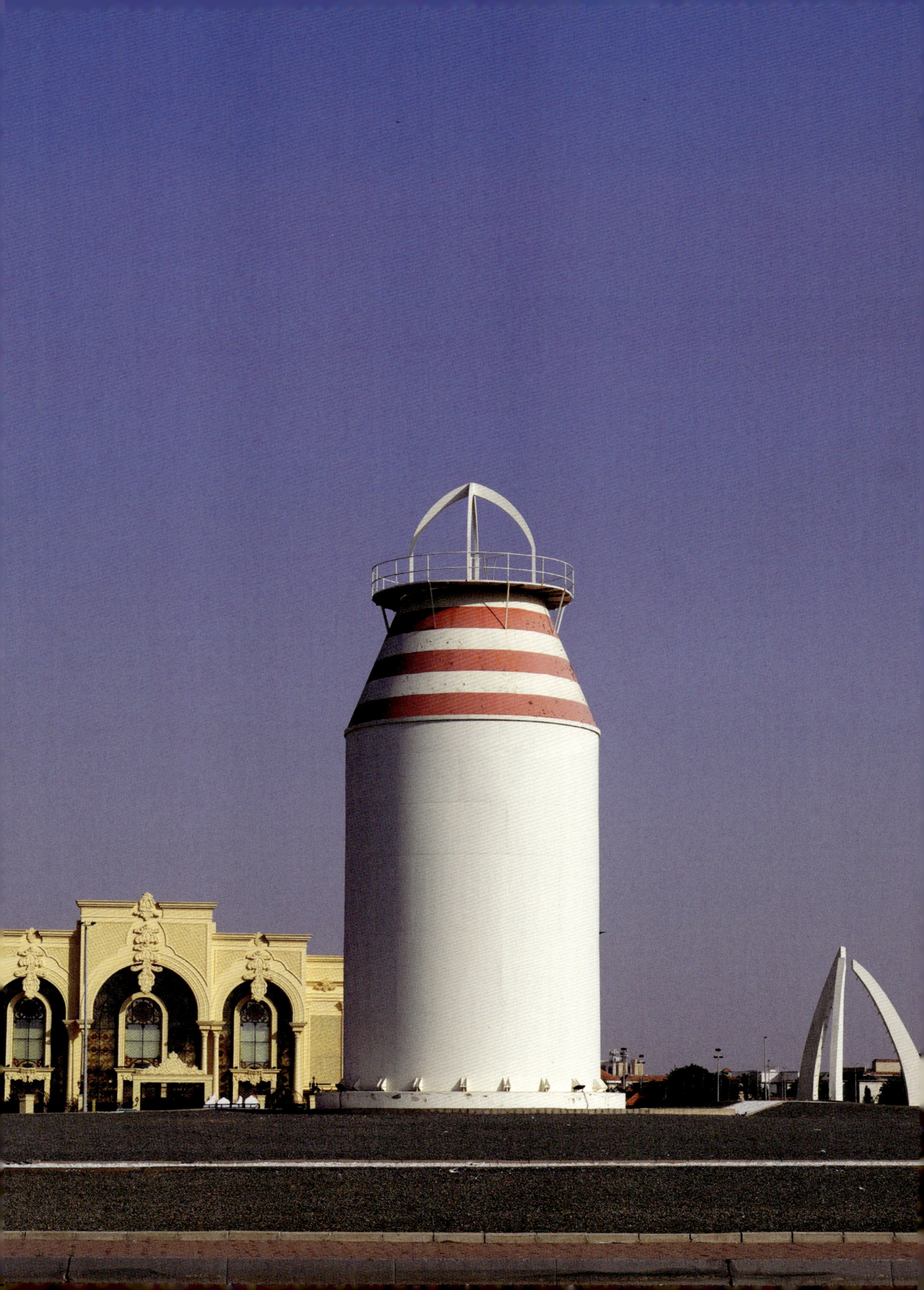

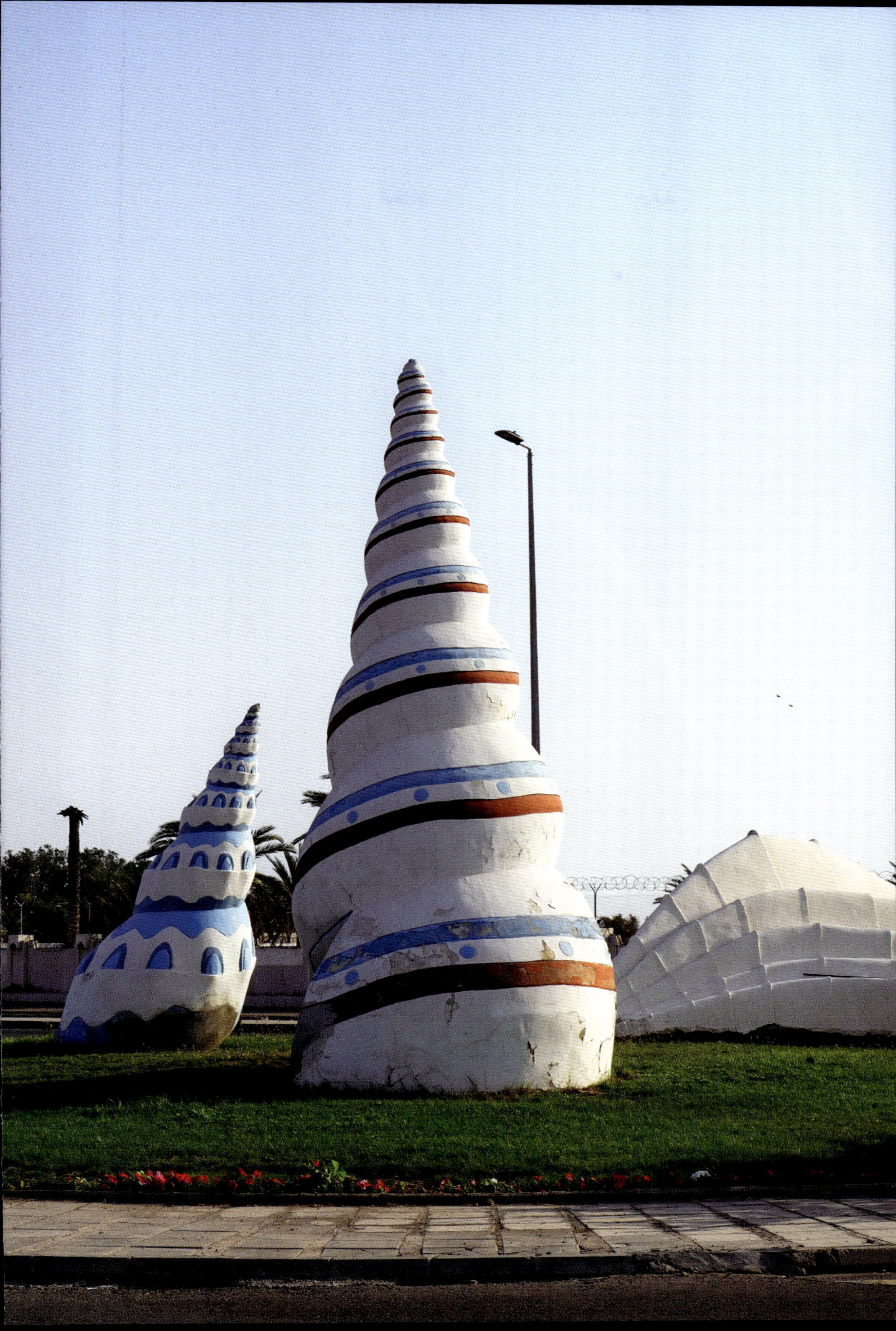

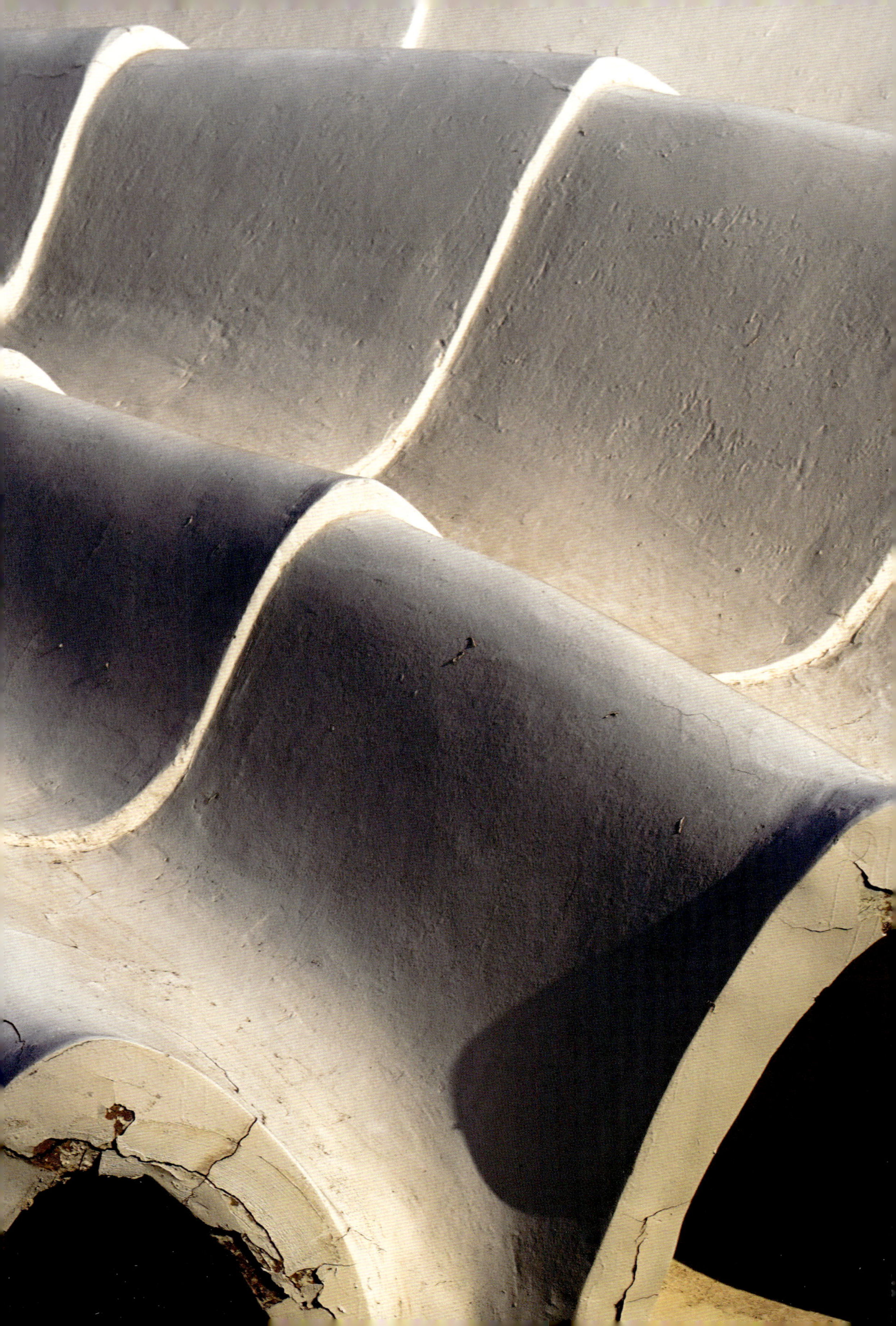

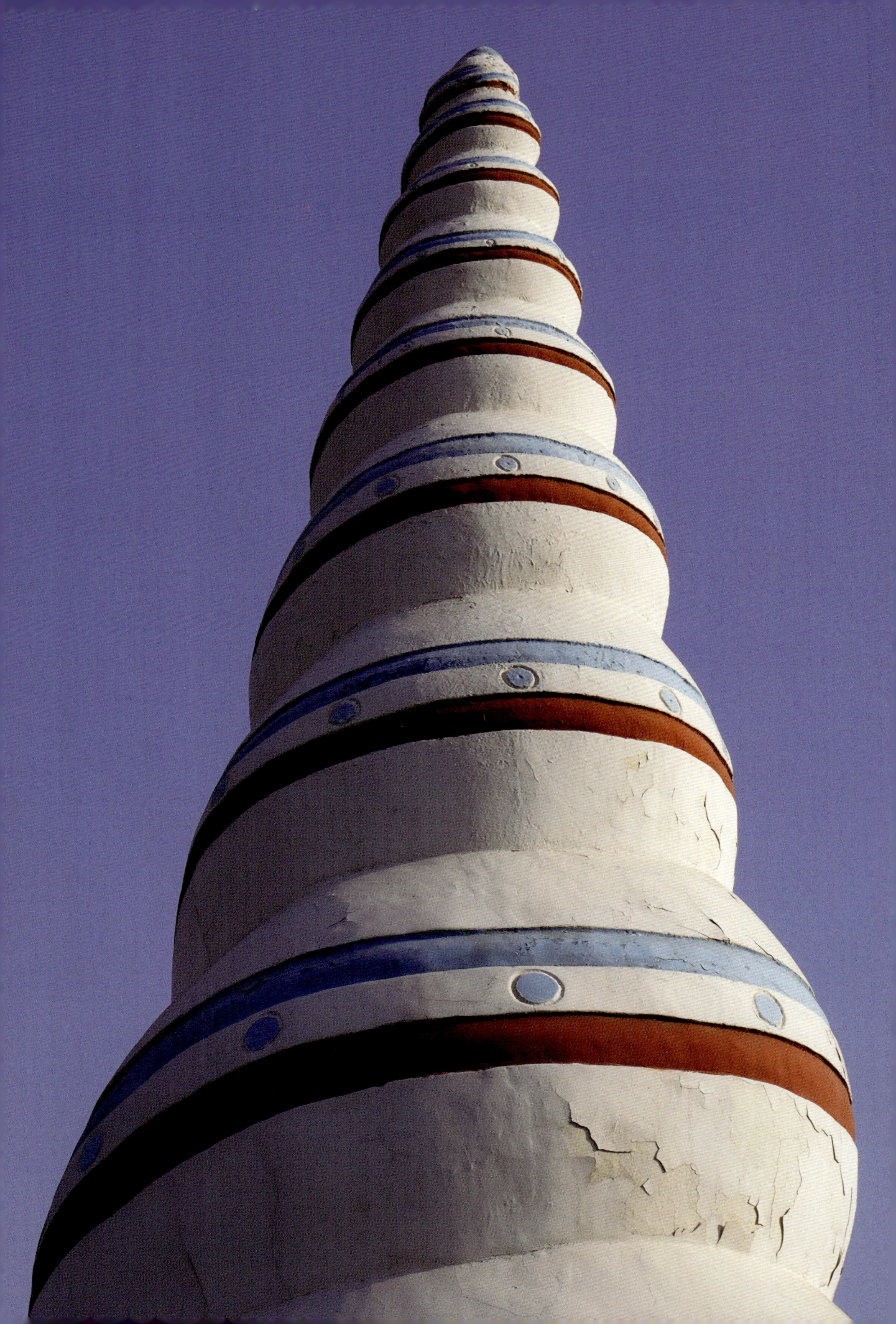

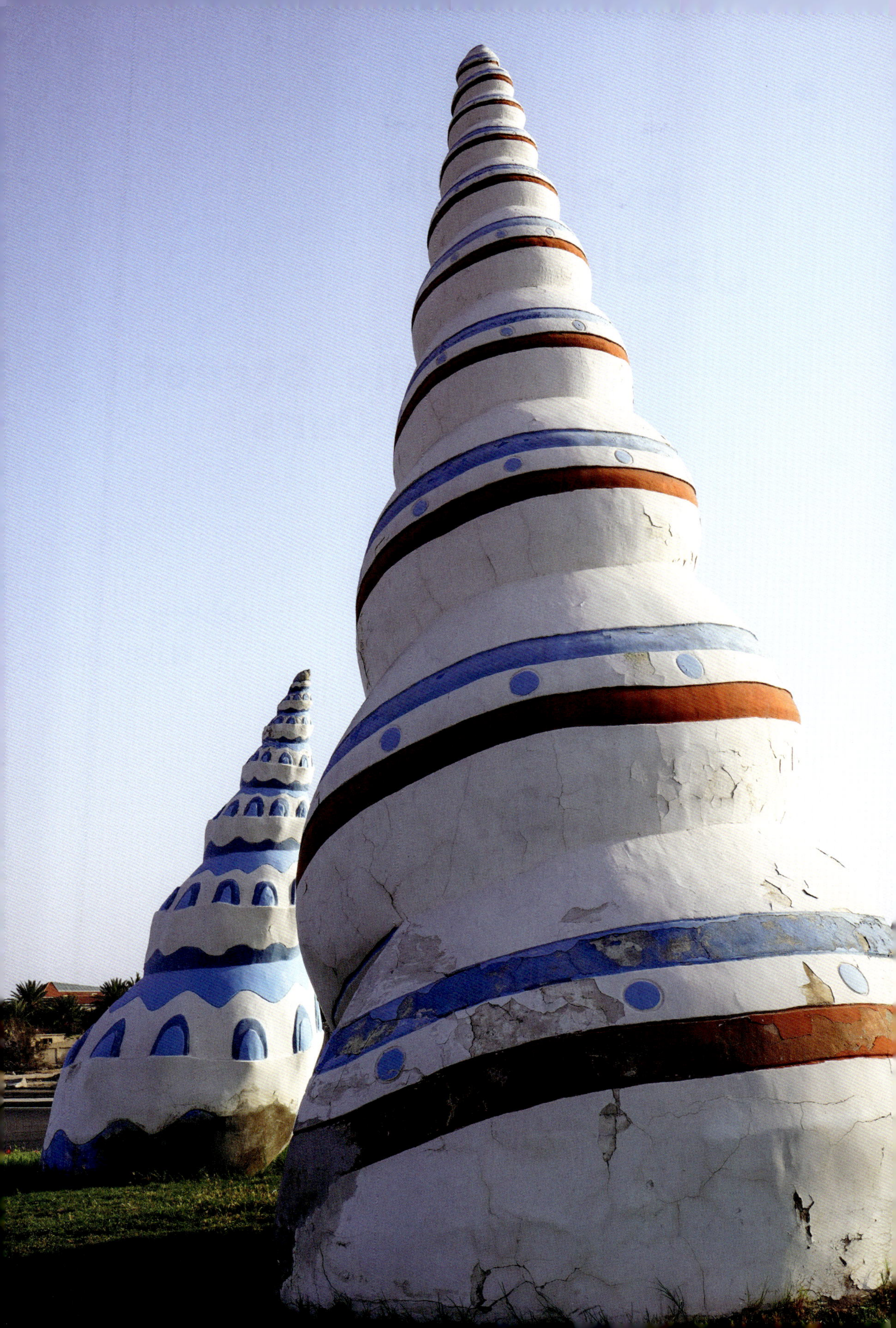

الشارع بين
الذاكرة والتحوّل

When the Street Became Ours

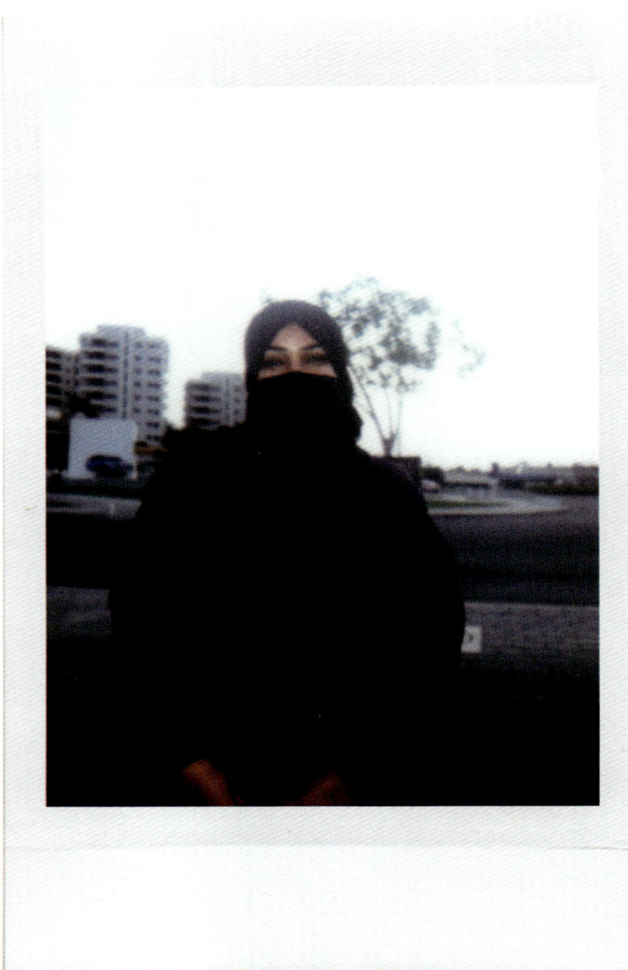

نسرين
Nisreen

Nouf Al-Harthi **How would you introduce yourself, Nisreen?**

Nisreen I'm Saudi, originally from Taif. After university, I settled in Jeddah. I studied Business Administration. When women were allowed to drive, I thought, Why not? I started working through ride-hailing apps. I love driving, it connects me to the city and its people.

Nouf **Did your career begin behind the wheel, or were you in another field before that?**

Nisreen I used to work in another sector, but I stopped about nine years ago. When women were permitted to drive[1], I felt I'd found my place. I bought a car, started driving, and thank God, I have a steady income.

Nouf **Take us back to that first moment of independence. How did your journey with driving truly begin, and when did that chapter happen for you?**

Nisreen It started in the United States. That's where I really learned to be independent. I was studying in Michigan and thought, "Why not buy a car and learn to drive"? My friends encouraged me, and soon I was driving them

نوف الحارثي **كيف تحبي تعرّفي عن نفسك نسرين؟**

نسرين أنا سعودية، أصلي من الطائف. بعد الجامعة استقريت في جدة. وانتهيت من الماجستير في إدارة أعمال. لما سمحوا للنساء بالقيادة قلت: ليه ما أجرب؟ وبدأت أشتغل عن طريق تطبيقات التوصيل. وأنا أحب السواقة، أحسها تقرّبني من المدينة والناس.

نوف **عملتي بشكل مستقل في السواقة ولا كنتِ في مجال ثاني؟**

نسرين كنت أشتغل في مجال ثاني، لكن وقفت من حوالي تسع سنوات. لما سمحوا لنا بالسواقة[1] حسّيت إن هذا مكاني. اشتريت سيارة وبدأت أسوق، والحمد لله عندي دخل ثابت من هذا الشغل.

نوف **رجّعينا لأول إحساس لك مع الطريق. كيف ومتى بدأت علاقتك الحقيقية بالسواقة؟**

نسرين البداية كانت في أمريكا. هناك تعلمت الاستقلال الحقيقي. كنت أدرس في ميشيغان وقلت أشتري سيارة وأتعلم أسوق لنفسي. صديقاتي شجعوني، وصرت أوصلهم للجامعة والمول، وأحيانًا أكسب فلوس كسوّاقة غير رسمية. التجربة أعطتني ثقة كبيرة. كان هذا تقريبًا سنة 2000.

to campus and to the mall, even making some good money as an informal driver. That whole experience gave me a lot of confidence. It was around 2000.

Nouf **And after you returned to Saudi Arabia, how did your relationship with the road evolve once the driving decision was made?**

Nisreen What motivated me was how organized the streets became. The monitoring systems, the discipline, and people's respect. Everything became structured and safer. This gave women a real chance to prove themselves. The number of female drivers is huge now[2].

Nouf **You've mentioned change. How would you describe the way Jeddah's streets themselves have transformed?**

Nisreen Completely. Before, there was only one road and constant traffic. Now there are bridges, tunnels, and exits. You can reach Mecca from different directions. The whole network is connected.

Nouf **When you're driving today, how do you perceive Jeddah?**

نسرين فرق كبير. قبل كانوا يتعبوا والله يعطيهم العافية بس اليوم القيادة سهلة وآمنة، وتعطيك إحساس بالقوة والتمكين.

نوف **وأنتِ تعبرين شوارع جدة يوميًا، كيف تتخيّلين مستقبل المدينة؟**

نسرين مو جدة بس، المملكة كلها. عدد السكان يكبر، ومعه لازم تكبر الطرق والخدمات. الطريق هو أساس الحياة اليومية؛ يربط الشغل بالبيت، والمدرسة بالحي، والناس ببعض. إذا كان التخطيط ذكي، تصير الحياة أسهل وأهدى. أنا متفائلة، لأن اللي نشوفه اليوم يدل إننا ماشيين بهذا الاتجاه.

نوف **أغرب موقف مرّ عليك؟**

نسرين كثير أجانب يستغربوا من الطرق. يقولوا: "شوارعكم مرة واسعة!" يتفاجأوا من عدد المسارات. هذا برأيي دليل على التطور اللي قاعد يصير بخدمات شوارعنا.

نوف **هل يخطر على بالك مواقف صعبة في عملك؟**

نسرين ولا شي كبير أو خطير، بس الزحمة ووقت الذروة، ولكن كمان هذا جدًا طبيعي.

نوف **نحن الآن في حي الحمراء، اللي كثير يشوفوه قلب جدة[3]. لكن إذا سألتك: كيف تقرئين ذاكرة المدينة من خلال معالمها؟**

Nisreen — It's totally different. Streets used to be narrow with one way in and out. Now you can choose your route. 70, 60, King Fahd, and King Abdullah roads. There's less congestion, and technology makes everything easier.

Nouf — **When women couldn't drive, the route and the ride were in someone else's hands. Now you control it. How does that shift feel?**

Nisreen — In the past, they struggled. Now everything is organized and safe, so driving is smooth and empowering.

Nouf — **Looking ahead, how do you imagine the future of Jeddah?**

Nisreen — Not just Jeddah, the whole Kingdom. With the population growing, everything must keep up, especially the roads. Roads are essential for work, school, and daily life. If planning is smart, life becomes simpler. I'm optimistic about the future.

Nouf — **Every driver has stories that linger. What's the strangest thing that's ever happened to you on the road?**

نوف — **وبعد رجوعك للسعودية؟ كيف تغيرت علاقتك بالطريق؟**

نسرين — اللي شجعني هو التنظيم. الشوارع صارت مرتبة، في أنظمة ومراقبة واحترام. كل شيء صار أوضح وأكثر أمان. هذا أعطى المرأة فرصة تثبت نفسها. واليوم شوفي عدد السواقات سواء كعمل أو بشكل شخصي كبير جدًا.

نوف — **كيف تشوفي تغيّر شوارع جدة؟**

نسرين — تغيّرت جدة بالكامل. قبل كان طريق واحد وزحمة دايم. اليوم في جسور وأنفاق ومخارج. تروحي مكة من أكثر من اتجاه. وشبكة المدن كلها مترابطة، وأعداد النساء اللي يسوقوا زادت بشكل كبير[2].

نوف — **ذكرتي التغيير في الشوارع ممكن تشرحي هذا أكثر؟**

نسرين — الشوارع كلها صارت مختلفة تمامًا. زمان أتذكر الشوارع ضيقة ومدخل ومخرج واحد. الآن أنتِ تختاري طريقك: السبعين، الستين، الملك فهد، الملك عبدالله. الزحمة أقل والتقنية عالأكيد سهّلت كل شيء.

نوف — **زمان المشوار كان بيد غيرك، بس اليوم أنتِ المتحكمة فيه. كيف توصفي هذا الإحساس؟**

Nisreen — Many foreign passengers are amazed by our roads. They say, “Your roads are huge”. They’re surprised by how wide the lanes are and compare them to their countries. They often say, ‘Seven lanes – we’ve never seen that. It’s proof of how far we’ve come.

Nouf — **And what about difficult moments? Any that stayed with you?**

Nisreen — Honestly, nothing major. Maybe just rush hour traffic, which is normal in any city.

Nouf — **We’re driving through Al Hamra now, a neighbourhood many consider the heart of Jeddah[3]. As someone who drives daily, how do you read the city through its landmarks and roundabouts?**

Nisreen — I love Al-Falak, the Engineers’ Tools, and the Camel in Obhur. Every roundabout has its own story. Passing them feels like entering another world. They’re part of Jeddah’s identity.

Nouf — **Tell me a story tied to one of these places.**

Nisreen — The Engineers’ Tools Roundabout has a memory I love. My father once hosted a big family gathering.

نوف — **نحنا قابلناك في المطار[4]، هل في نساء غيرك يشتغلون في نفس المجال؟ وكيف تجربتهم؟**

نسرين — أكيد، مو بس أنا. كل وحدة لها طريقتها وقصتها الخاصة. بعضهم يمرون بتجارب سهلة، وبعضهم أصعب، لكن بالنهاية كلنا نسوق ونعيش الشارع كل يوم.

نوف — **وهل مشاويرك بس في جدة؟**

نسرين — أغلبها جدة ومكة، لكن رحت ينبع، المدينة، الليث، القنفذة، والطائف. أول مرة سقت في ينبع انبهرت بالتنظيم. التطور هناك مو بس في جدة ومكة.

نوف — **استخدمتي عبارة «تجربة الشارع» أكثر من مرة، بس إيش تعني لك هذي التجربة بالأساس؟**

نسرين — الشارع زي البيت. شفتي كيف تلاقي في البيت راحة وأمان، الطريق لازم يكون كذا. لأننا نقضي فيه وقت طويل. إذا ما كان آمن، ما بتقدري تسوقي بثقة. لما يكون منظم، تحسي براحة. والحمدلله اليوم الشارع يعطيني ثقة وأمان.

نوف — **واضح معالم المدينة تعني لك كثير. بس كيف تشوفيها؟**

We were on our way, and I called him, saying, “Baba, I’m at the Engineers’ Tools Roundabout.” He didn’t know the name. I reminded him it’s the one with the compass and triangle, and he laughed. These sculptures shape how we remember the city.

Nouf **As the city evolves, how does that affect the way you navigate it and the way you remember it, too?**

Nisreen Some places remind me of the old days. At the same time, Jeddah has grown so much. Some neighbourhoods didn’t exist before. Even though I live here, some places still feel new to me. My experience is a mix of familiar and new. People ask if I’m afraid to drive at night. I tell them not to be afraid, explaining that the roads are safe and well-lit.

Nouf **We first met you at the airport[4]. Are there many other women who share this line of work with you?**

Nisreen Of course. Every woman has her own story. Some have it easier than others, but we’re all out here driving every day.

نسرين معالم جدة تحكيها قبل شوارعها. دواراتها، مثل الفلك، والهندسة، والجمل في أبحر، كلها محطات في الذاكرة. كل معلم وكل شارع له قصته الخاصة. وأنتِ تمرّين فيها تحسين وكأنك تدخلين عالم مختلف في كل مرة. كل معلم وشارع له قصة، وكلها جزء من هوية جدة.

نوف **قلتي لكل شارع ومعلم موقف مرتبط فيه، وش المواقف اللي ممكن تفكري فيها الآن؟**

نسرين فيه قصة مضحكة مرتبطة بدوار الهندسة. مرة كنت رايحة عزيمة عائلية وكلمت أبوي قلت له: أنا عند الهندسة. قال: ما أعرفه. قلت له: يا بابا، اللي فيه مثلث وبرجل قياس، وقعد يضحك قال: آه تذكرته. سبحان الله رمزية المجسمات هذي تثبت في الذاكرة.

نوف **ومع تغيّر معالم المدينة، كيف توصفي تجربة تذكرها؟**

نسرين التغييرات تأثر. في أماكن تذكرني بالأيام القديمة، وبنفس الوقت جدة صارت مرة كبيرة. فيه أحياء ما كانت موجودة، وإذا مشيت فيها أحس نفسي أتعلمها من جديد، حتى وأنا ساكنة هنا. أحيانًا أحد يقول لي «أنا ساكن هنا» وأرد «والله ما أعرف المنطقة». تجربتي صارت مزيج بين أماكن قديمة أعرفها وأماكن جديدة قاعدة أكتشفها. الناس يسألوني: «ما تخافين تسوقين بالليل؟» أرد: «أخاف من إيش؟ الطريق منوّر وآمن». وهذا خلّى تجربتنا كنساء أسهل وأجمل مع التغيّر.

Nouf **Do you mostly work in Jeddah?**

Nisreen Mostly Jeddah and Mecca, but I've also driven to Yanbu, Medina, Al Lith, Al Qunfudhah, and Taif. I was amazed the first time I drove in Yanbu. The streets and signals were well organized. Development isn't just in Jeddah and Mecca.

Nouf **You've spoken beautifully about "the street experience." What does that phrase mean to you personally?**

Nisreen The street, to me, is as essential as home. Home gives comfort and security, and the road should, too. We spend so much time on it. If it doesn't feel safe, you can't drive confidently. When the road is smooth and organised, you feel at ease. For me, the street gives a sense of confidence and safety.

Nouf **As we pass these roundabouts, I can see how much they mean to you. How do you interpret them - their sculptures, their presence?**

Nisreen Maps only come alive through streets, lines, and edges. My mom always asks why I drive so much. I tell her she doesn't know how much I enjoy being

اليوم التقنية سهّلت علينا الوصول، لكن الهوية ما اختفت. صارت تظهر في سلوكنا داخل الشارع: في احترامنا للطريق، وفي تعاملنا مع بعض. ديننا وثقافتنا حاضرين حتى في التفاصيل الصغيرة، مثل حرص الناس على النظام والنظافة.

نوف **وكأن السيارة نفسها أصبحت جزءًا من هذا التعبير؟**

نسرين بالضبط. السيارة صارت امتداد للشخص. أهل جدة يهتمون بسياراتهم لأنها تعكسهم. أنا مثلاً أغسل سيارتي كل يومين، لأن السيارة المتسخة تزعجني. كثير من الزوار يلاحظون هذا الشيء. ما يهم إن السيارة تكون جديدة أو فاخرة، الأهم تكون نظيفة ومهتم بها. هذا نوع من الاحترام، للنفس وللآخرين.

نوف **هل هذا الاهتمام يولّد ضغطًا اجتماعيًا أحيانًا؟**

نسرين ممكن، لكني أشوفه غالبًا كمنافسة صحية. لما أشوف شخص مرتب، ما أحس بضيق، بالعكس أتحفّز أكون أفضل. جدة فيها هذه الروح؛ ناسها راقية ومنفتحة وتهتم بالتفاصيل. وهذا ينعكس على الشارع، وعلى شكل المدينة، وعلى الإحساس العام فيها.

نوف **إحنا الآن في طريق الملك. كيف تشوفيه؟**

نسرين طريق الملك هو عمود جدة الفقري. يوصل كل شيء مهم. أكثر شيء يأثر فيني هنا هو دوار الكرة الأرضية. كل مرة أمره أتأمل عظمة الله.

on the road. Even during rush hour, I'm happy. The roundabout sculptures, Astronomy, Science, Accident, and Camel, are etched in my memory. We navigate by roundabouts, not street names. Prince Majid Square feels like a work of art in the middle of the city. Art is everywhere, even if we don't notice it. And when people talk about Jeddah, the first thing they mention is the sea. I love going to the roundabout called "where boats gather in the evening."

Nouf **You talk about this place with a lot of feelings. What's your personal story with it?**

Nisreen I love this area. This is where Jeddah truly captures me, the boats, the sea. I can't imagine living away from it. For me, the sea is oxygen. Taif is beautiful, but Jeddah is something else. It's unique, with its people and its character. Many people call it Beverly Hills.

Nouf **That's a striking comparison. Why do you think people use it?**

Nisreen Because people believe we can be even better. The Kingdom is incomparable. Our development is authentically Arab identity. We preserve our

نسرين الخريطة حياتها بالشوارع. أمي دايم تقول لي: ليه تسوقي كثير؟ أقول لها: ما تعرفي قد إيش أحب الطريق. حتى في الزحمة أكون مبسوطة. ومعالم جدة من دوارات الفلك، التصادم، الجمل...محفورة في ذاكرتي. ونحنا نتحرك بالدوارات أكثر من أسماء الشوارع. ميدان الأمير ماجد كأنه لوحة فنية. والفن حولنا حتى لو ما انتبهنا. ولما الناس تذكر جدة، أول شيء يذكروه البحر والسمك. شوفي هذا الدوار أحبه، تجمع الزوارق في المساء.

نوف **مرة حابة كيف قاعدة تحكي عنها بإحساس.**

نسرين أحب المنطقة هذه. هنا جدة تمسّني فعليًا. البحر والمراكب. ما أقدر أتخيل نفسي بعيد عنها. البحر بالنسبة لي أكسجين. الطائف جميلة، بس جدة شيء ثاني. كثير ناس يقولولي إنها «بيفري هيلز».

نوف **عادي أسألك ليش ممكن يكون معيارنا «بيفري هيلز»؟**

نسرين لأنهم يشوفوا إننا نقدر نكون أفضل. طبعًا نحنا تطورنا بهوية عربية. ونحافظ على عاداتنا ونمشي للأمام. والتطور مو بس مباني بس بكل شي بالحياة.

نوف **ذكرتِ مسألة الحفاظ على الهوية. كيف تشوفين انعكاس الهوية في شوارع المدينة؟**

نسرين أجدادنا كانوا يهتدون بالنجوم ويعرفون الطريق من العلامات الطبيعية.

traditions while moving forward. Real development isn't just about buildings.

Nouf **We've spoken a lot about place and memory. How do you personally define identity, and how do you see it reflected in the city's streets?**

Nisreen Our grandparents lived simple lives, using the stars and compasses to find their way. Today, navigation is easier, but our identity remains in how we treat each other and respect the road. I lived in the United States and saw the difference. Here, our faith and culture guide us. Even though people care for their cars, it reflects our identity. From how we dress to how we behave to how the city looks, it's all connected.

Nouf **Cars are such a big part of the city's rhythm. How easy is it to find a good, clean car here? And what does "new and clean" mean to you?**

Nisreen People in Jeddah care about their cars. It's part of who they are. I wash my car every two days. A dirty car feels unpleasant. Many visitors notice how clean the cars are. And no, it doesn't have to be brand new. Although many people frequently change cars due to job-related offers. Cars are part of how people present themselves, and here, presentation matters.

Nouf **Do you think that culture around appearance creates pressure, or does it fuel something else?**

Nisreen It has an effect, but it's more like healthy competition. When I see someone well put together, I feel inspired to be better, not less. Jeddah has that energy. People are cultured, open-minded, and care about details. It shows in their clothes, speech, and behaviour.

Nouf **We're now on King Road, one of Jeddah's most well-known streets. From your perspective as a driver, how does the city reveal itself here?**

Nisreen King Road is like the spine of Jeddah. It connects everything important: hotels, hospitals, restaurants, and malls. What moves me most is the Globe Roundabout at the end. Every time I pass it, I reflect on God's greatness.

Nouf **Are there other places in the city that give you the same feeling?**

Nisreen The Camel Roundabout reminds me of our roots and heritage. It symbolizes our journey from camels and horses to cars today. I always imagine what travel was like back then. We're not far from the Corniche now. Do you ladies want to get out?

Nouf **Fourteen years behind the wheel is a long journey. How would you describe what it's given you?**

Nisreen Fourteen years is a collection of experiences that taught me something new at every stage. My personality grew with the road. I've lived through the late eighties, the early 2000s, and now 2025. I've witnessed massive change. Change can build you or break you. Driving is my comfort and my escape. I play music, open the window, and breathe. It has also become a way to connect with people. I've had many meaningful encounters with strangers. Every one of these years has made me love the road more.

Nouf **Before we wrap up, tell me about your road soundtrack. What's your road song?**

Nisreen That's easy. It's not Arabic. It's called Mirror[5]. It feels like part of the journey now. The lyrics touch me. The road becomes a mirror, reflecting my mood. The moment it plays, I feel like I'm entering another world. Mirror is the sound of the road.

وكيف بسط لنا هذه الأرض وسخرها لنا.

نوف **هل فيه أماكن ثانية تعطيك نفس الإحساس؟**

نسرين دوار الجمل يذكّرني بأصلنا. من الجِمال للسيارات. أتخيل كيف كان السفر والتنقل زمان والمشقة اللي فيهم.

نوف **14 سنة سواقة، إيش أعطتك؟**

نسرين 14 سنة تجارب. شخصيتي كبرت مع الطريق. عشت الثمانينات، الألفينات، واليوم 2025. شفت تغيّر كبير. السواقة راحتي وهروبي. أشغّل موسيقا، أفتح الشباك، وأتنفّس. وأيضًا صارت هي وسيلة تواصلي مع الناس. قابلت ناس كثير وكوّنت ذكريات جميلة. وكل سنة خلّتني أحب الطريق أكثر.

نوف **لو فيه أغنية الطريق ممكن ترشيحها وش بتكون؟**

نسرين سهلة. بس ترا مو أغنية عربية. اسمها Mirror[5]. أحسها جزء من الرحلة. الطريق يصير مرآة لمزاجي. أول ما تشتغل أحس إني دخلت عالم ثاني. Mirror هي صوت طريقي.

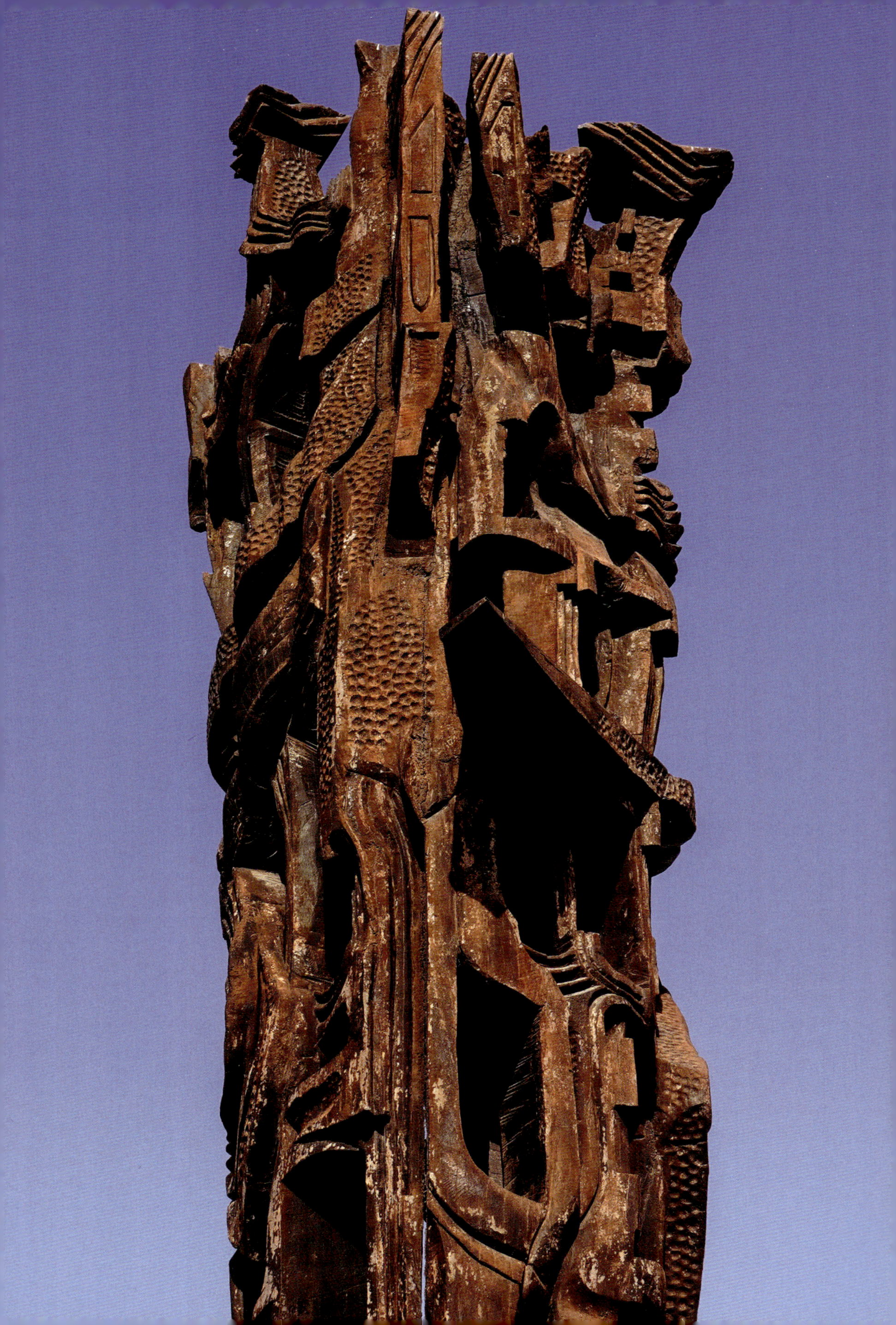

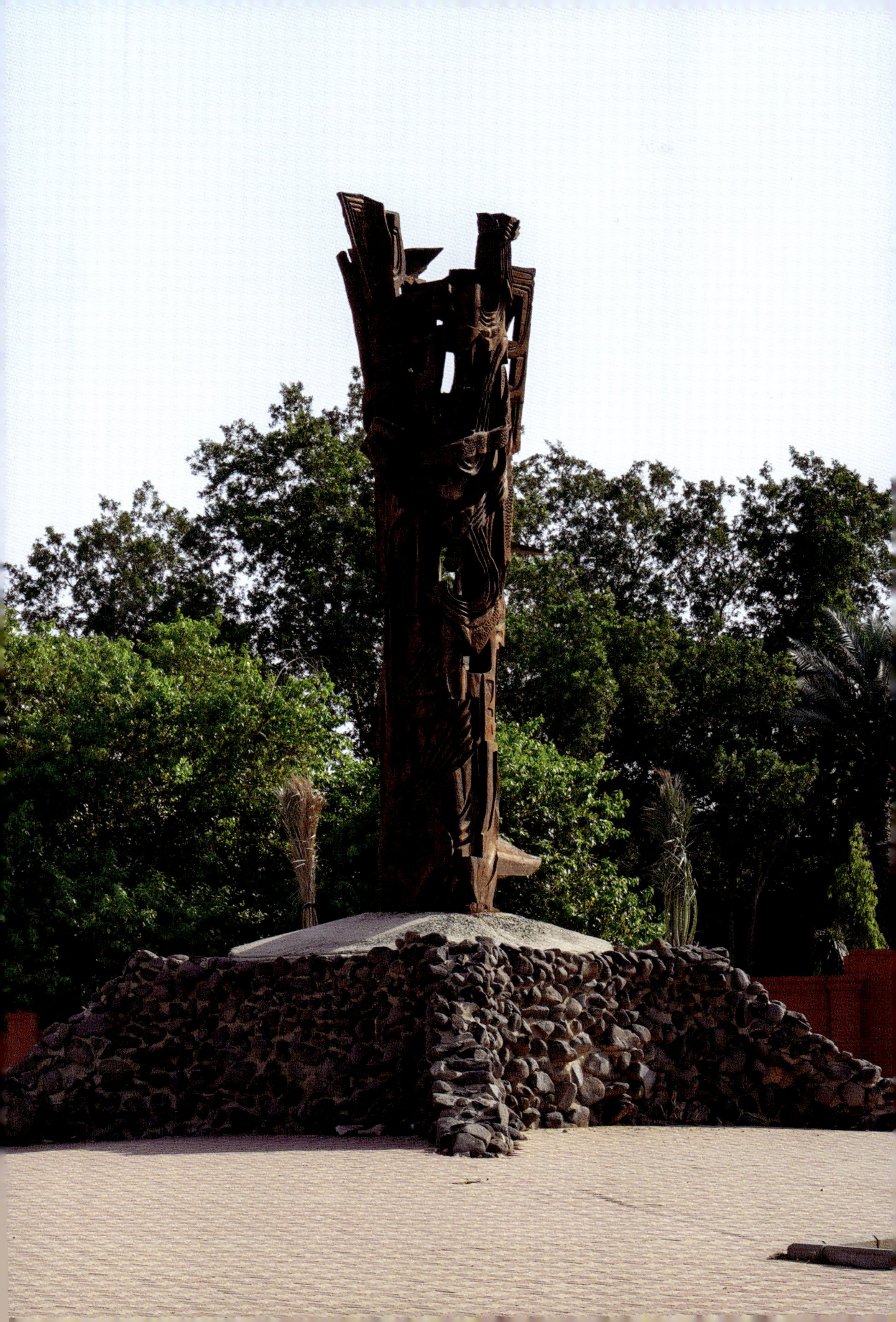

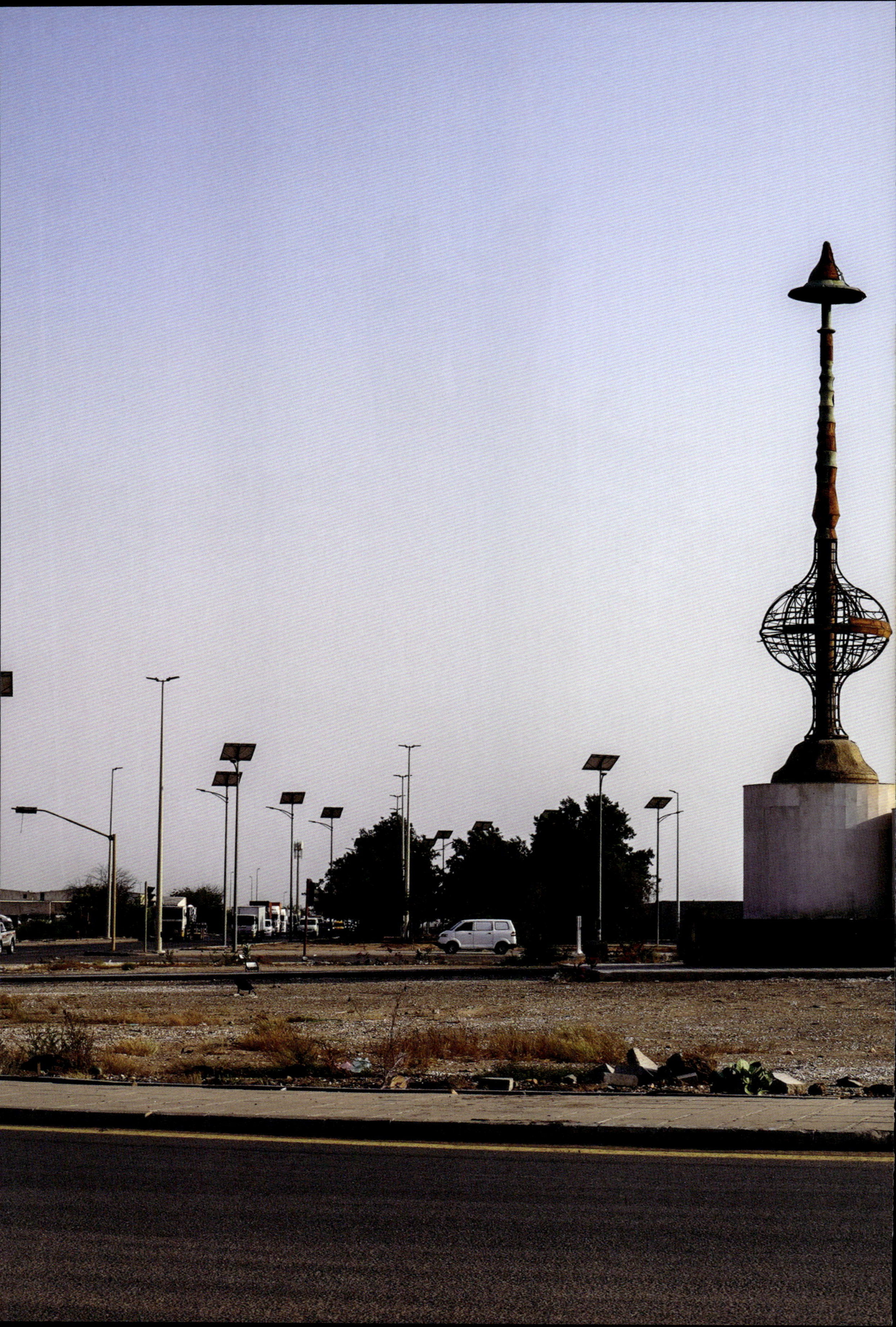

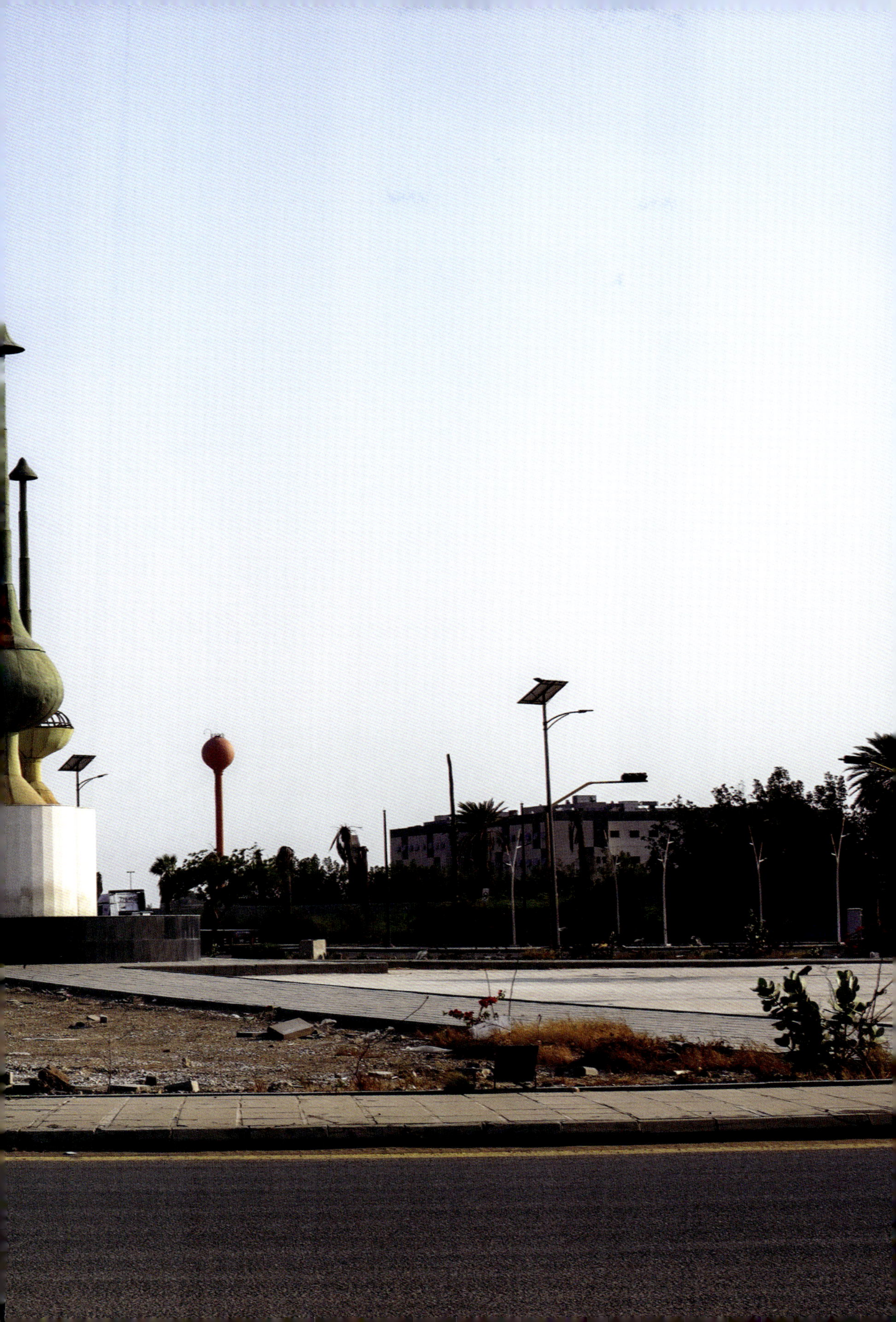

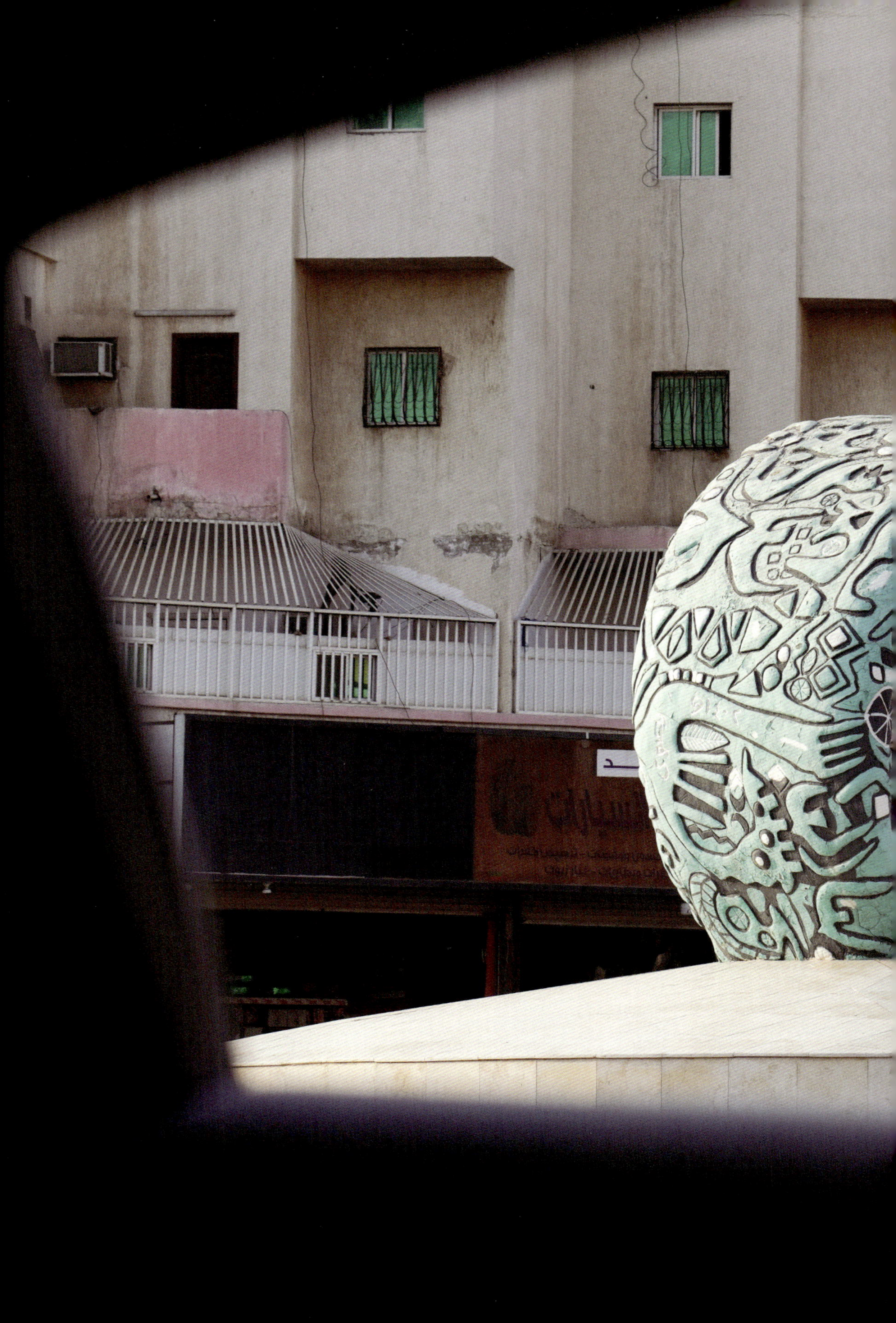

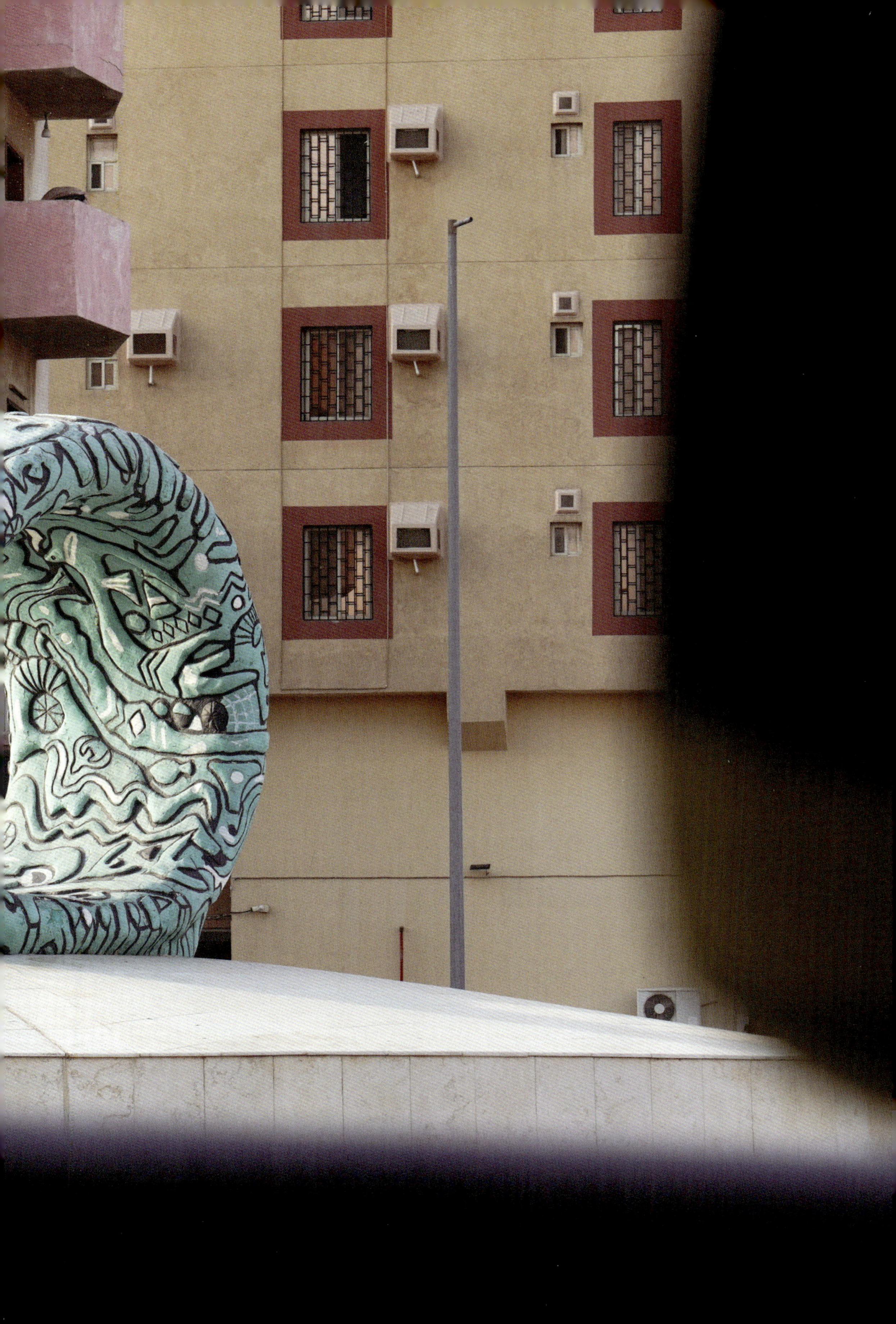

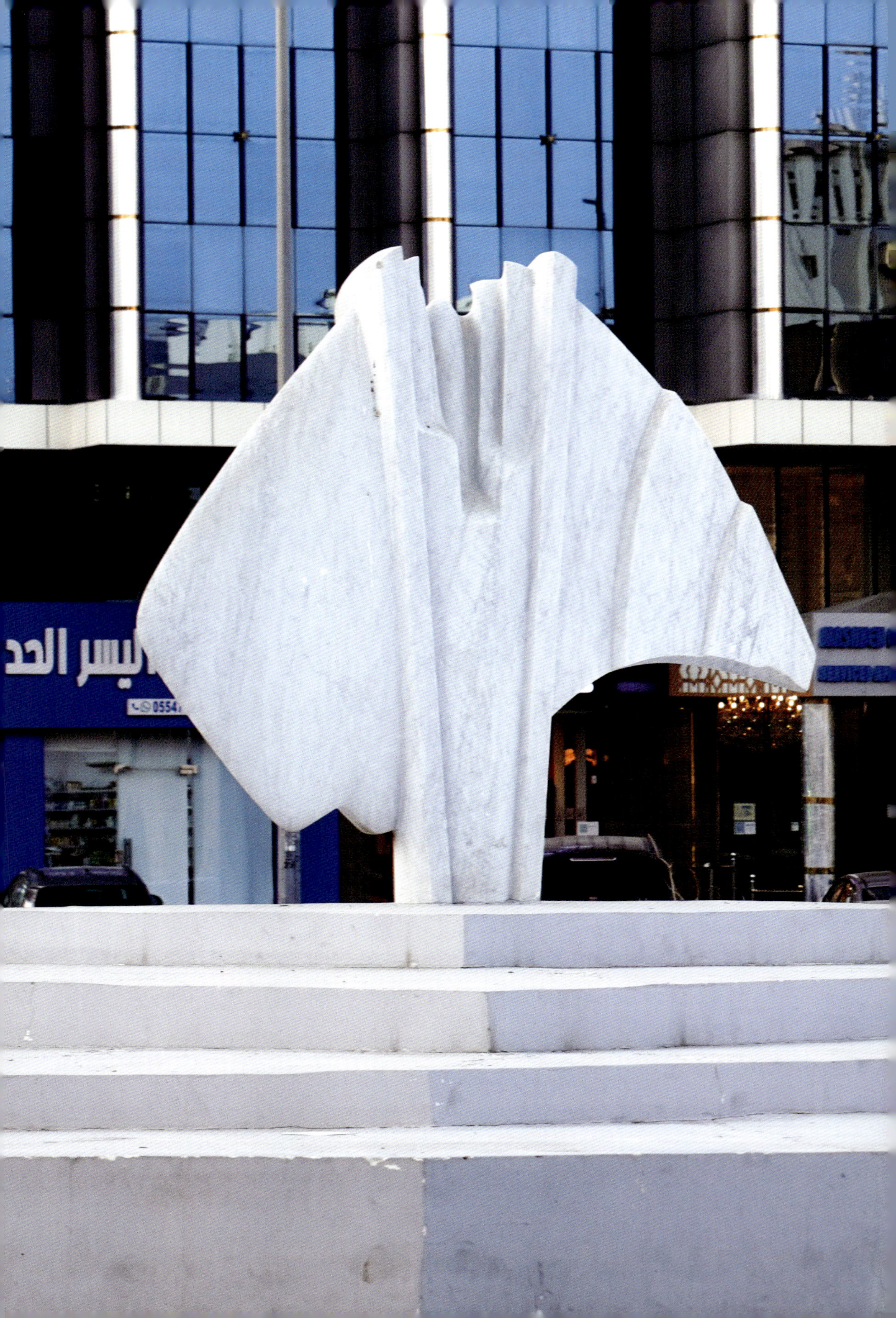

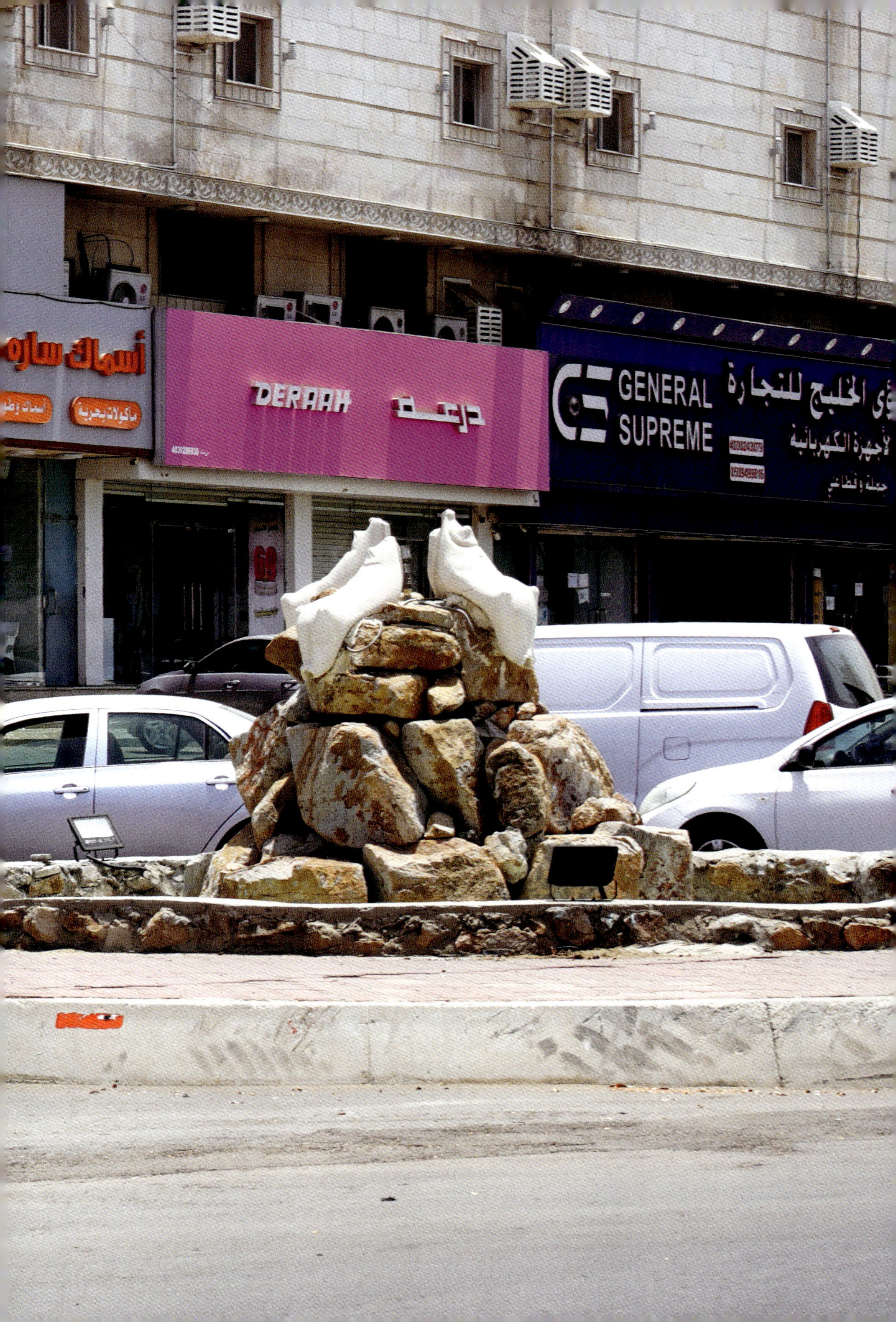
أسماك ساره
DERAAK
GENERAL
SUPREME
الأجهزة الكهربائية

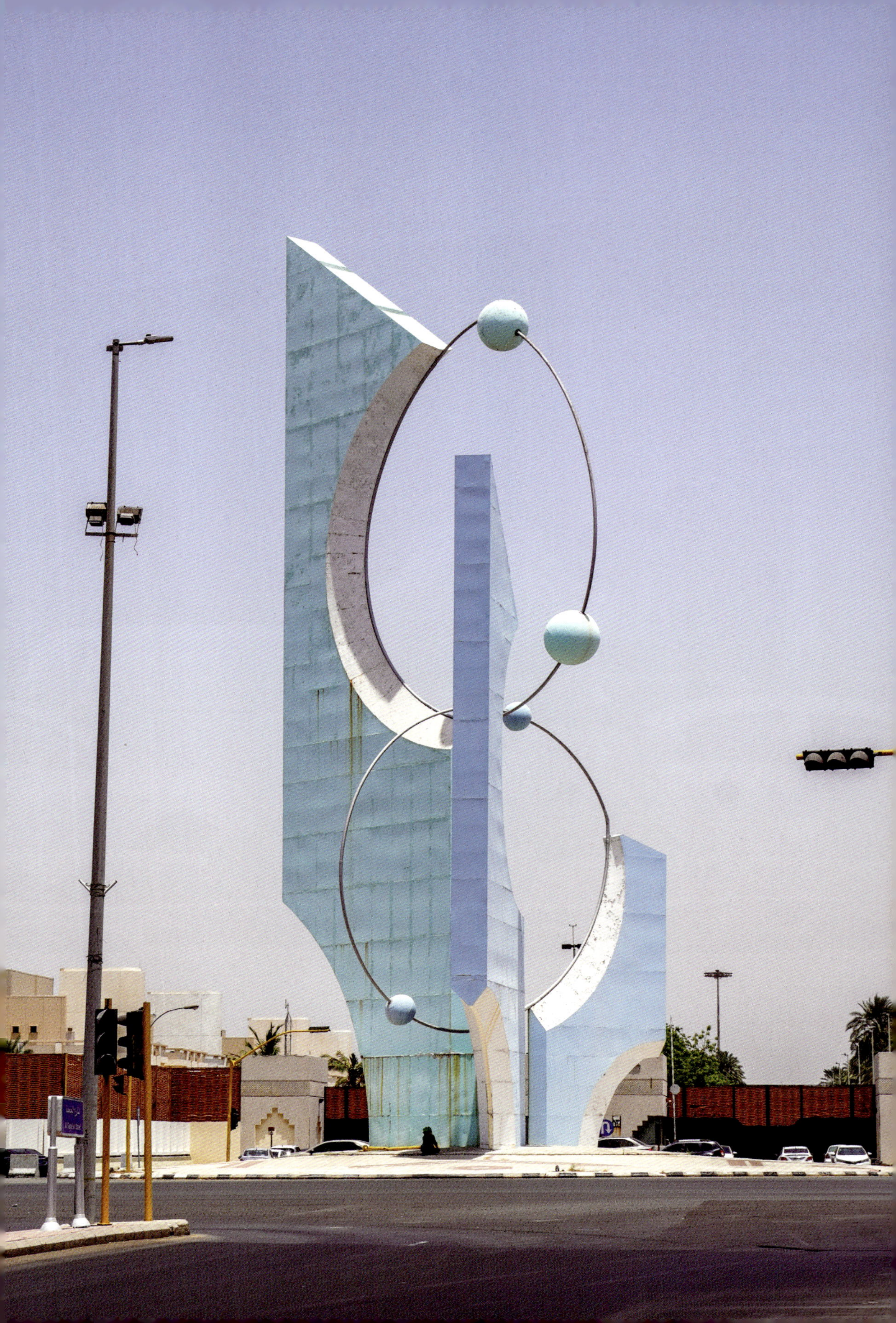

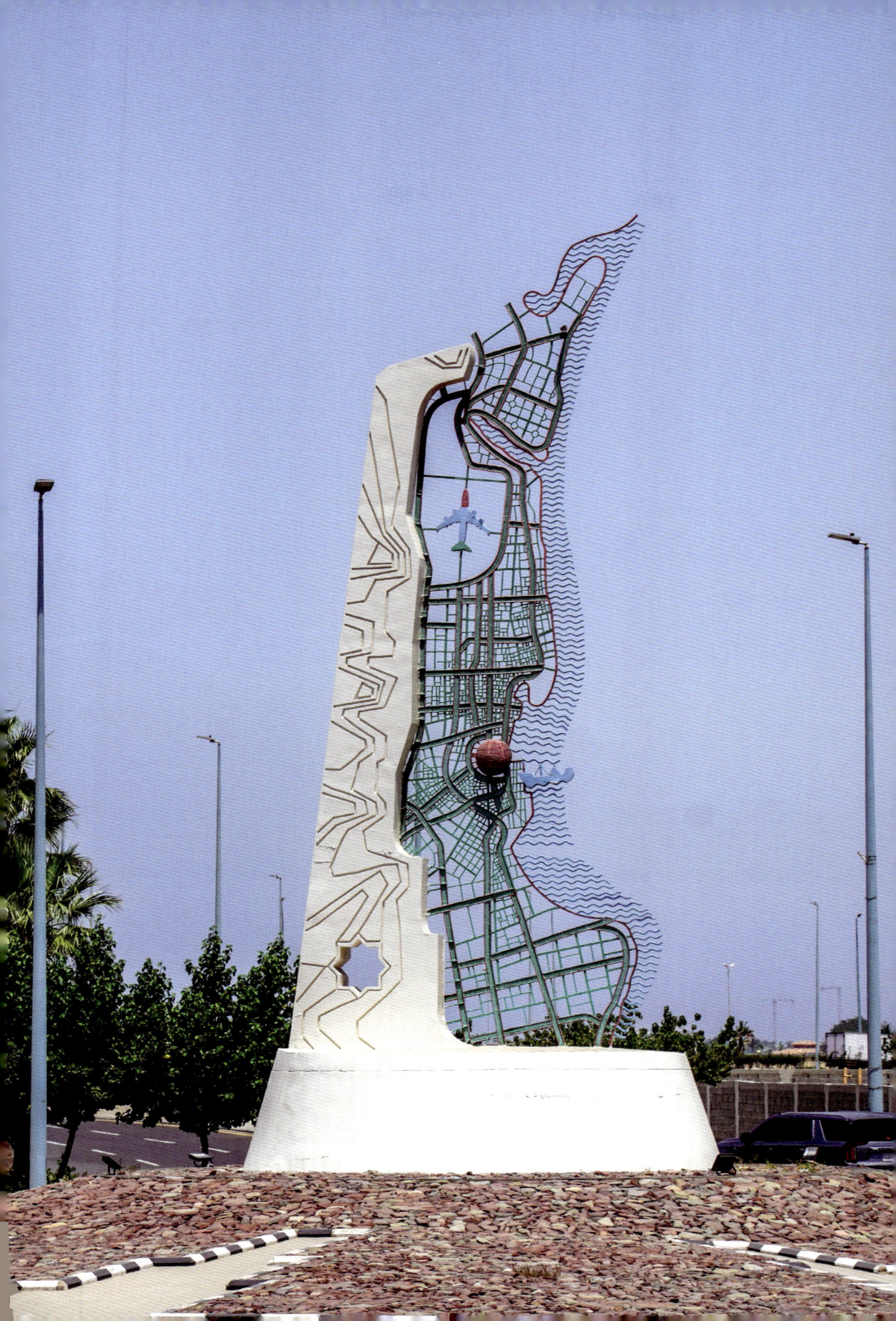

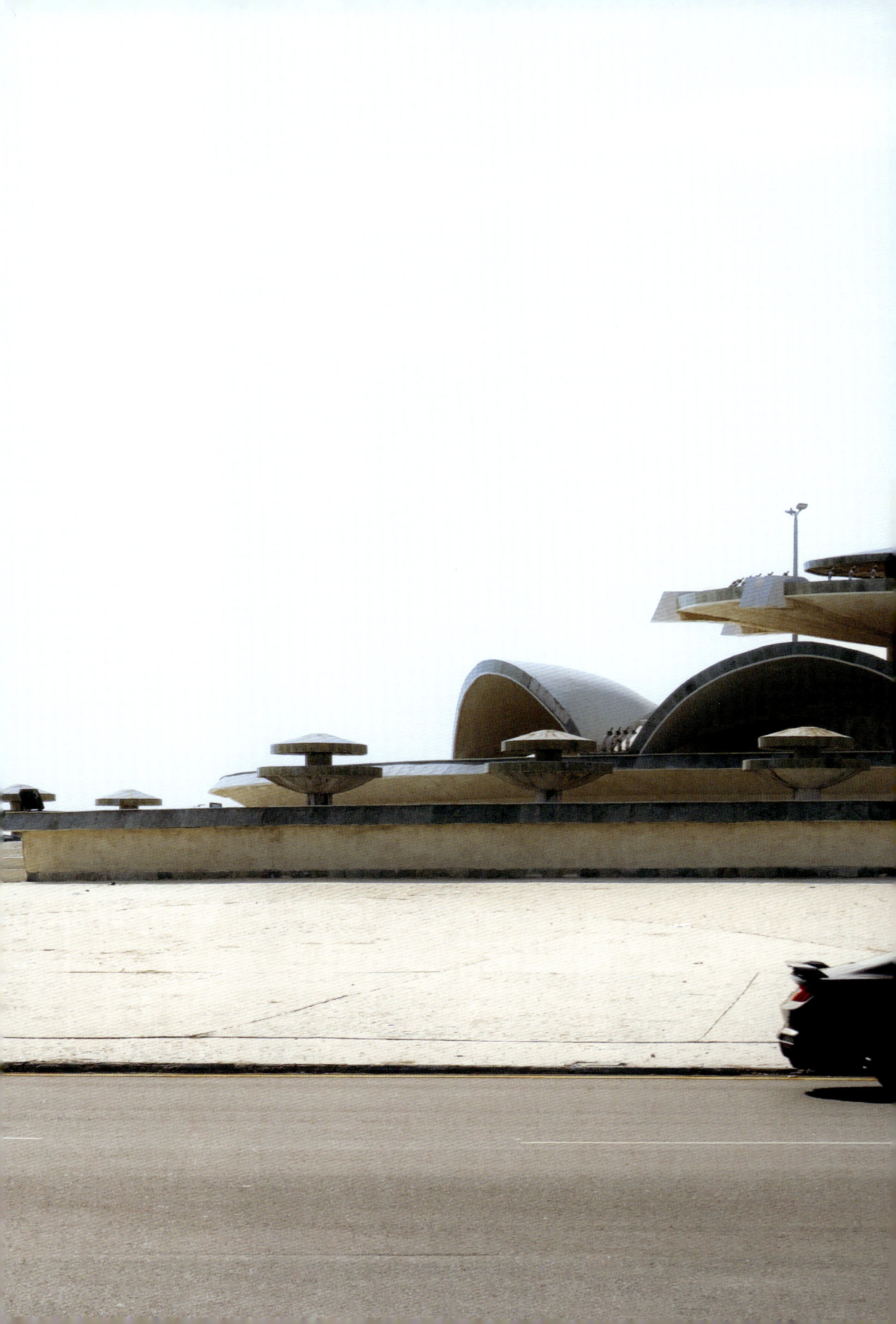

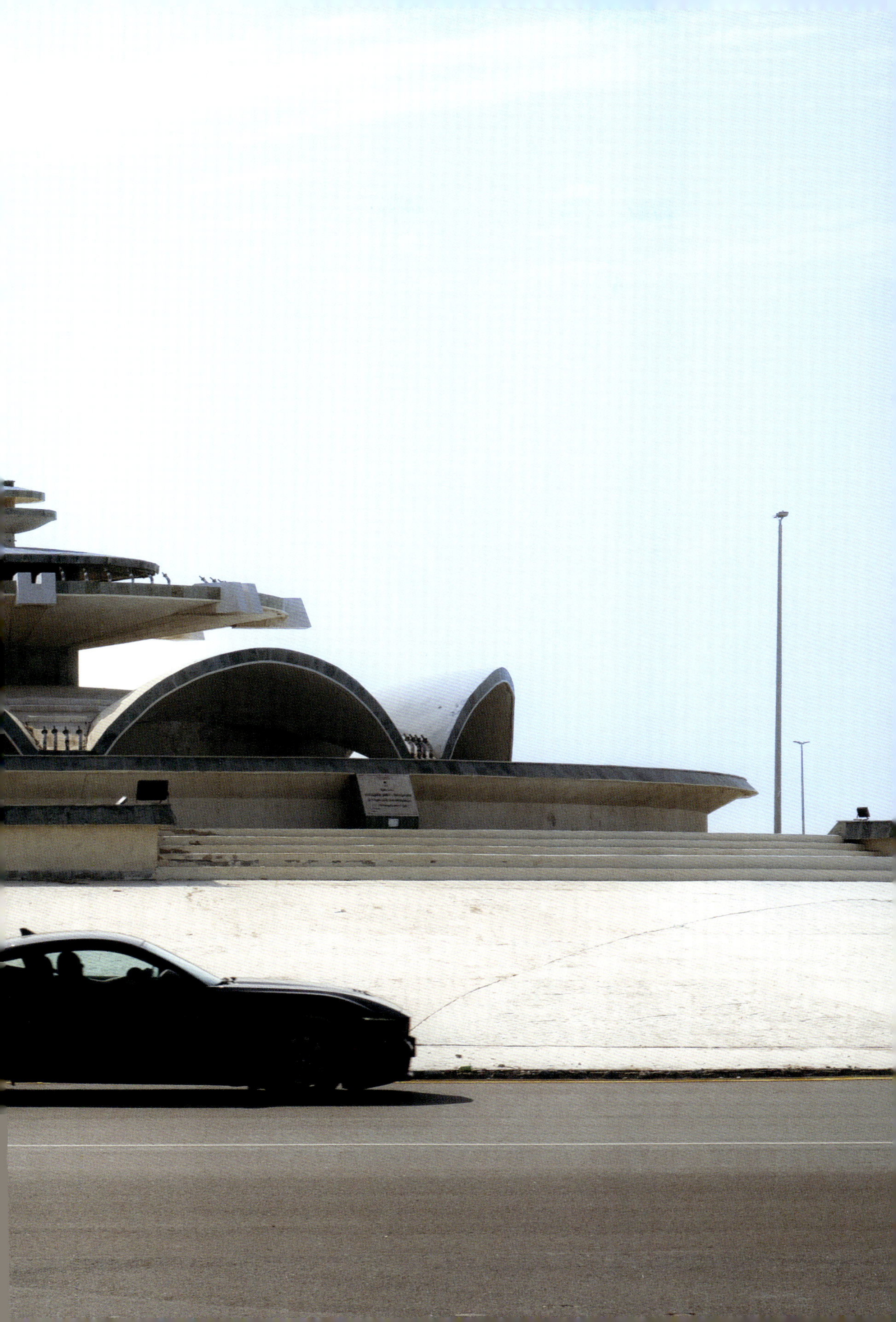

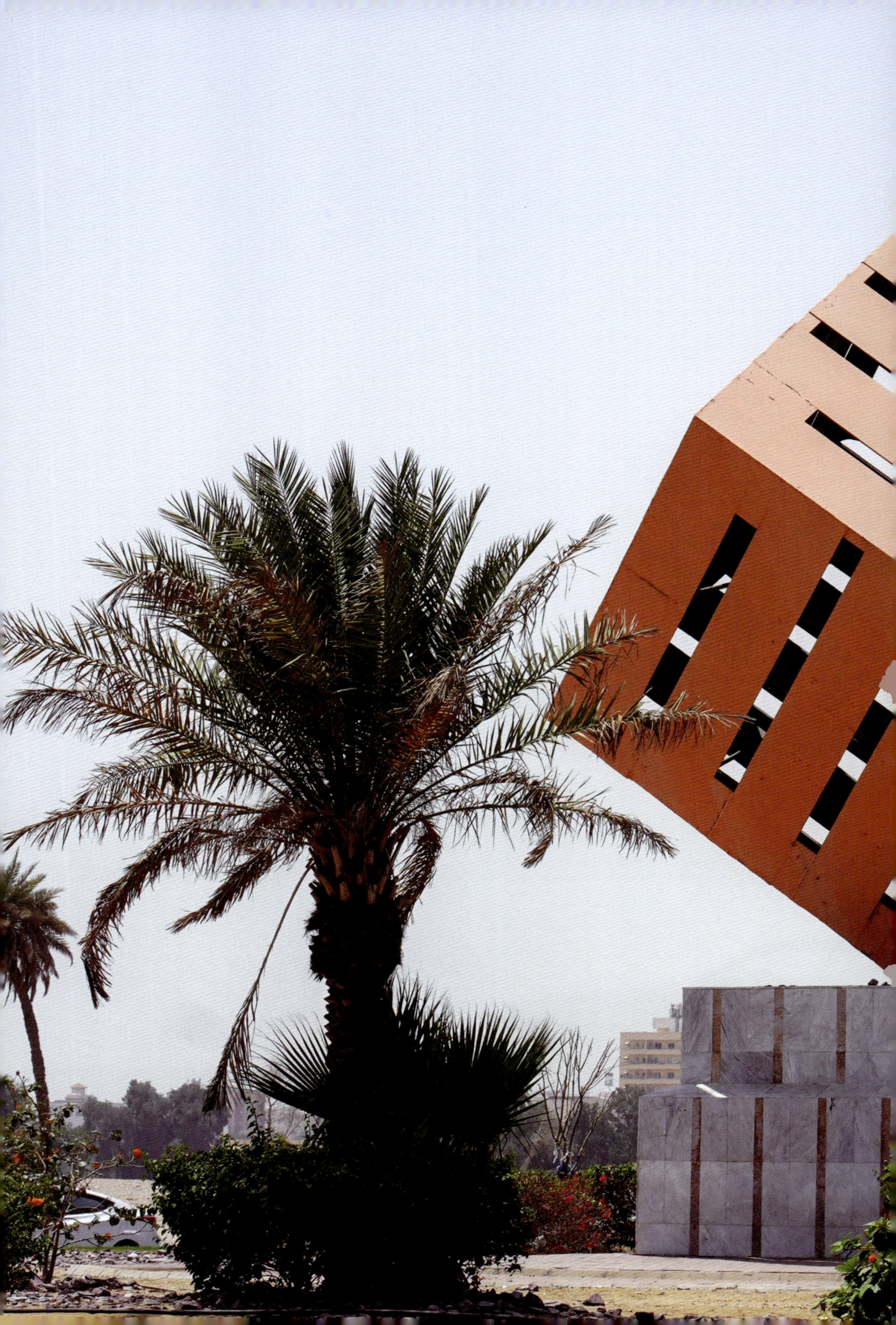

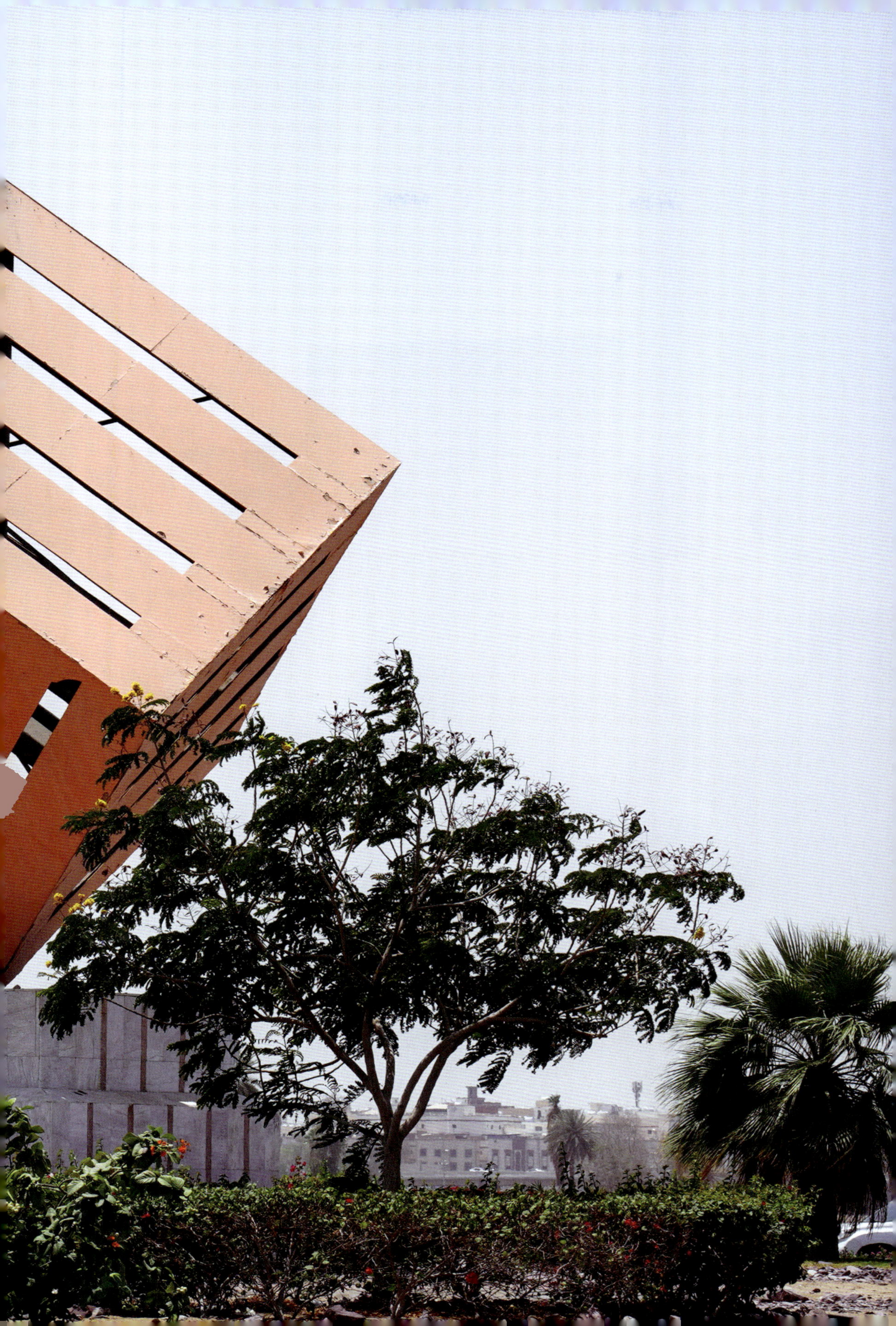

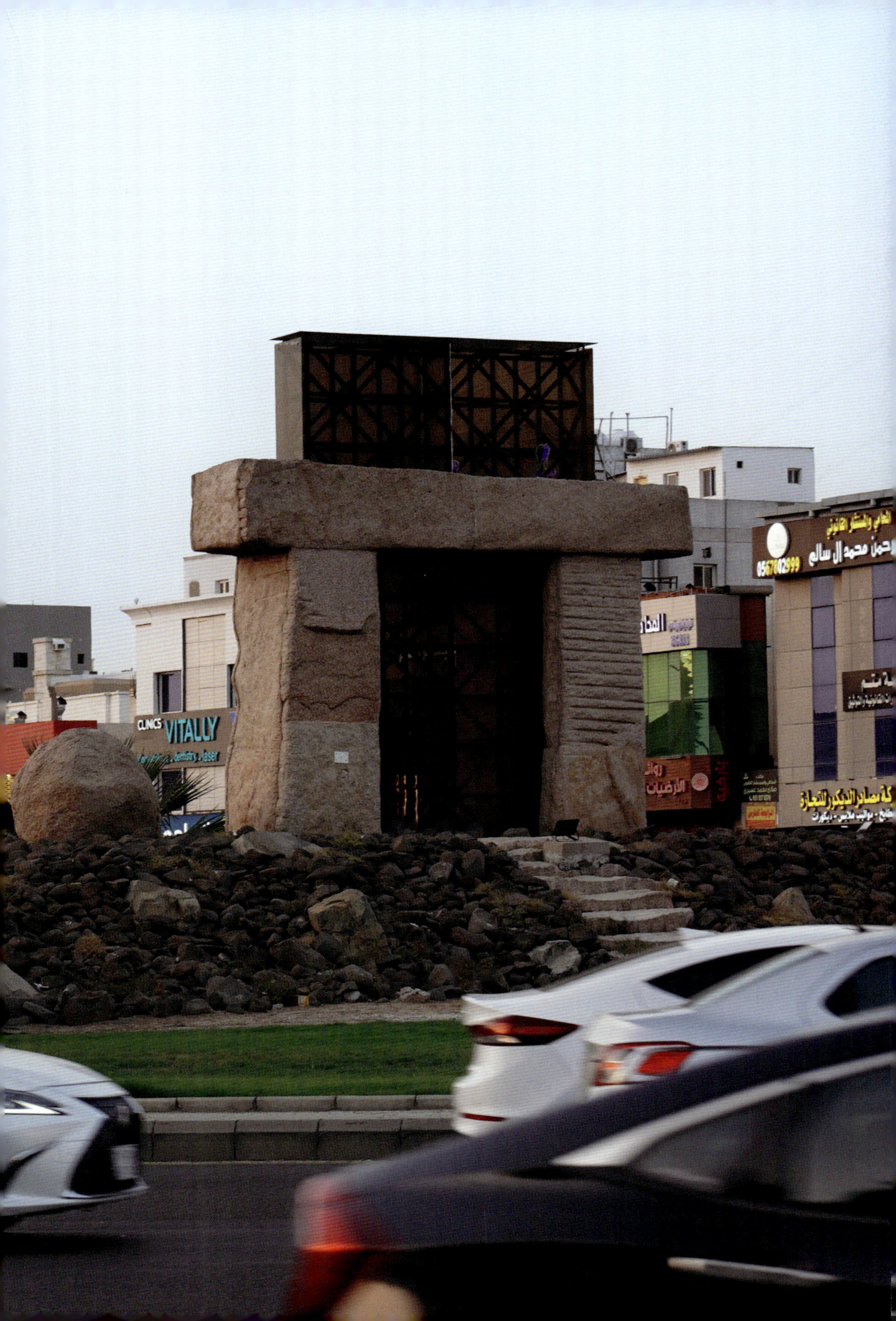
CLINICS VITALLY

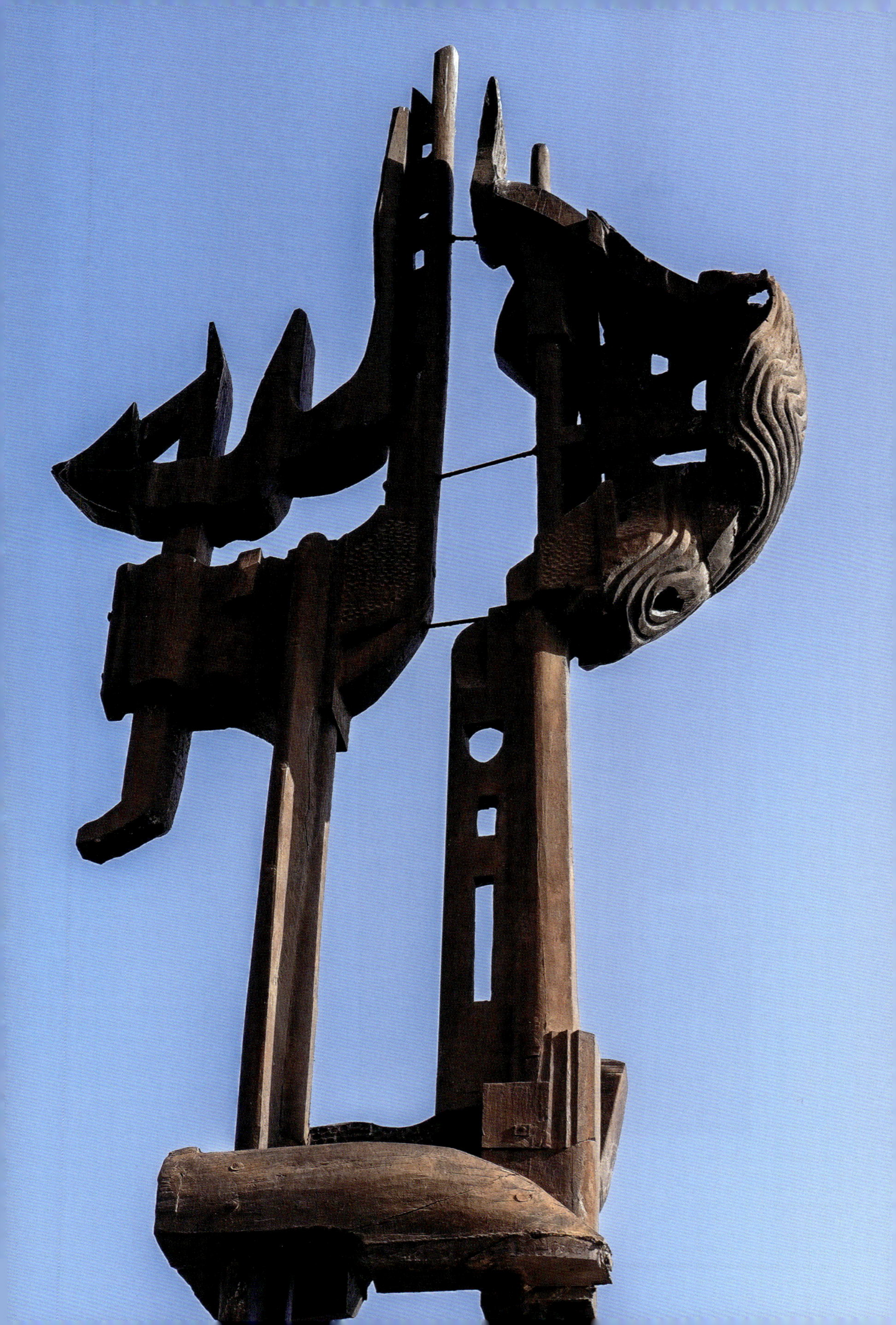

الوطن في شوارع جدة

Finding Home on Jeddah's Streets

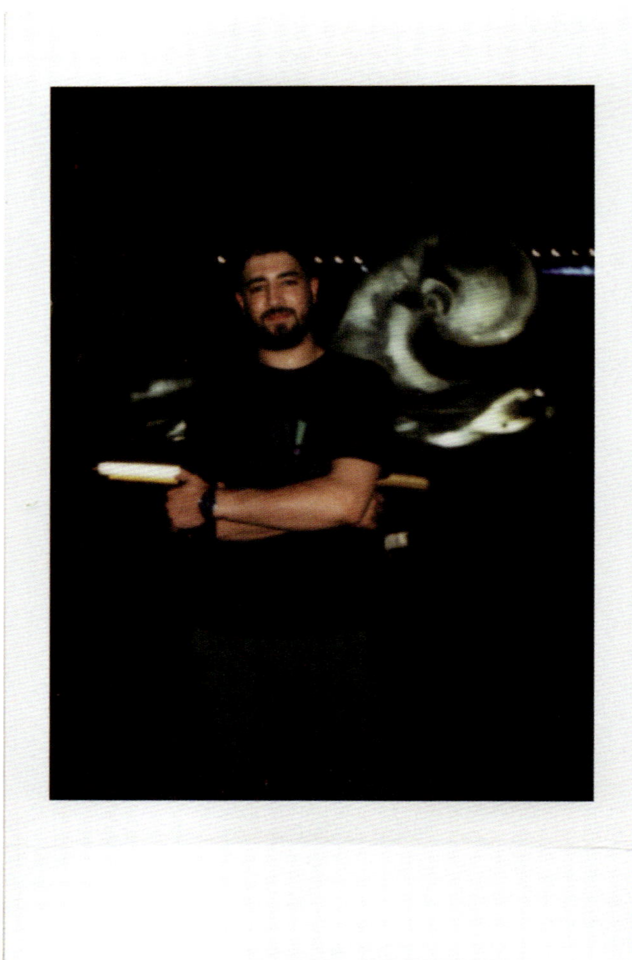

محمود

Mahmoud

Mahmoud

My name is Mahmoud Mohammed Najem, a 29-year-old Syrian-born and raised in Jeddah. About three years ago, I started working for myself after struggling to find a stable, well-paying job. There were opportunities, but none that fit, so I began driving, taking employees, students, and airport passengers. I studied dentistry in Sudan for two years, but had to stop because of financial difficulties.

Nouf Al-Harthi

Is that when you decided to focus on driving for income?

Mahmoud

Before I had a car, I took any job I could find. Fortunately, once I got my own car, I started driving for work. I began with apps like Uber, and things were going well for a while, but later the platforms became limited to Saudi nationals[6]. Some people used other people's names to get around that, but I chose not to. I always say, 'As a stranger, be polite.'

Now I work independently, driving employees, students, and sometimes doing airport trips.

محمود

اسمي محمود محمد نجم، عمري ٢٩ سنة، سوري، اتولدت وتربيت في جدة. قبل تقريبًا ثلاث سنوات قررت أشتغل لحالي، لأني تعبت وأنا أدور على وظيفة ثابتة براتب كويس. كانت في فرص طبعًا، بس ولا وحدة كانت مناسبة. فبدأت أشتغل سواق، أوصل موظفين وطلاب وأحيانًا مشاوير المطار. درست طب أسنان في السودان سنتين، بس اضطريت أوقف بسبب الظروف المادية.

نوف الحارثي

وهنا قررت تعتمد على السواقة كمصدر دخل؟

محمود

زمان ما كان عندي سيارة كنت أشتغل أي شغل يطلع لي. الحمد لله، لما اشتريت سيارة، بدأت أشتغل عليها. في البداية اشتغلت مع تطبيقات زي أوبر، وكانت الأمور ماشية تمام، بس بعدين هذي التطبيقات قصروا الشغل على السعوديين[6]. في ناس طبعًا استخدموا أسماء أصحابهم السعوديين عشان يسجلوا فيها، بس أنا ما حبيت الطريقة هذي. دايمًا أقول: «يا غريب كن أديب».

دحين أشتغل لحالي، أوصل موظفين وطلاب، أحيانًا أوصل للمطار. مو دايم الشغل نظامي ١٠٠٪، بس هذا رزقي. لو أحد وقفني واتفقنا على سعر، تمام، ما اتفقنا أكمّل طريقي.

نوف

بما إنك كبرت هنا، كيف تتذكر جدة أول والحين؟ وكيف تشوف مستقبلها؟

It's not always by the book, but it's how I make a living. If someone waves me down and we agree on a price, great; if not, I just move on.

Nouf — **Since you grew up here, how do you remember Jeddah then and now? And how do you see its future?**

Mahmoud — I remember Jeddah through its landmarks. I see its future as even more beautiful than Dubai in a few years. My whole life has been here; I've traveled abroad, but nowhere feels like Jeddah. It's a city that never stops changing, always becoming something new.

Nouf — **How do you see that change reflected in your driving experience?**

Mahmoud — I've loved cars since I was a kid; they've always been my passion. I'm not into football like most people; for me, cars are everything. Driving clears my head and teaches me patience. Over time, I've learned to slow down and take things as they come. I used to lose my temper in traffic, but now I try to stay calm. The street reminds you that "in patience there is safety, in haste there is regret." I'm still learning that lesson every day.

نوف — **وإحنا في وسط جدة الحين، كيف تشوف التغييرات حولك وايش المناطق المفضلة واللي ما تنساها؟**

محمود — جدة تغيّرت كثير، وكلها للأحسن. أي واحد عاش فيها زمان يلاحظ الفرق: أحياء، شوارع، جسور، إشارات. كل شي جديد ومنظم. جدة اليوم غير جدة أول. وصارت مدينة ترحب بالجميع أكثر وأكثر: سياح، أجانب، عرب. أي أحد يقدر يعيش فيها براحة. مو زي الرياض، هناك الوضع أغلى (يضحك). جدة بسيطة وناسها طيبين. وهنا كل شي يصير علامة. تقول «عند عزيز مول» أو «دوار العلم» والكل يفهمك. حتى الزوايا الصغيرة هي نقاط معروفة. أنا أحب جهة دوار الأندلس عند الأندلس مول، واسع ومريح. بس المفضل عندي دايم كان دوار الجمل. وقت ما تخلص المدرسة وتبدأ الإجازة، لما نشوفه بالسيارة نعرف إننا قرّبنا من البحر، من الفرح، ومن شاطئ الإسكندرية.

نوف — **ومع الطرق الجديدة، كيف تحس لمّا معلم يختفي؟**

محمود — الشوارع القديمة مليانة ذكريات. أفتكر الإشارات والزحمة كيف كانت. شارع السبعين مثلاً[7]، كان كله إشارات، دحين كله جسور. القديم له طعمه أكيد، بس الجديد أريح وأسرع. لمّا معلم يختفي رح نقول "عزيز مول سابقًا". الاسم يبقى حتى لو المكان راح. في الصفا

Nouf **When you talk about patience and learning, does a particular story come to mind?**

Mahmoud *(laughs)* Once, I was driving a passenger from the airport to the north terminal, but his flight was actually from Terminal 1. He told me, "Just hurry!" I warned him there might be undercover traffic police, but I crossed the yellow line anyway. Sure enough, we got stopped, three tickets at once. I learned my lesson; everything I'd earned that week disappeared right there.

Nouf **Since we're now in the city center, how do you see the changes around you?**

Mahmoud Jeddah has changed a lot and always for the better. Anyone who's lived here long can tell: the neighborhoods, the roads, the bridges, the traffic lights, everything is new, modern, and organized. Jeddah today is nothing like the Jeddah of before. It's a city that welcomes everyone: tourists, foreigners, Arabs. Anyone can live here comfortably. Not like Riyadh, it's more expensive there *(laughs)*. Jeddah is simple, and its people are kind.

Here, everything becomes a landmark and a memory, not just a roundabout. Say "near Aziz Mall"

محمود أتذكر جدة من معالمها. وأشوف مستقبلها بعد كم سنة أجمل حتى من دبي. أنا عشت كل حياتي هنا، سافرت برا صحيح بس ولا مكان حسّيته زي جدة. مدينة تعيش فيك، وتتغير ويصير فيها أشياء جديدة بس دائمًا تعيش فيك.

نوف **كيف التغيير هذا ظهر معاك في السواقة؟**

محمود أنا أحب السيارات من وأنا صغير وهي شغفي. ما أحب الكورة زي أغلب الناس، السيارات عندي كل شي. وأشوف السواقة تريحني وتعلمني الصبر. مع الوقت تعلمت أهدي وأمشي الأمور على مهلي. قبل كنت أعصب في الزحمة، دحين أحاول أكون هادي. الشارع يعلمك إن «في التأني السلامة وفي العجلة الندامة». ولسه أتعلم الدرس هذا كل يوم.

نوف **في موقف معين تستحضره علّمك الصبر؟**

محمود (يضحك) مرة كنت أوصل واحد من المطار للشمالي، بس رحلته كانت من صالة واحد. قال لي: «يلا استعجل!» قلت له ترا فيه مرور سري، وعدّيت الخط الأصفر. طبعًا وقفونا، ثلاث مخالفات مرة وحدة. كل تعب الأسبوع راح في لحظة، دفعته لتسديد المخالفات. درس ما أنساه.

or “by the Flag Roundabout,” and everyone knows exactly where you mean. Even tiny corners turn into reference points. Personally, I like the Andalus Roundabout near Andalus Mall. It’s big and open. But my favorite was always the Camel Roundabout. When school ended and vacation started, seeing it meant we were close to the beach, to joy, to childhood, to Alexandria Beach.

Nouf **You mentioned the new roads. How have they changed your experience behind the wheel, especially when a landmark changes or disappears?**

Mahmoud The old streets hold memories, no doubt. I remember where the traffic lights used to be, and how bad the congestion was. Take Al-Sabeen Street[7], for example, it used to be full of lights, and now it’s all bridges. The old version had its charm, but today everything is smoother and faster. We simply say, “Aziz Mall, formerly.” The name stays even if the place doesn’t. In Al-Safa, for example, there used to be the Al-Zahra Roundabout near Ridan. They removed it, but we still say “by the old Al-Zahra Roundabout.” With time, the old names fade, but we keep using them anyway.

Nouf **Can you explain the difference? How does that change feel to you?**

محمود السواق يشوف كل شي: حوادث، مواقف غريبة، ناس من كل الأنواع. قبل ما يكون عندي سيارة، كنت أركب مع ناس كثير مجانًا، بس أشاور في الشارع ويطلعوني. ولما صار عندي سيارة، ما نسيت هذا المعروف. أحيانًا أشوف واحد ما معاه حق المشوار، وأقول: «هذا أنا زمان». أوديه ببلاش. حتى لو أنا والله محتاج فلوس بنزين. لو وحدة كبيرة في السن أو واحد رايح مستشفى، ما أقدر آخذ منه فلوس. مو دايمًا طبعًا، بس لما قلبي يقول كذا. أرد الجميل قد ما أقدر.

نوف **أي طرق هي اللي تقطعها غالبًا في جدة؟**

محمود أتجنب الكورنيش، زحمة خاصة الويكند. بس حسب الطلب: طريق المدينة، الخطوط السريعة، أحيانًا المطار بس دحين أتجنبه بسبب المخالفات[8]. طريق الملك عالم ثاني، دايم حي. أحب أشوف السيارات الفخمة والتجمعات فيه. كنا نروح عند دوار الرضاعة[9]، طريق الملك، البترجي، بس نتفرج عليهم.

نوف **تغيّر الوضع الحين؟**

محمود كثير. أغلب أصحابي سافروا، وصار هذا كله ذكريات. كنا نجلس على الرصيف، نجيب سناكات وشيشة، نتفرج ونحلم: "يوم من الأيام بشتري وحدة كذا أو بسوي شي كذا".

Mahmoud — Before, you always knew exactly where the traffic jams would be. Now, with all the new bridges, everything flows much more smoothly. Still, the past has its sweetness. Sometimes I catch myself thinking, “Look how much it’s changed.” Every year, Jeddah transforms. Honestly, I talk about Jeddah more than I talk about my own country. I’m like a fish in water here. If I leave, I feel like I can’t breathe.

Nouf — **Is that just nostalgia speaking?**

Mahmoud — Not at all. Anyone who’s lived in Jeddah would understand. It’s my home, my world. I grew up here, and my friends are here. When I leave, I feel like a stranger; when I’m here, I’m at peace. It’s just the truth.

Nouf — **You studied in Sudan and worked different jobs before getting your car, right? How long have you been driving?**

Mahmoud — Since I was a kid, even before I had a license. But as a full-time job, it’s been three years.

Nouf — **In those three years, what stories stay with you?**

مثلاً، كان في دوار الزهراء عند ريدان، شالوه، بس لسه نقول «عند دوار الزهراء القديم». الأسماء القديمة تروح مع الوقت، بس إحنا نتمسك فيها.

نوف — **كيف تحس بالفرق؟**

محمود — أول كنت عارف الزحمة فين ومتى. دحين مع الجسور، الحركة أسهل. بس زمان له حلاوته كمان. أحيانًا أقول: «شوف قد إيش تغيّرت». كل سنة جدة تتغير. صراحة أتكلم عن جدة أكثر من بلدي. أنا هنا زي السمكة في الموية. لو أطلع، أحس نفسي أختنق.

نوف — **هل هذا حنين بس؟**

محمود — لا والله. أي واحد عاش في جدة يفهم. هي بيتي وعالمي. كبرت هنا وأصحابي هنا. لما أطلع أحس نفسي غريب، ولما أرجع لها أرتاح.

نوف — **من متى تسوق؟**

محمود — من وأنا صغير، حتى قبل الرخصة. بس كشغل، لي ثلاث سنوات.

نوف — **هل فيه مواقف تستحضرها من خلال هالثلاث سنوات؟**

Mahmoud — Anyone who drives sees everything: accidents, strange situations, people from all walks of life. I remember one thing clearly: before I owned a car, I used to hitch rides, and many people gave me lifts for free. When I finally had my own car and started working, I remembered that kindness. Sometimes I see someone who can't afford a ride, and I think, "That used to be me." So I drive them for free. Even if I need fuel myself, it feels like paying kindness forward. If I'm driving an elderly woman or someone going to the hospital, I can't take money from them. Not always, but when my heart tells me to, I do it. Whenever I can repay the good I once received, I do.

Nouf — **What routes do you usually drive?**

Mahmoud — I avoid the Corniche, it's too crowded, especially on weekends. My routes depend on requests: Medina Road, the highways, sometimes the airport, though I avoid it now because of fines[8]. King Road is another world; it's always alive. I like watching the supercars and the gatherings there. We used to go near the Marine Science Roundabout[9], King Road, and Al-Batarji just to watch the cars.

محمود — ما تضايقني كثير لأني أعرف الطرق. زحمة جدة مو زي الرياض. غالبًا ٢٠–٣٠ دقيقة. بس من كثر السواقة صرت أطفش شوية (يضحك). قبل كنت أحب أطلّع أهلي، دحين مرة أكسّل وأأجل مواعيدها.

نوف — **وبعد الإزالات، كيف تغيّرت الحركة؟**

محمود — بعد الإزالات بالجنوب، ناس كثير نقلوا لشمال جدة[11]. بالبداية كانت فوضى وزحمة. بعدين الأمور ضبطت. وأنا أعرف الطرق بس أستخدم GPS عشان أتجنب الزحمة. ما يهمني أزيد ٥ أو ١٠ كيلو، أهم شي أمشي وما أعلق فيها. الصباحات كانت سيئة مع المدارس والدوامات، بس مع الشوارع الجديدة والجسور الوضع تحسن.

نوف — **المنطقة هذي دايم زحمة؟**

محمود — في جسر تحت الإنشاء بين الأربعين وصاري، بيريح شارع السبعين. دوار الهندسة قريب، دايم فيه حوادث. بس إن شاء الله الوضع يتحسن. المدينة قاعدة تتغير بسرعة.

نوف — **لاحظت زيادة في عدد النساء العاملات في التوصيل مثلك؟**

محمود — صحيح، بس أول مرة طلبت أوبر وجت وحدة، توترت مرة

Nouf **How was that experience? Has it changed?**

Mahmoud It's changed a lot. Most of my friends traveled, so now it's mostly memories. We used to sit on the sidewalk with snacks and shisha, watching cars go by. It was fun, just dreaming, saying, "One day, I'll have one like that."

Nouf **Where did your friends go?**

Mahmoud Most went abroad, to Turkey and Egypt, to continue their studies. Now we meet maybe once a year. They're my childhood friends from Al-Safa, between Al-Safa and Al-Marwah. I studied in Sudan for two years, just like them, before coming back.

Nouf **Did you come back because of the recent events in Sudan[10]?**

Mahmoud No, I came back in 2017. I couldn't afford to continue studying. I froze my university file instead of withdrawing completely; maybe I'll return one day.

Nouf **You mentioned Alexandria Beach earlier; where is it now?**

نوف **فين راحوا أصحابك؟**

محمود تركيا ومصر، يكملوا دراسة. ونحنا نشوف بعض يمكن مرة في السنة. أصحاب طفولة من حي الصفا والمروة. وأنا طلعت درست في السودان سنتين زيهم بس رجعت.

نوف **رجعت بسبب الأحداث الأخيرة[10]؟**

محمود لا، رجعت ٢٠١٧. ما قدرت أكمل دراسة بسبب ظروفي المالية. لكنّي جمّدت ملفي ما سحبته، أقول يمكن أرجع بيوم من الأيام.

نوف **قبل شوي ذكرت شاطئ الإسكندرية، وينه الحين؟**

محمود اسمه دحين كوكيان، بس الناس لسه تقول الإسكندرية. نفس الشي. كان فيه براميل زرقا والناس تسبح حولها. وتصدقي ذكرتيني بدوار الكرة الأرضية، هذا كنا نروحه كل ويكند. برضو سيارات، وتجمعات. كل ما أشوف الكرة أفكر في الدنيا، في الطريق، وإننا عايشين على كوكب زيها وكيف الأرض مبسوطة لنا. لحظة تفكر وسط الزحمة.

نوف **وكيف تشوف الزحمة اليوم؟**

Mahmoud — It's now called Kokiyan Beach, but people still say Alexandria. Same idea, people remember the old names, not the new ones. It used to have blue barrels, and people would swim around them. And you reminded me of the Globe Roundabout, we used to go there every weekend. Cars, gatherings, energy. Every time I see that globe, I start thinking, how the roads stretch, how we live on a sphere. A moment of reflection, right there in traffic.

Nouf — **Since you mentioned the roads, tell me about traffic and movement. How do you see Jeddah's traffic today?**

Mahmoud — Traffic doesn't bother me much because I know how to navigate. Jeddah's traffic isn't like Riyadh's. Here, it's usually twenty or thirty minutes at most. But honestly, since I started driving every day, I've begun to dislike it a bit, haha. I used to love driving my family around, but after facing jams every day, I sometimes postpone or cancel trips.

Nouf — **After all the recent changes, how do you think people's movements across the city have shifted?**

Mahmoud — After the demolitions in the south[11], people from

نوف — **فكرة المشروع كانت «فضفضة بالسيارة»؟**

محمود — إيوا، كنت أفكر ليه أدور ناس؟ اللي يحتاجني يجي. ونطلع مشوار وكلام.

نوف — **عجيب! كلمة أو فكرة أخيرة؟**

محمود — والله قاعد أفكر في طريق الملك وذكرياتي هناك.

نوف — **تعرف ثمة أغاني طريق الملك؟**

محمود — (يضحك) تامر عاشور[12].

نوف — **هذا يخليني أختم بنفس السؤال، إيش تسمع بالعادة وأنت تسوق؟**

محمود — كل شي. أجنبي، هاوس، ريمكسات. وأحيانًا الصمت. لو لحالي أحتار، بس لو مع أحد هو يختار. في أغنية جات في بالي: «يبغالها فلوس»[13]. تعرفيها؟

all backgrounds moved north. At first, traffic was unbearable. But gradually, it got better. I know the roads well, but I still use GPS to check where traffic is and avoid it. I don't mind adding five or ten kilometers, as long as I keep moving. I like open roads. In the beginning, it was chaos; people were trying to get used to new neighborhoods. Morning traffic was terrible. But after the new roads and bridges opened, everything started to flow again.

Nouf **Is this area usually crowded?**

Mahmoud There's a bridge under construction between Al-Arbaeen and Sari that should ease traffic on Al-Sabeen Street. The nearby Engineering Roundabout often has accidents, people rush, and there's no signal. But once the bridge is done, things will improve. The city's changing fast.

Nouf **Speaking of change, I didn't realize there are so many female drivers now. How do you see that shift?**

Mahmoud The first time I ordered an Uber, a woman showed up, I panicked, and sat in the back! It was new to me. But now it's normal. Some women drive really well; others are still learning, especially at roundabouts, where they sometimes

وجلست ورا! بس دحين عادي. في بنات يسوقوا ممتازين، وفي لسه يتعلموا، خاصة في الدوارات، أفضل أكون قدامهم (يضحك) عشان ما يصدموني. طبعًا مو تعميم، في بنات أحسن من سواقة الرجال. وأكيد الشارع يوريك كل شي.

نوف **بما إنك تسوق في وسط المدينة وبين المدن، وش الفرق بين سواقتك في الخطوط السريعة والمدينة؟**

محمود الخط أحيانًا أبطأ، حادث يوقف كل شي. المدينة صحيح مليانة إشارات بس توصل أسرع. في النهاية كلها تعلمك الصبر.

نوف **وإحساسك فيهم؟**

محمود الشوارع داخل المدينة تحسسني بالأمان. لو صار شي، المساعدة قريبة. الخط السريع لا، بتقعد تنتظر وطبعًا بتدفع مبلغ وقدره على السطحة. لكن داخل المدينة كل شي أسرع وأسهل.

نوف **عندي فضول، وافقت على فكرة المقابلة بسرعة، ليش؟**

محمود حسّيتها قريبة مني. كنت متخيل فكرة مشروع شي زي كذا. واحد يركب، يحكي، يفضفض. ولما جيتوا قلتوا لي قلت خلاص هذي هي.

enter without looking. I prefer to drive ahead of them, just in case. I'm not generalizing, some women drive better than men. The street shows you everything.

Nouf **What's the difference for you between highways and city streets?**

Mahmoud Highways can be slower; accidents stop everything. City streets have lights, but I usually get there faster. In the end, it's about patience. I choose between constant lights and heavy jams; either way, you need calm.

Nouf **You talk about roads technically, but what about emotionally?**

Mahmoud I'm not great at expressing feelings, but city streets make me feel safe. If something happens, there's always help nearby. On the highway, you're alone, waiting for a tow truck, paying for every small thing. In the city, you can fix things fast; on the highway, everything costs time and money.

Nouf **When I first told you about this interview idea, you agreed immediately. Many others were hesitant. Why did you say yes so fast?**

Mahmoud I felt the idea was close to me. I'd imagined something like this, someone riding with me, talking, venting. When you explained it, I thought, "That's exactly what I've been thinking about." It's new, different, fun, why not? I like to try new things.

Nouf **And the idea of "venting in the car," where did that come from?**

Mahmoud From different ideas I've had. Why should I look for people? Let people come to me. Instead of wasting time, I can just be here, and whoever needs me, whether for a ride or a chat, can find me.

Nouf **We're nearing the end of our ride. Anything you'd like to add?**

Mahmoud I was just thinking about King Road and all my memories there.

Nouf **Have you heard the stereotypes about songs on King Road?**

Mahmoud (laughs) Tamer Ashour[12].

Nouf **Since we're talking about music, what's your driving soundtrack?**

Mahmoud I don't have a favorite song. I listen to everything, mostly English, house music, remixes, for hours. Sometimes I drive in silence. If I'm alone, I never know what to play. But if I have someone with me, they choose. Oh, there's one song that just came to mind: "Yebghalha Floos"[13] it means "It Needs Money." Do you know it?

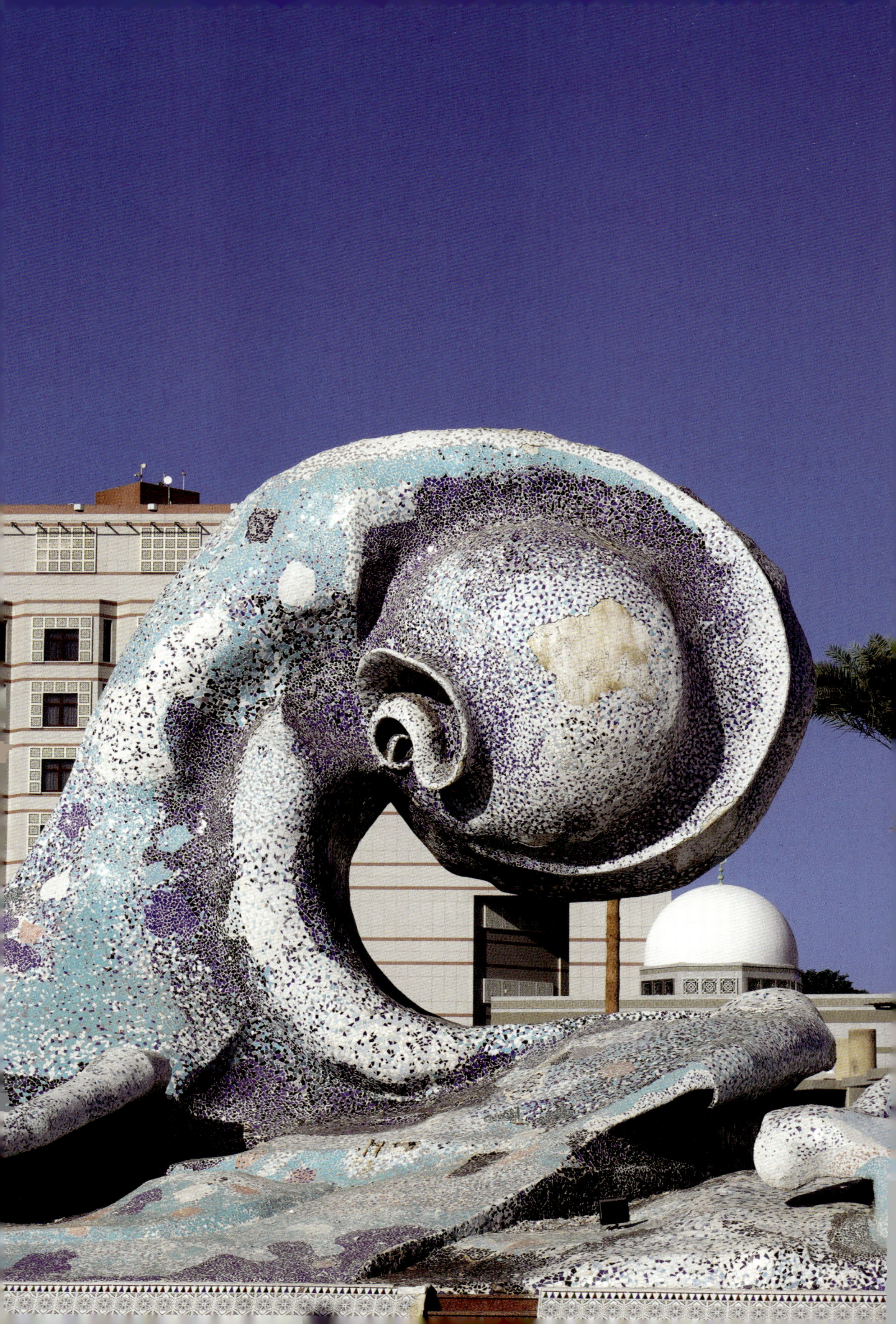

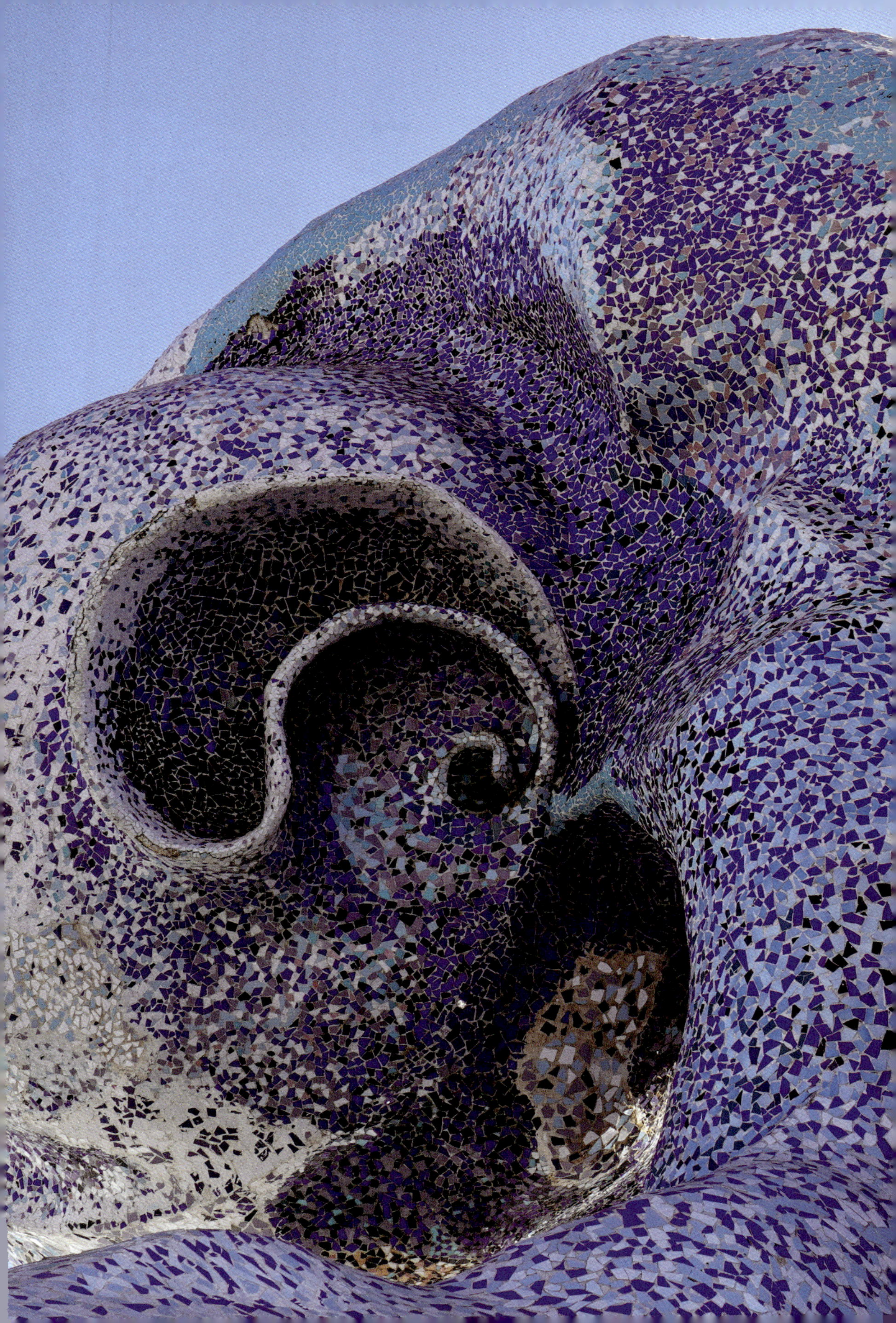

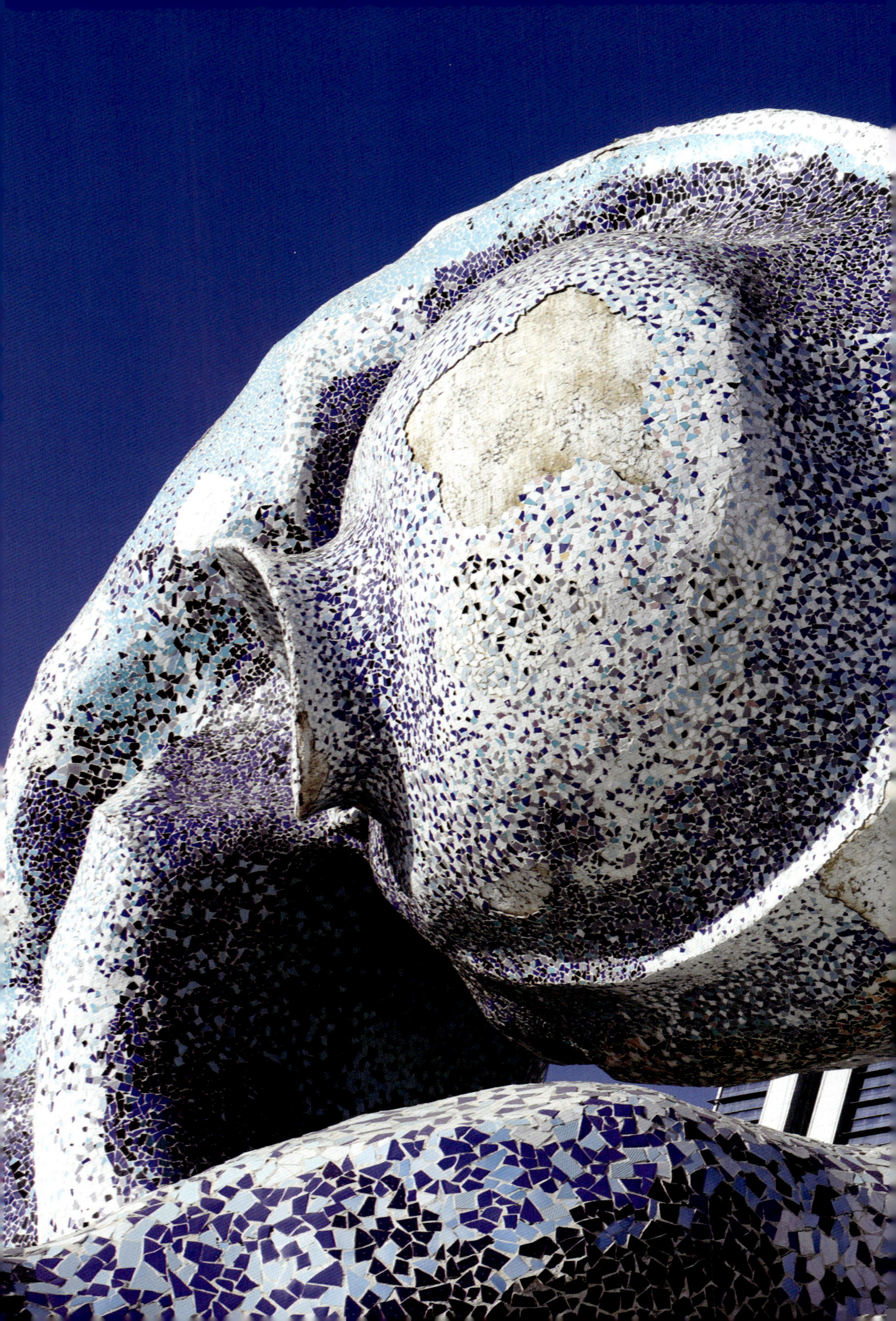

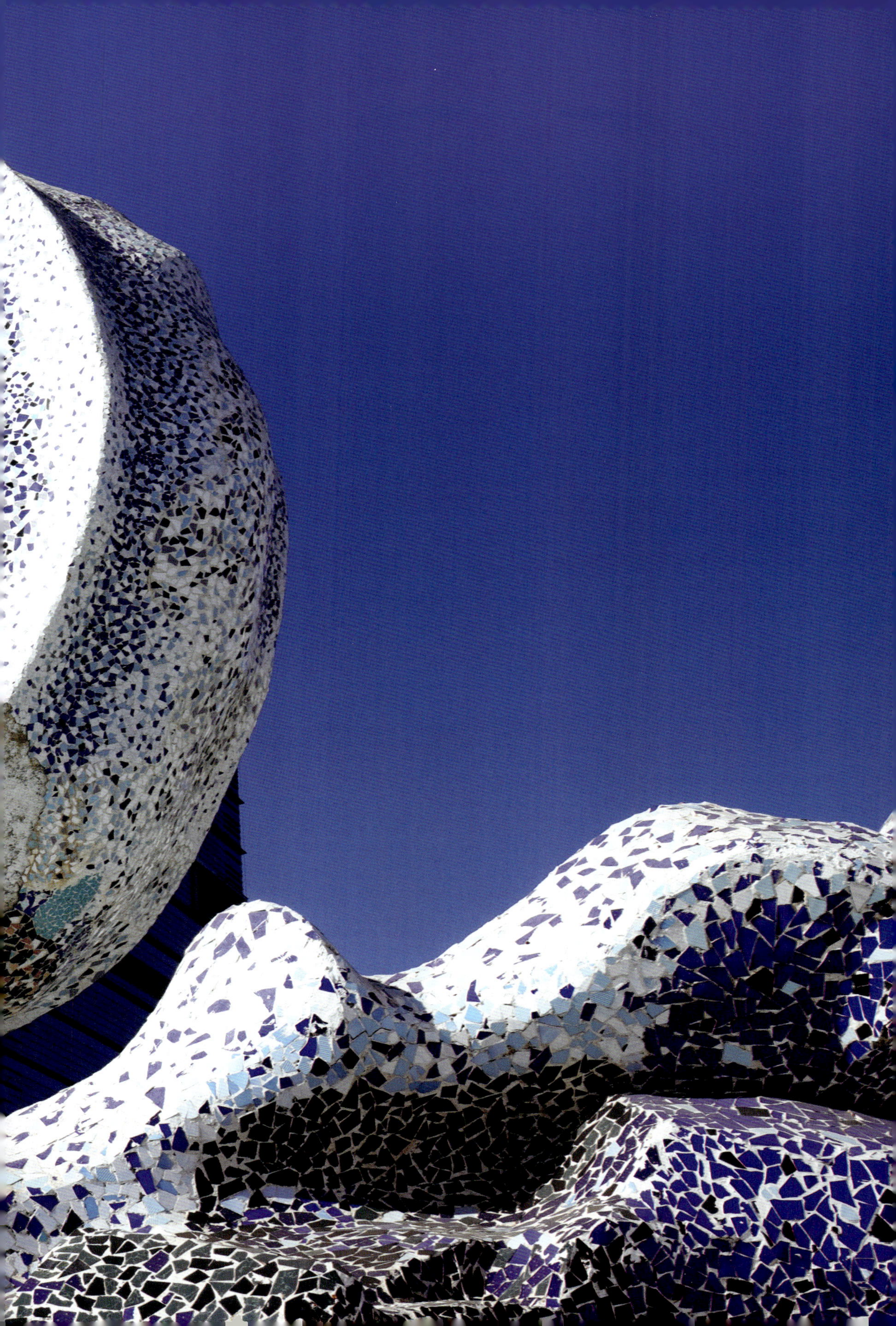

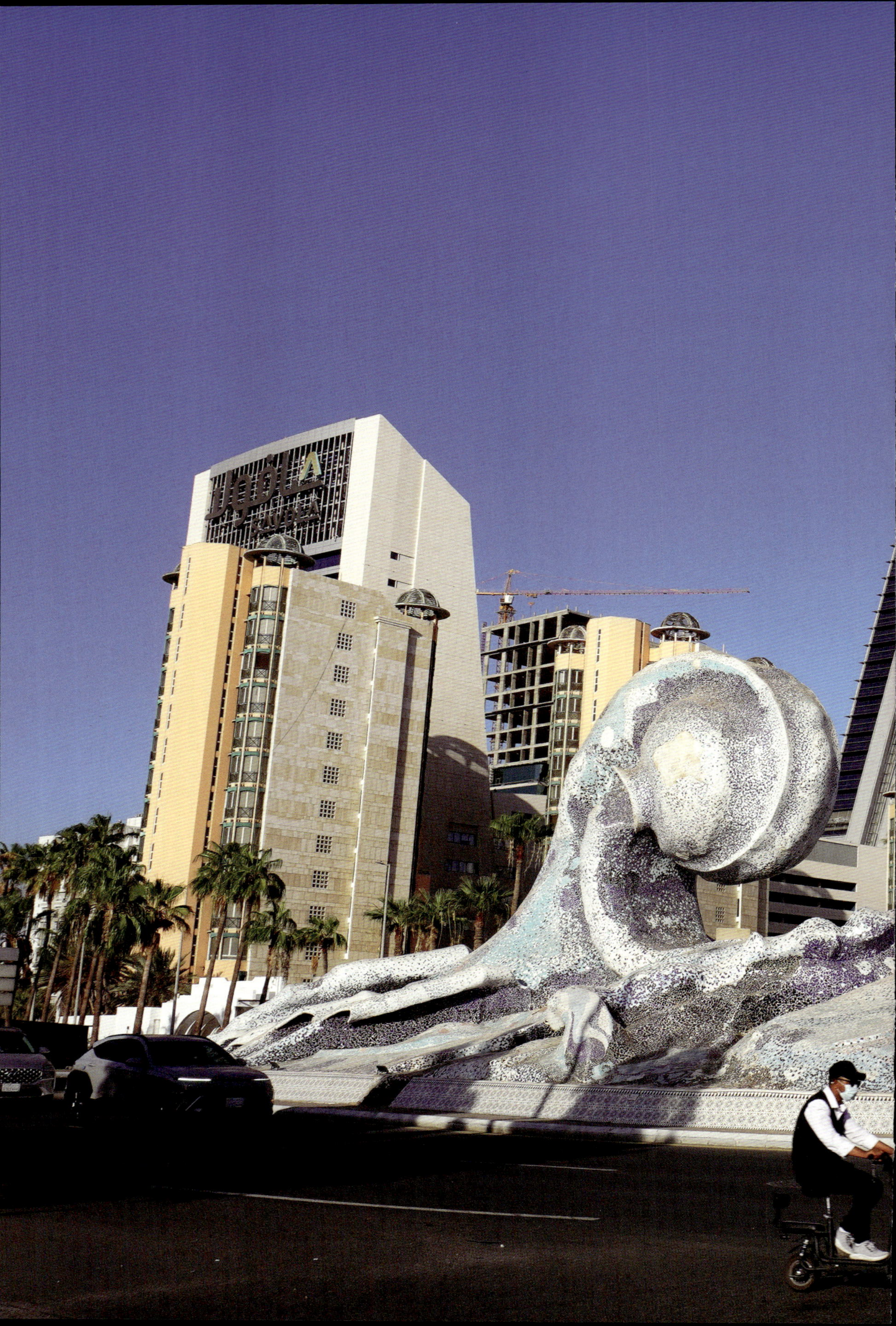

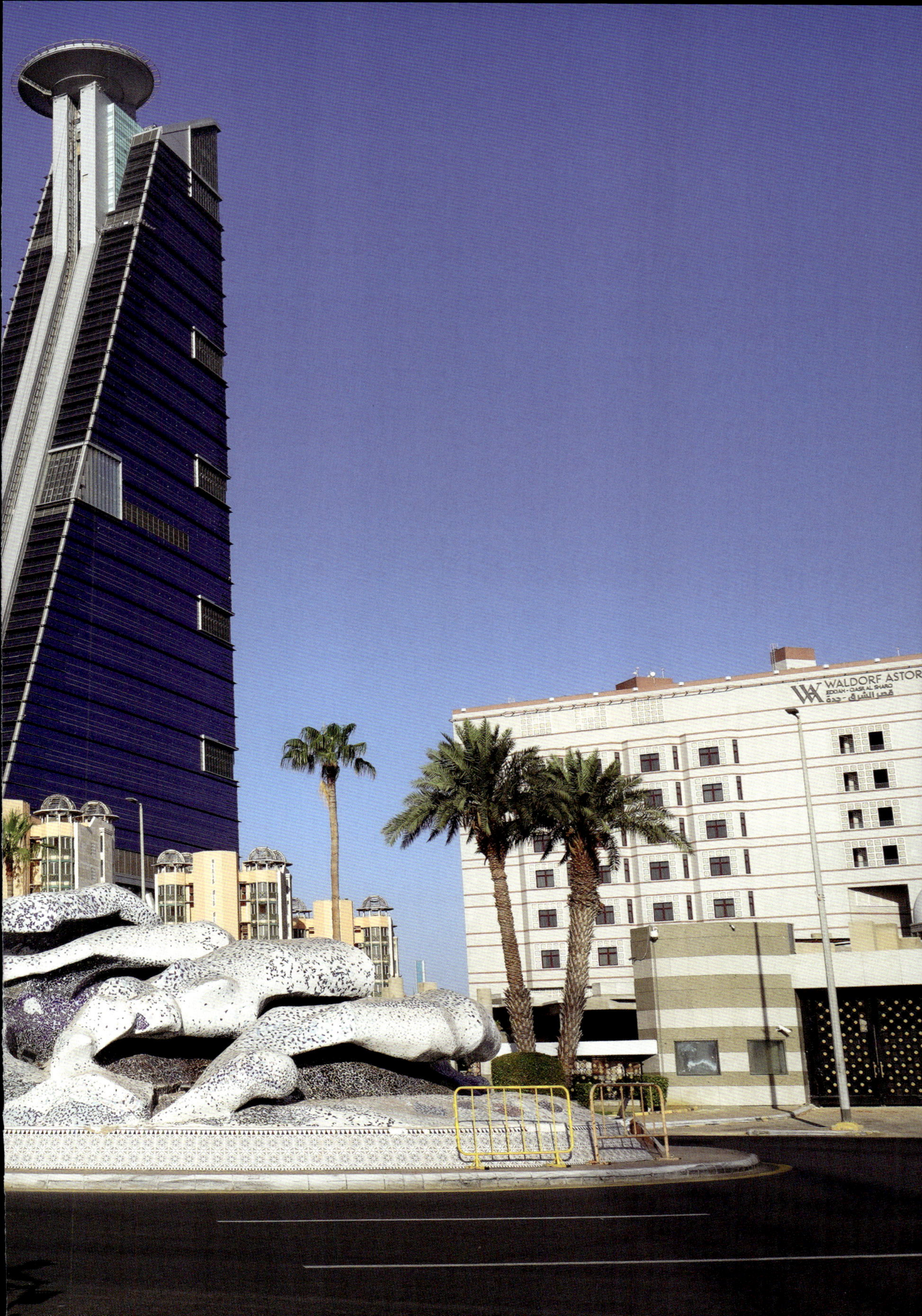
WALDORF ASTOR
EDDAH - QASR AL SHARQ
قصر الشرق - جدة

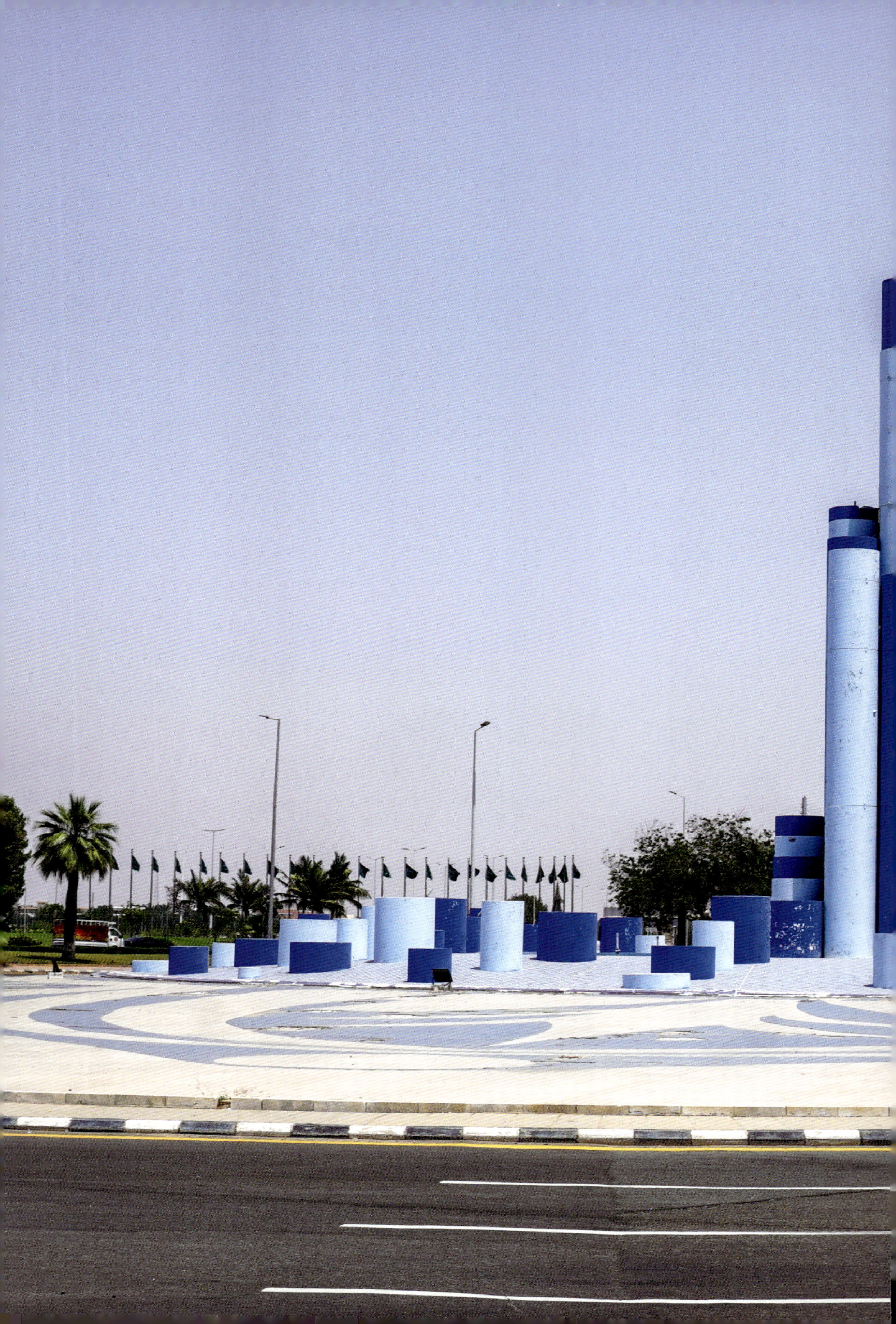

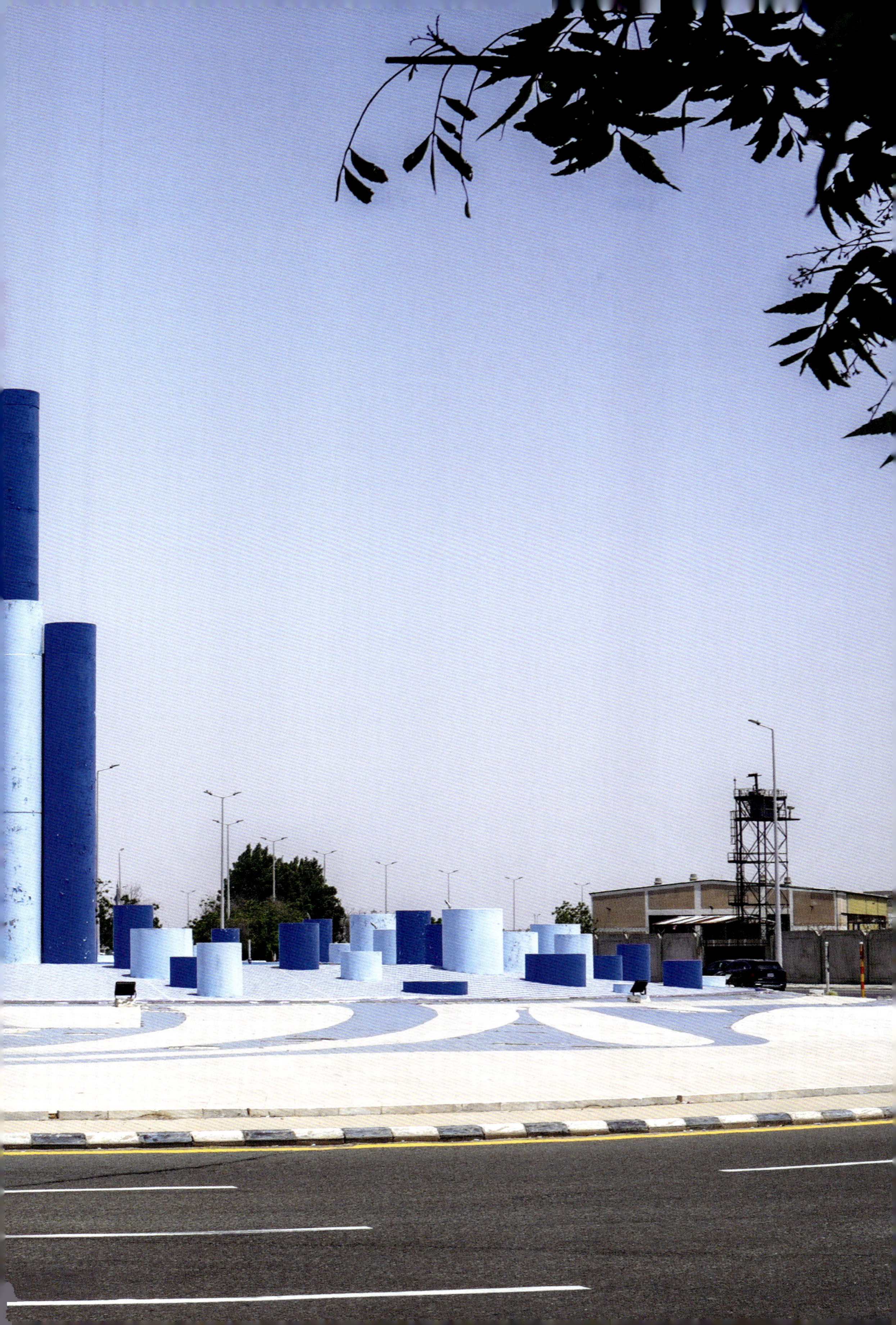

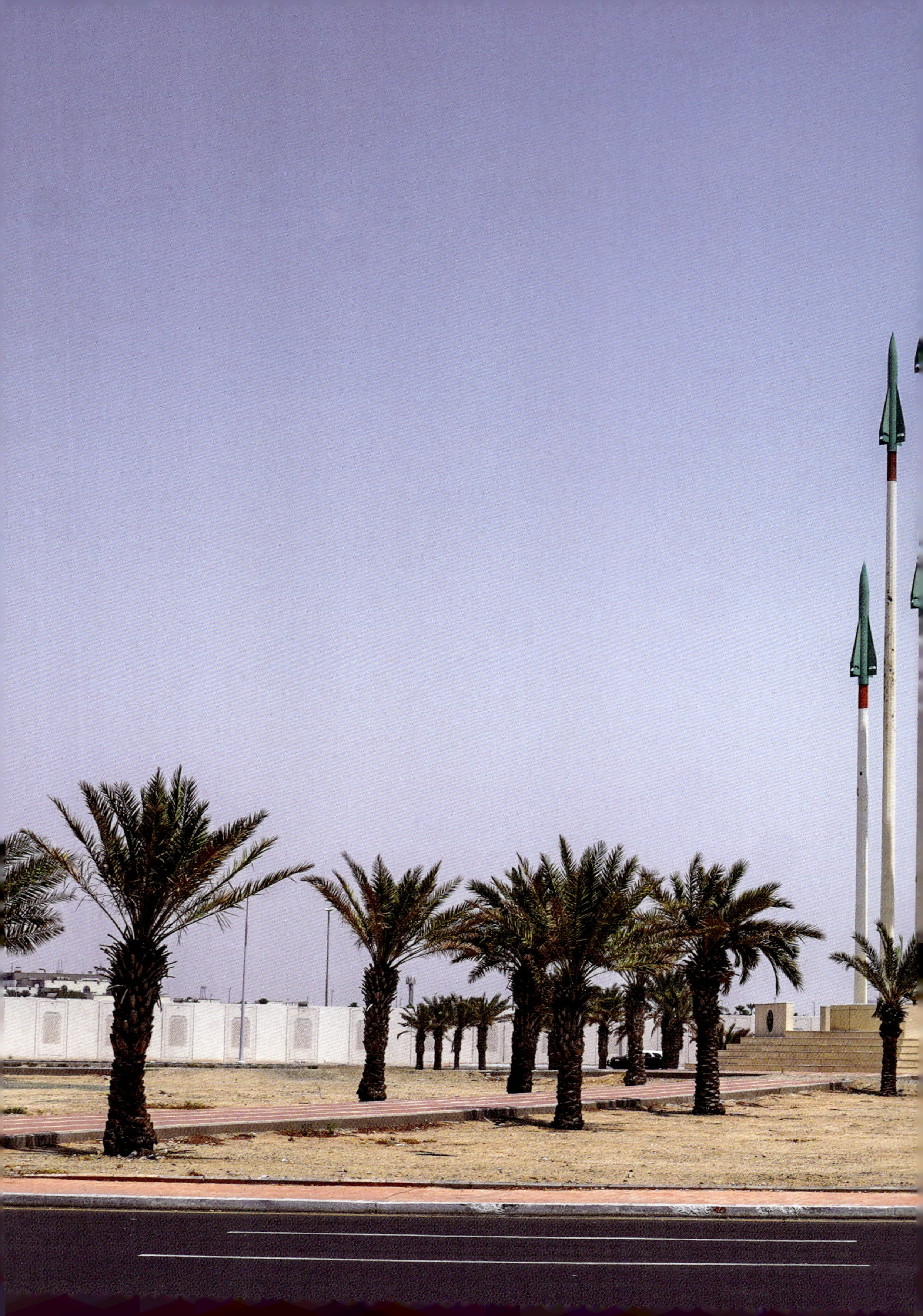

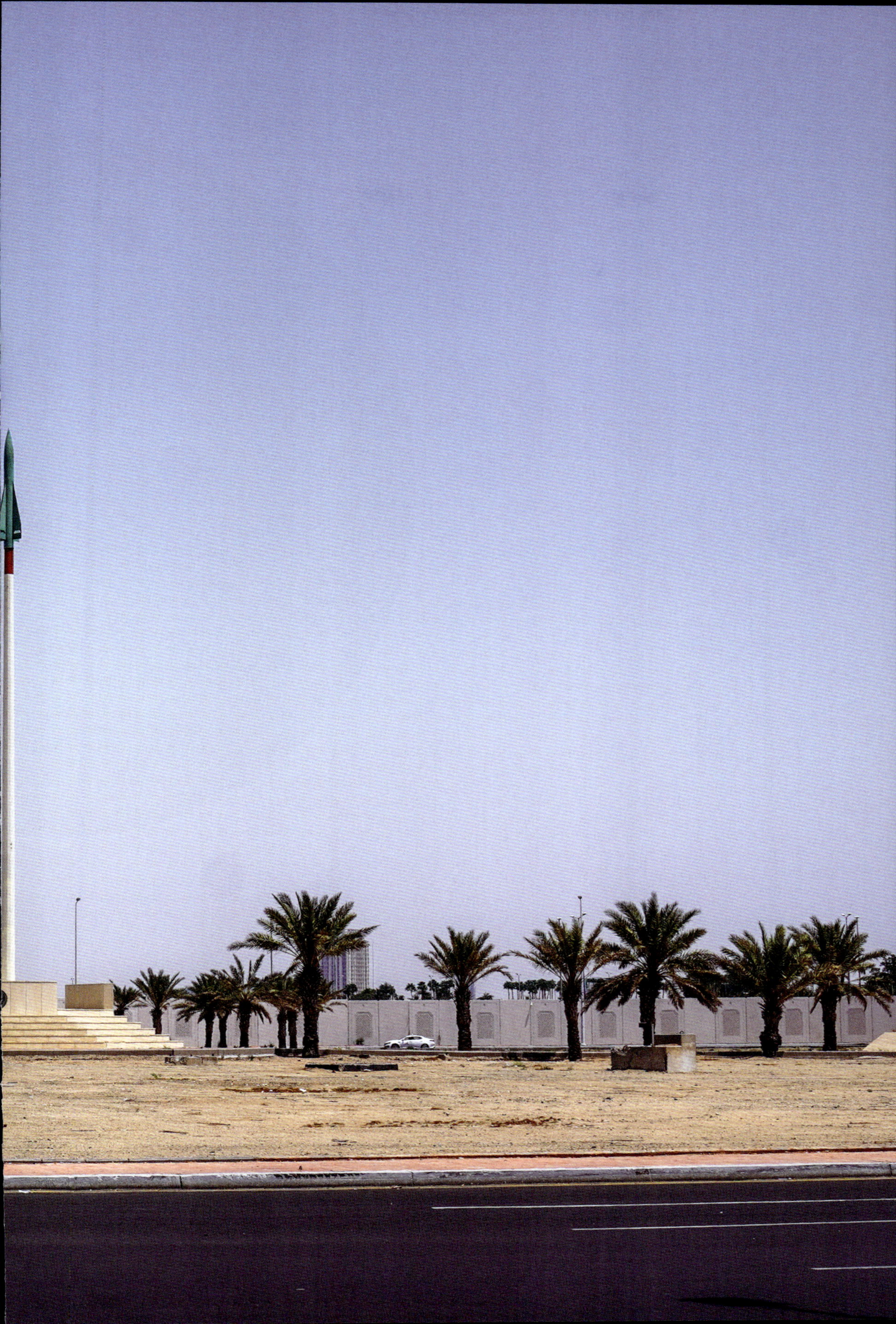

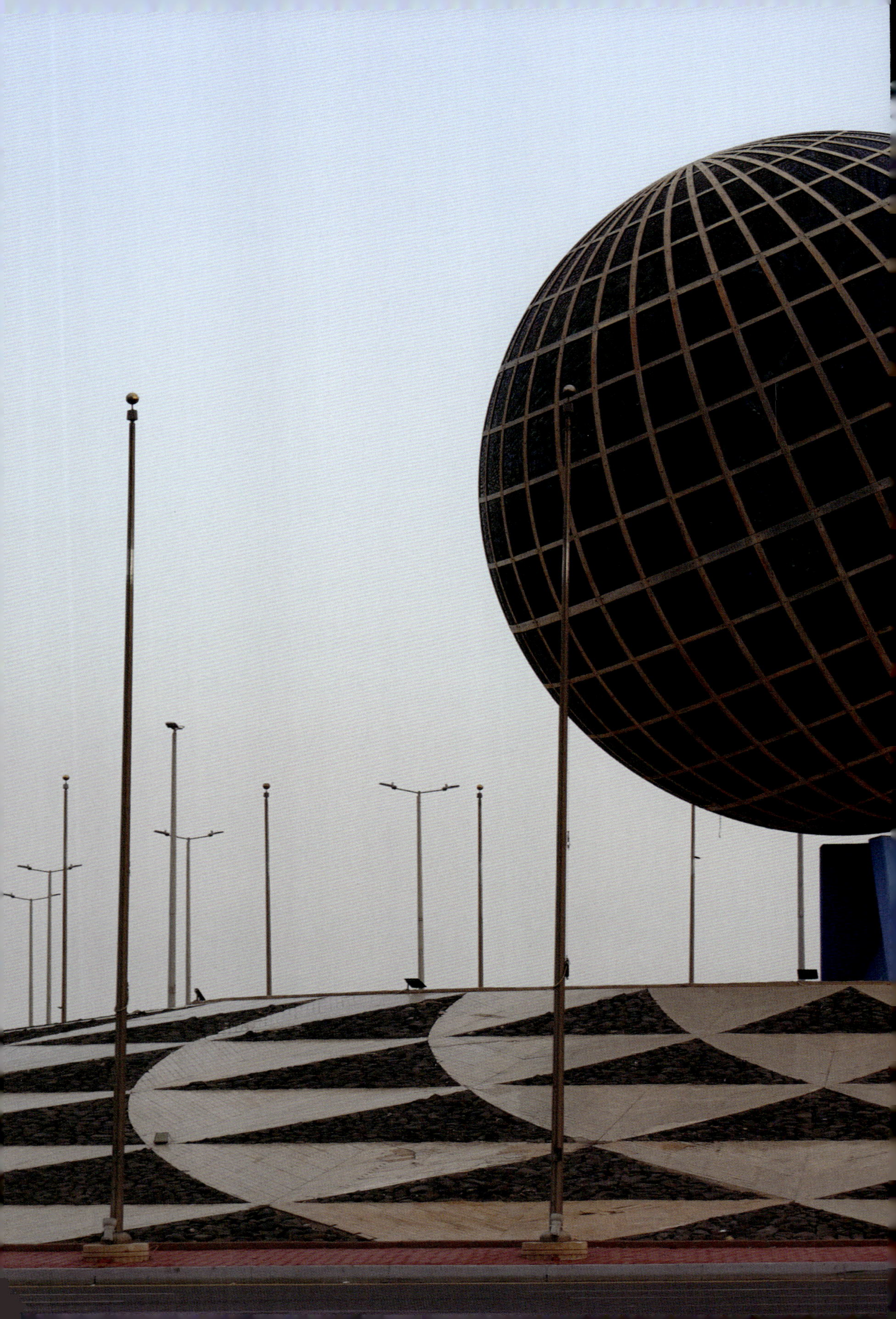

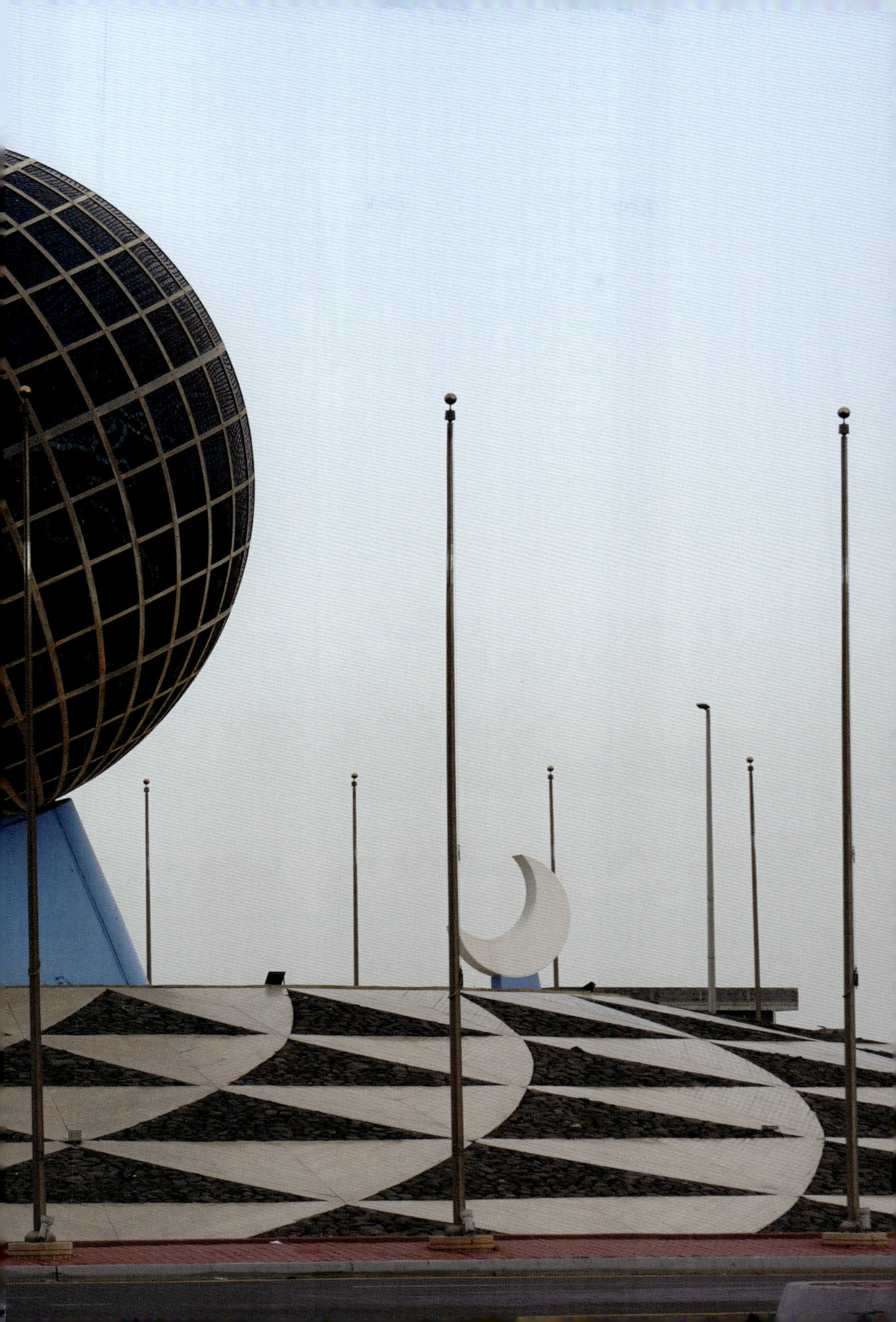

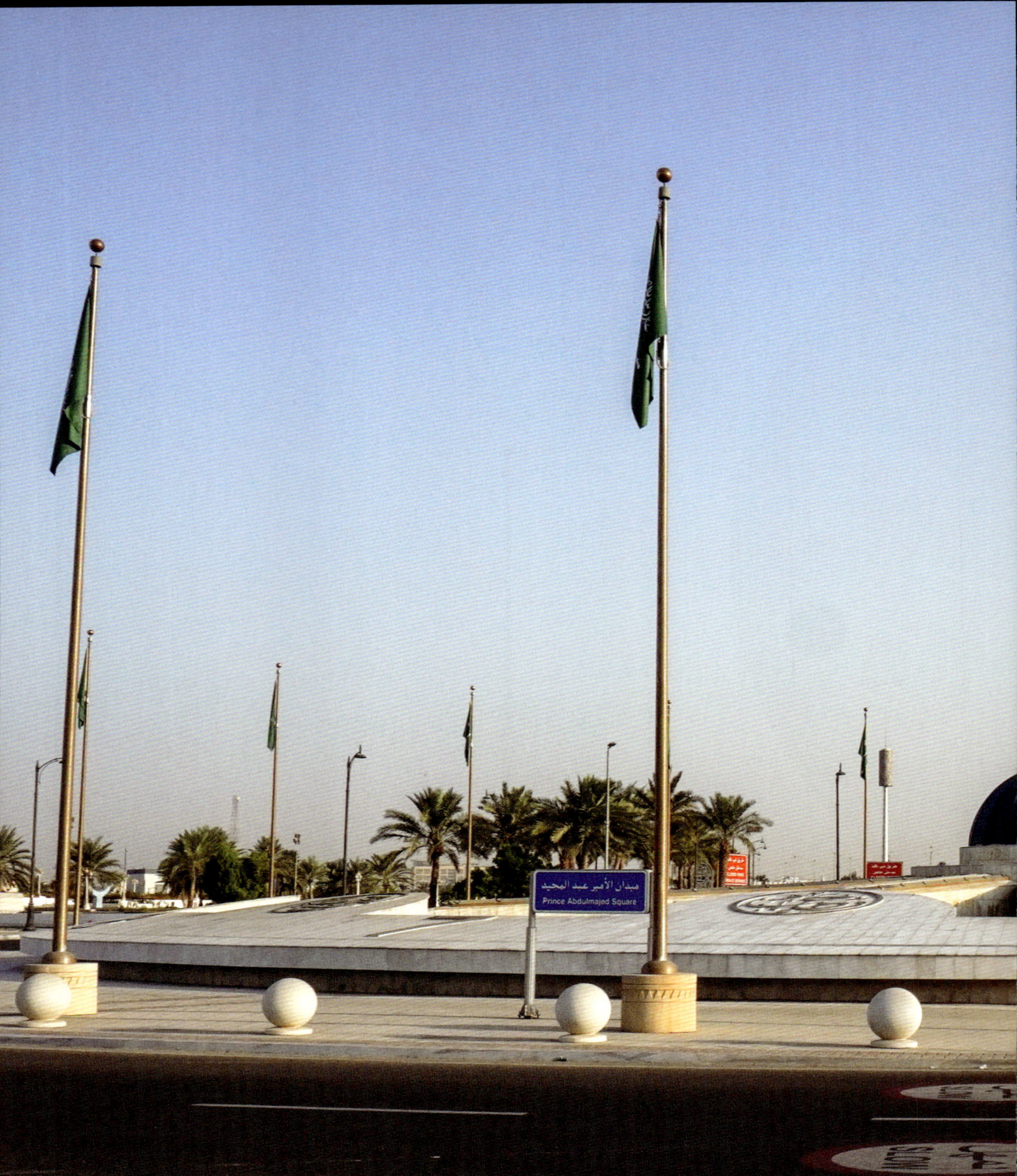
ميدان الأمير عبد المجيد
Prince Abdulmajed Square

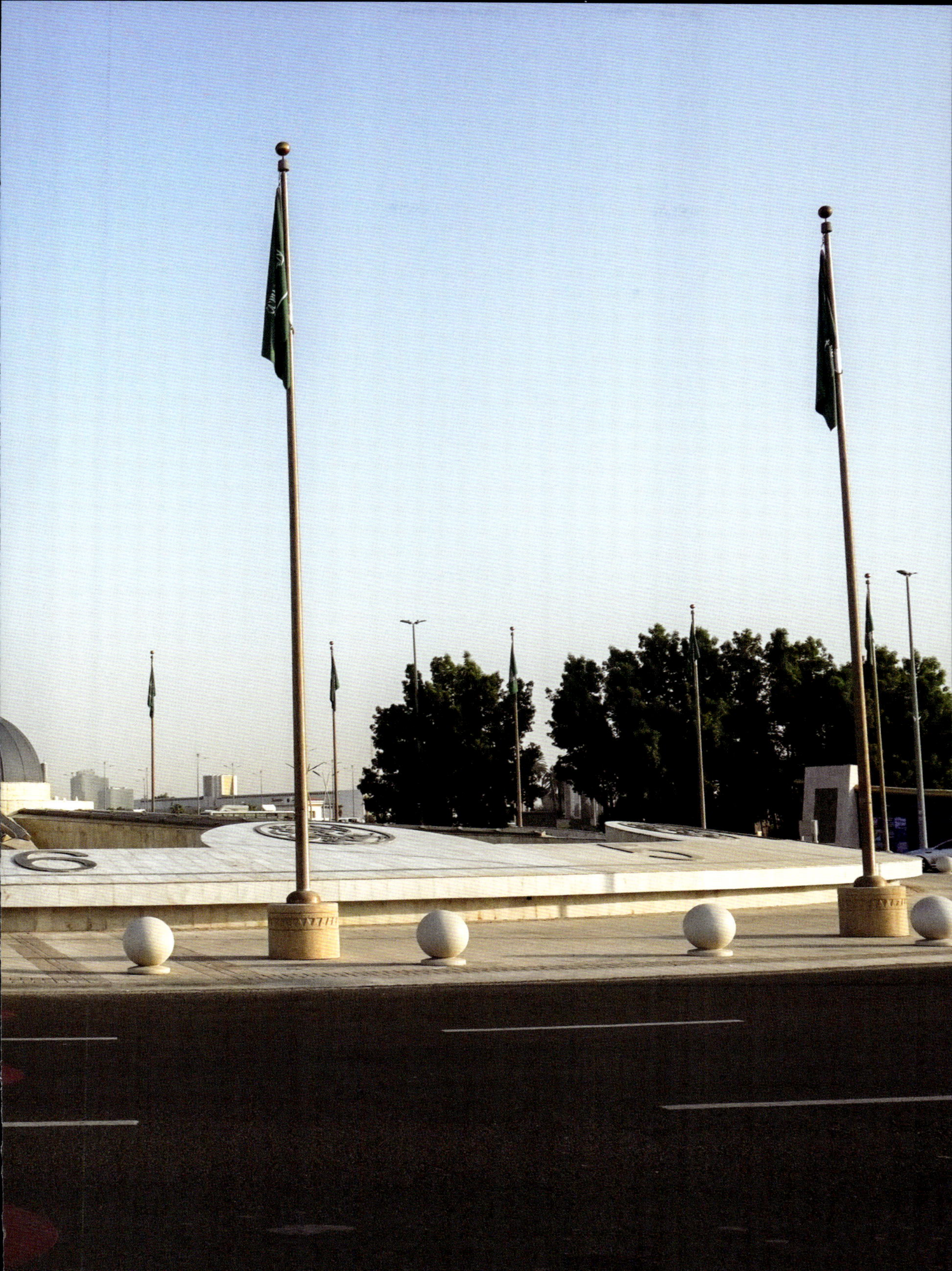

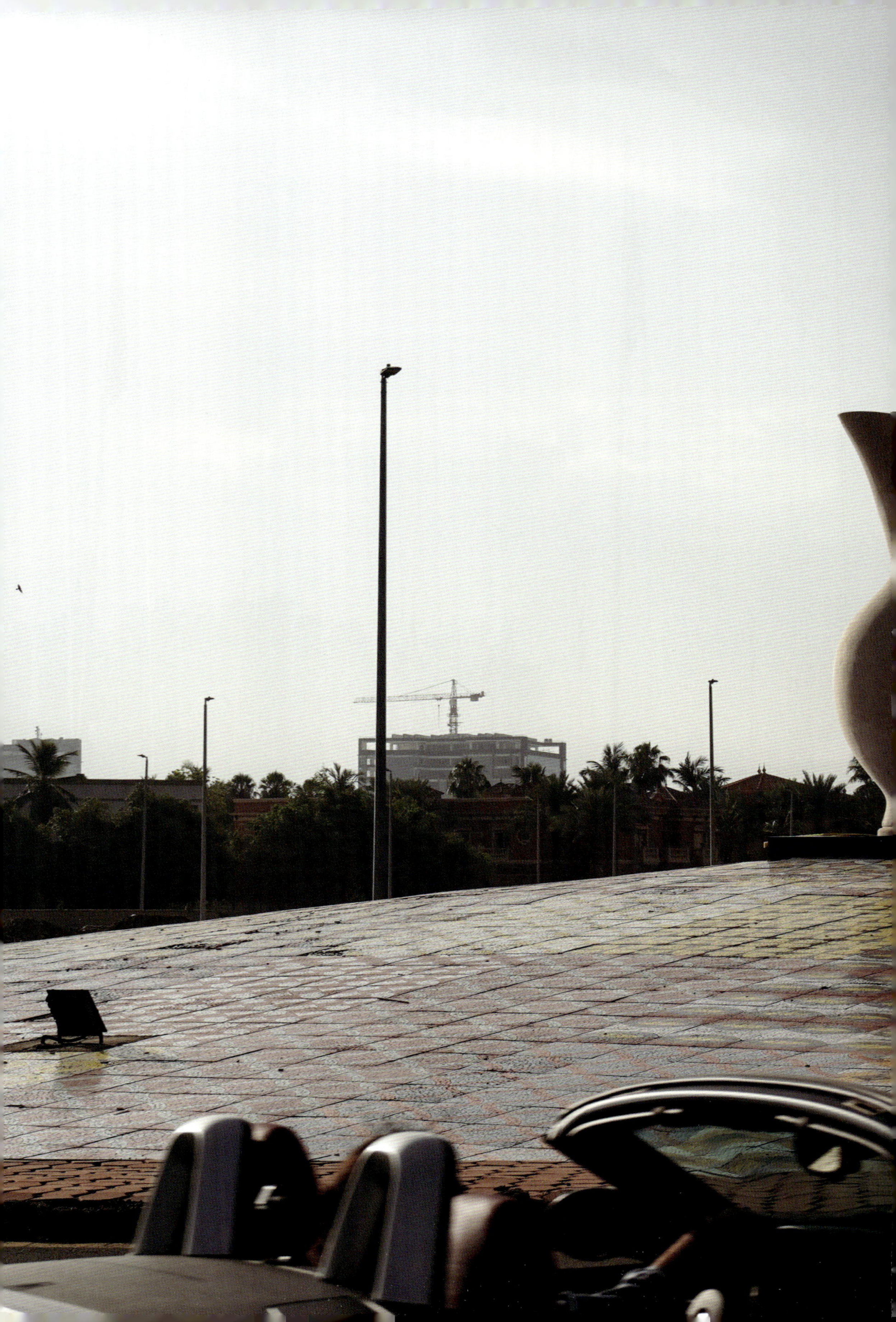

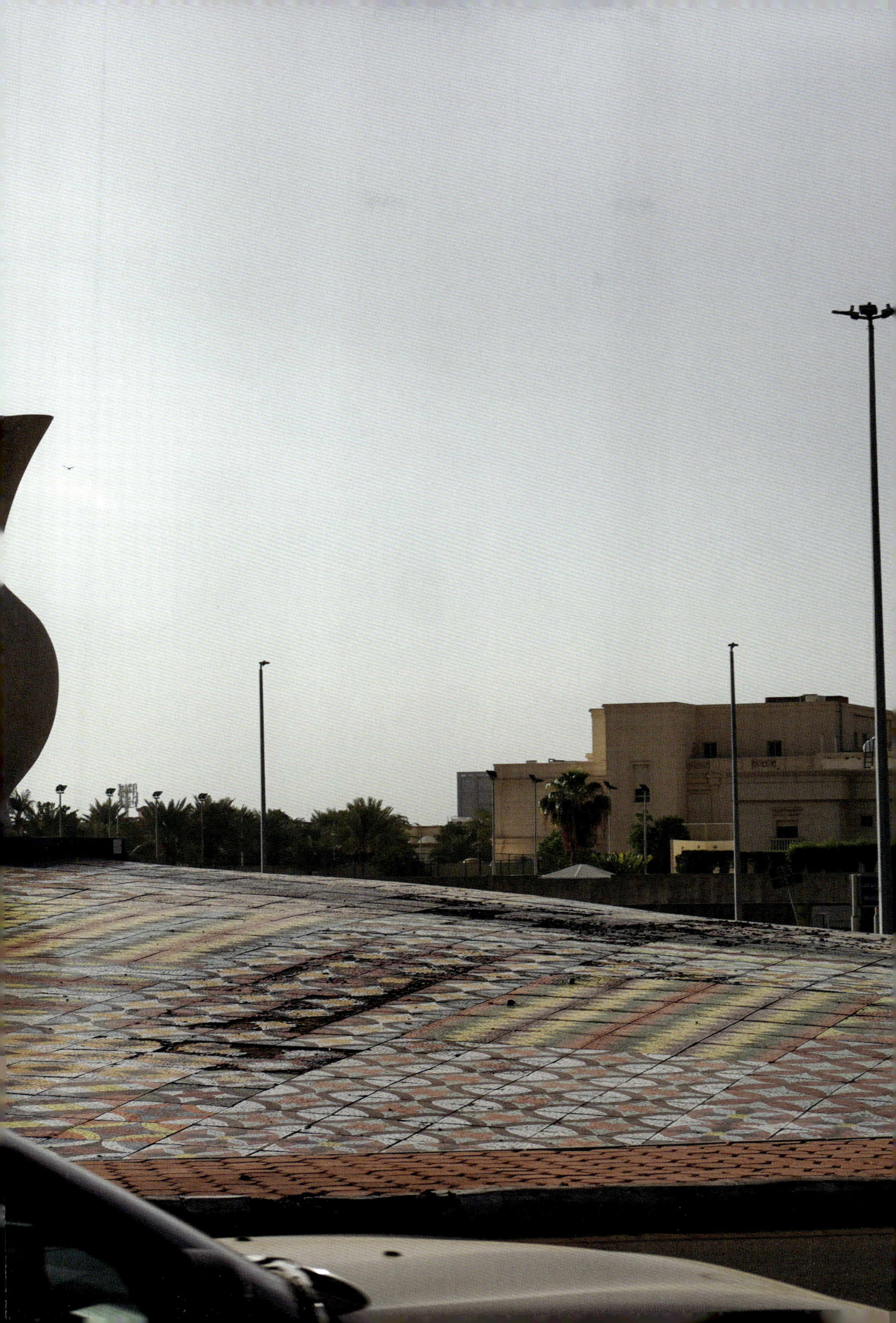

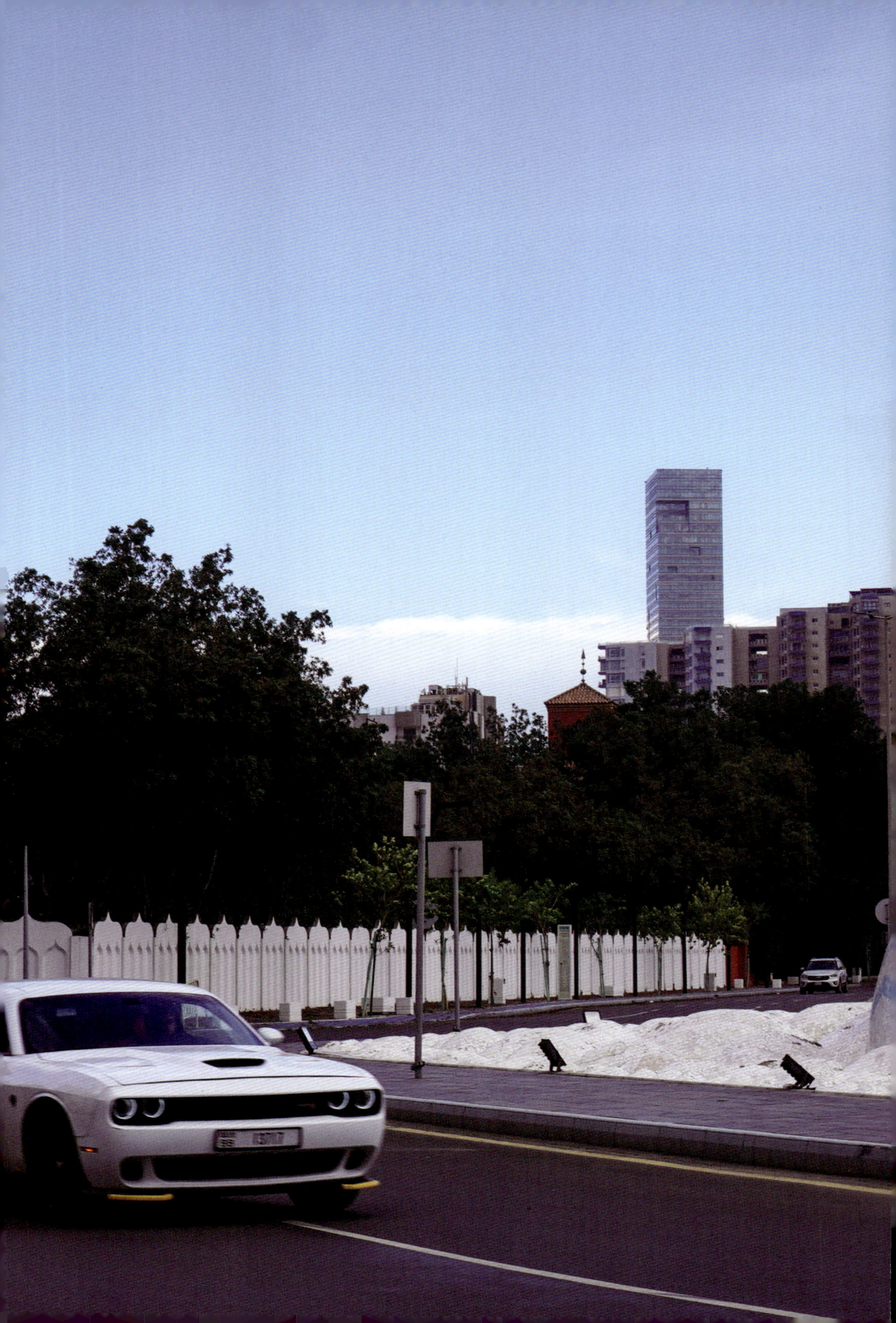

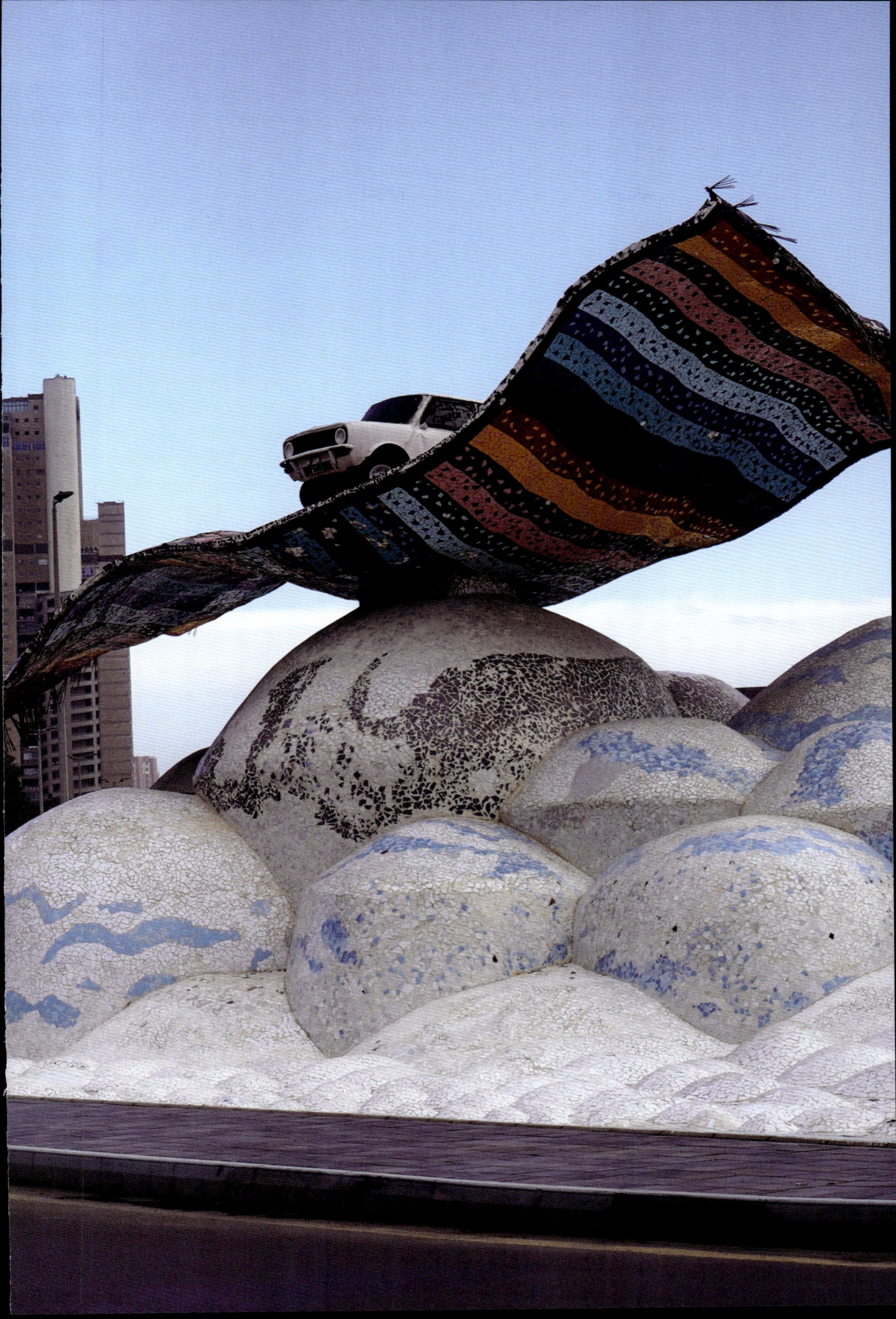

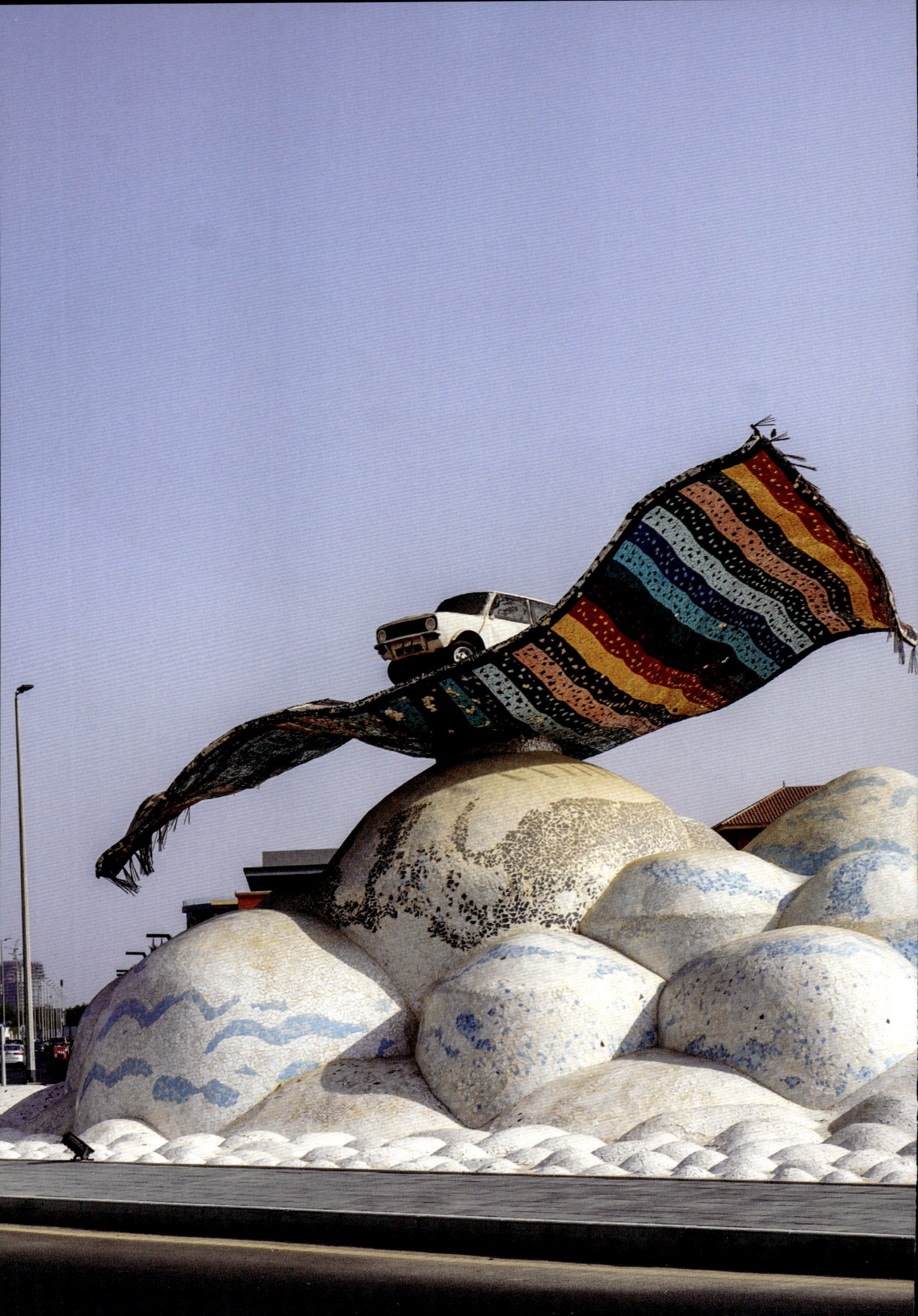

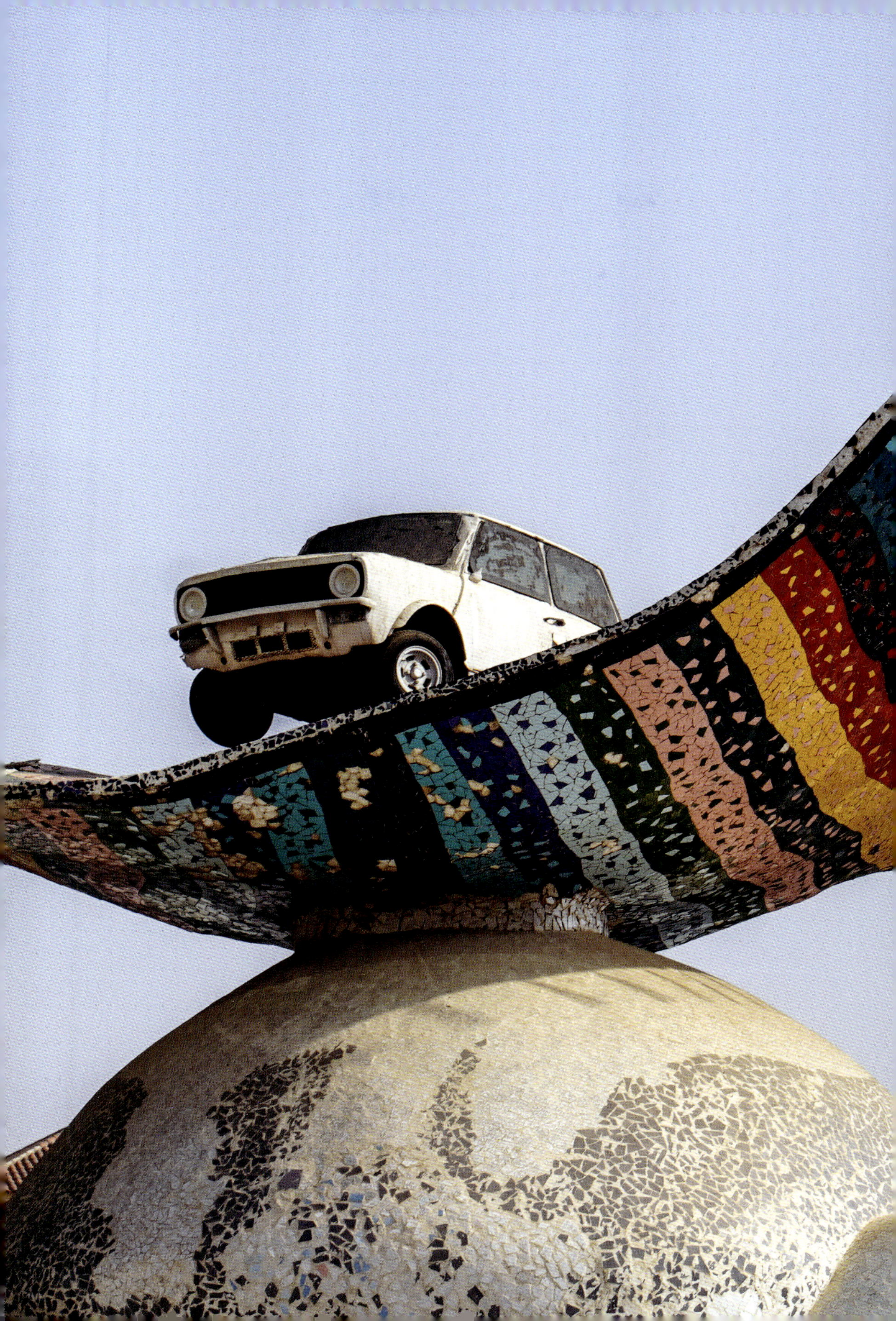

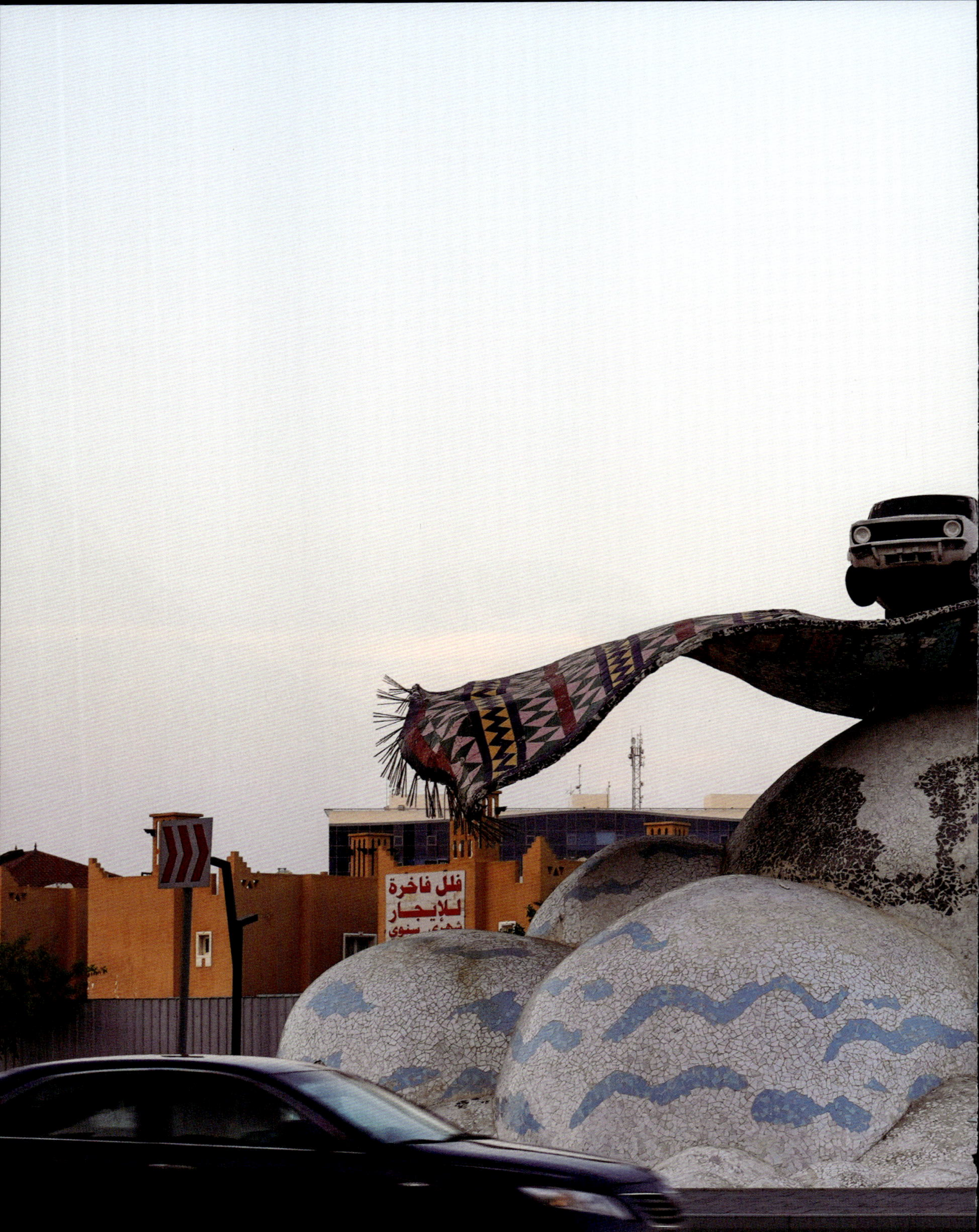

فلل فاخرة
للإيجار
سنوي

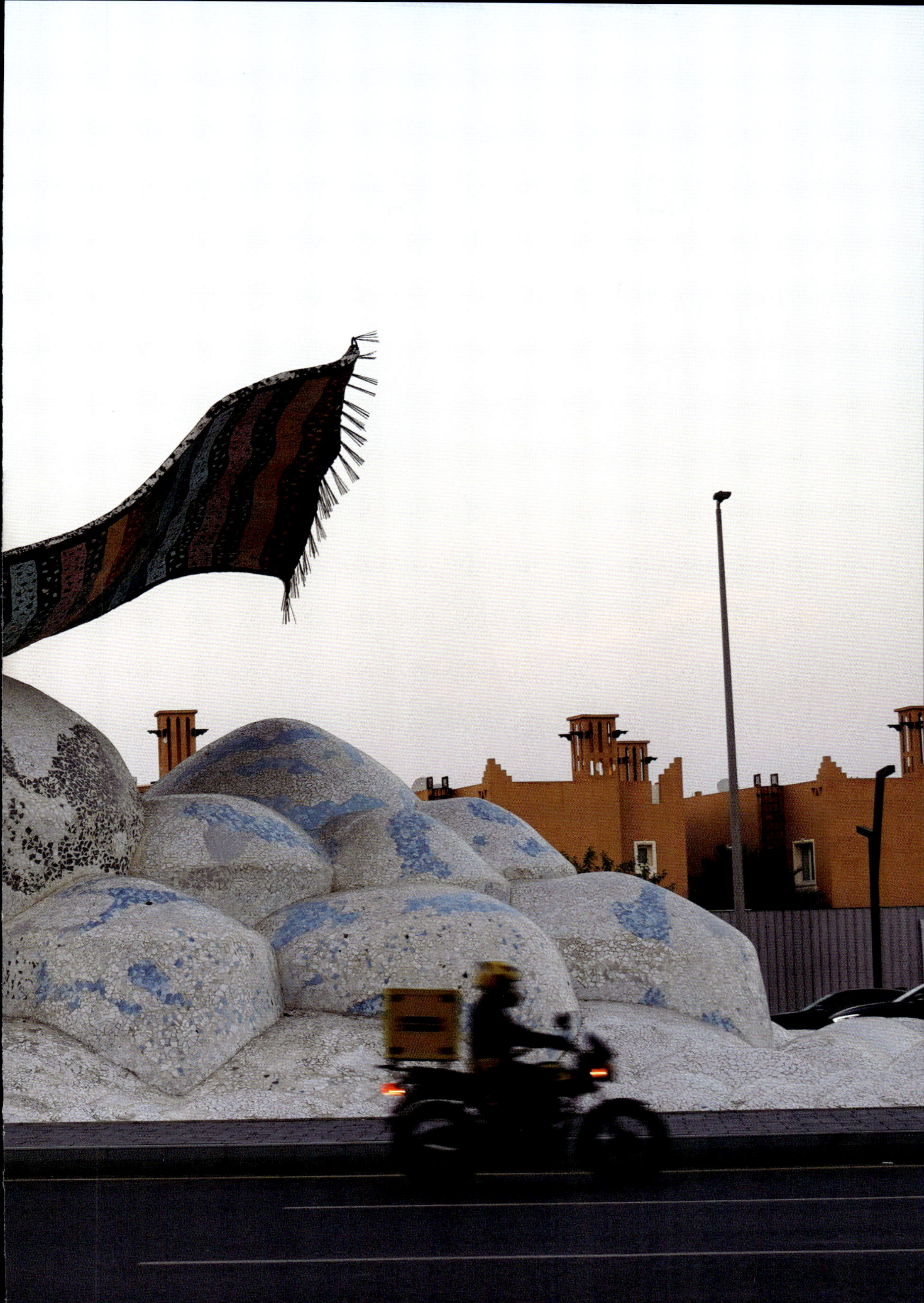

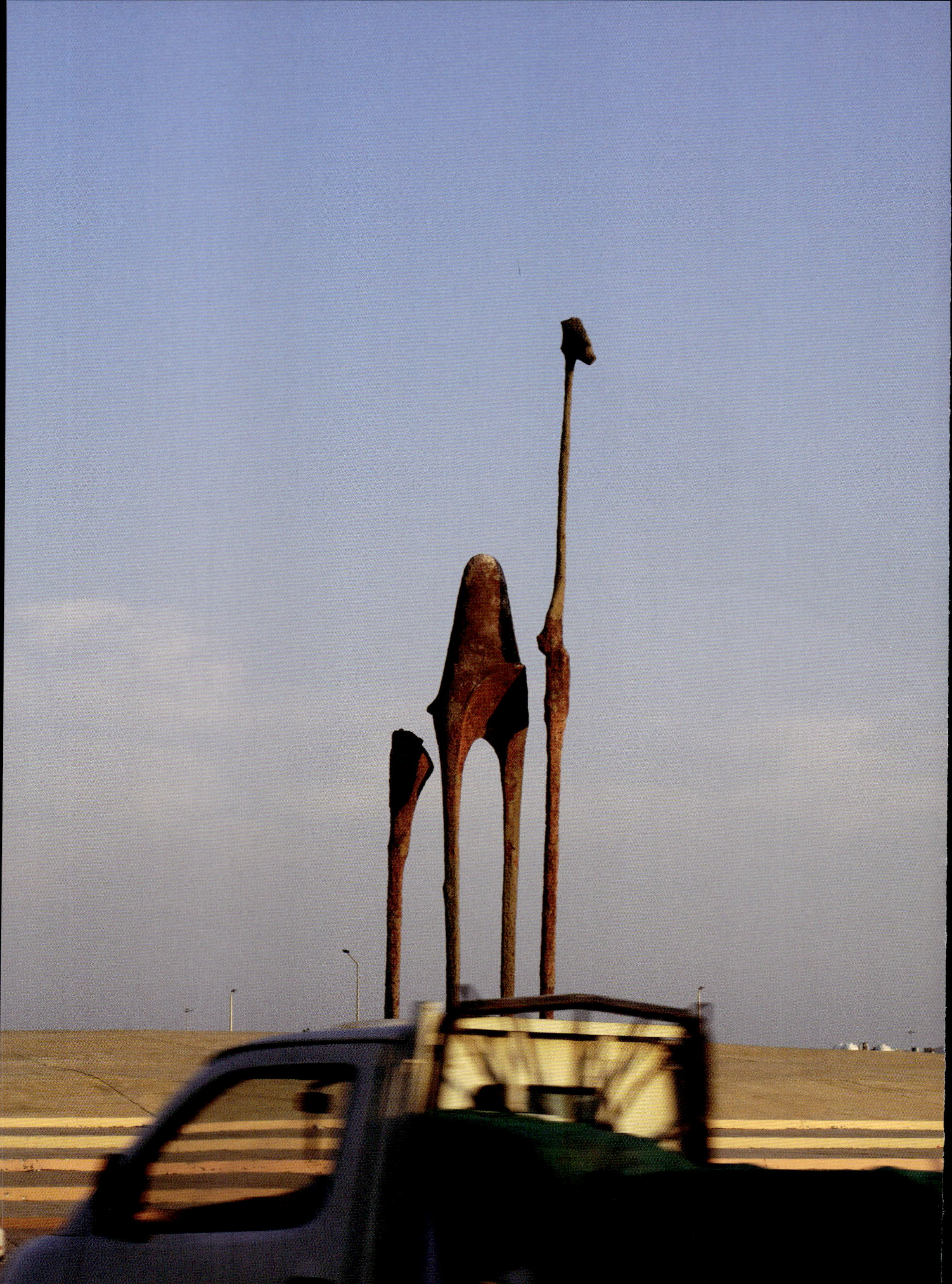

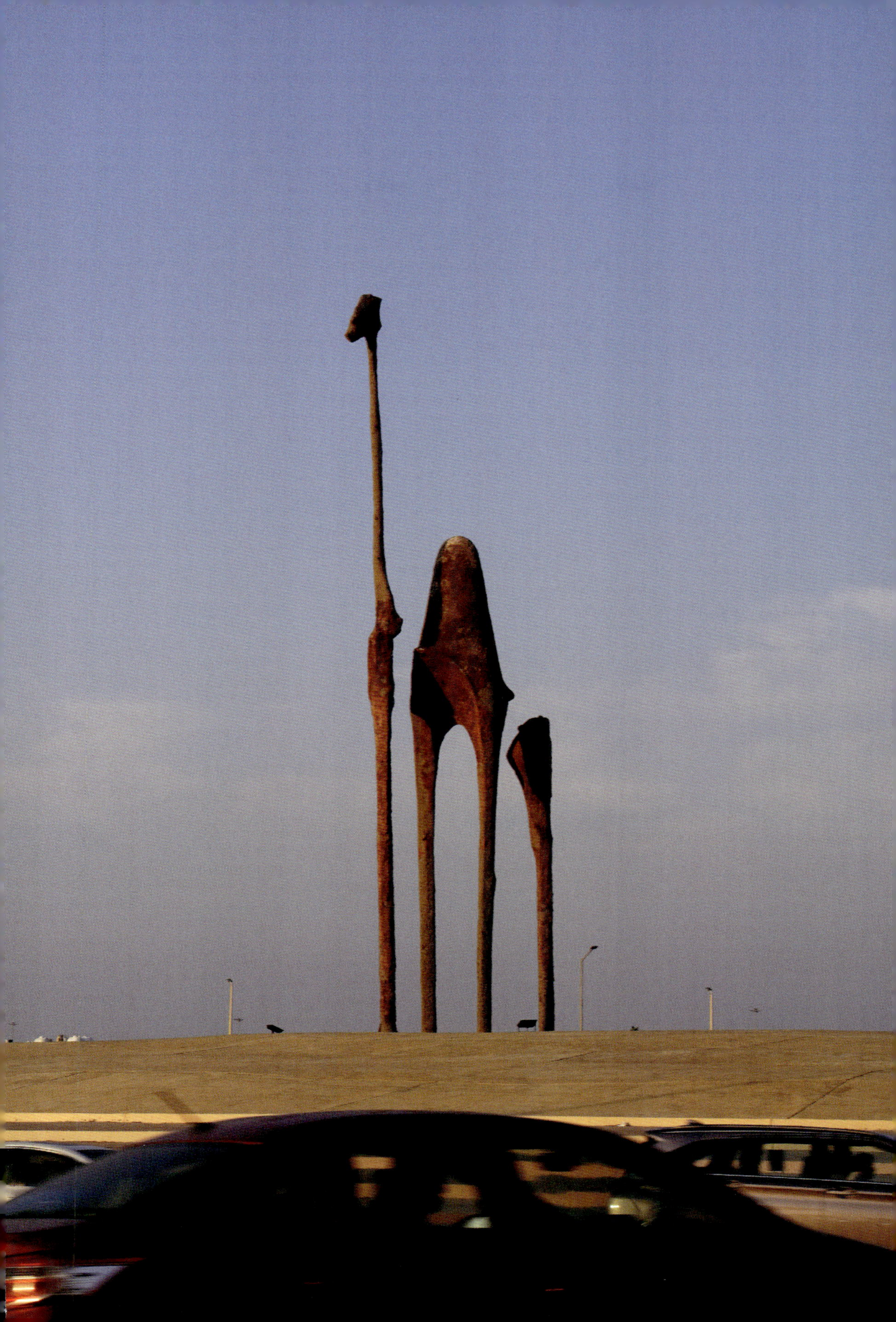

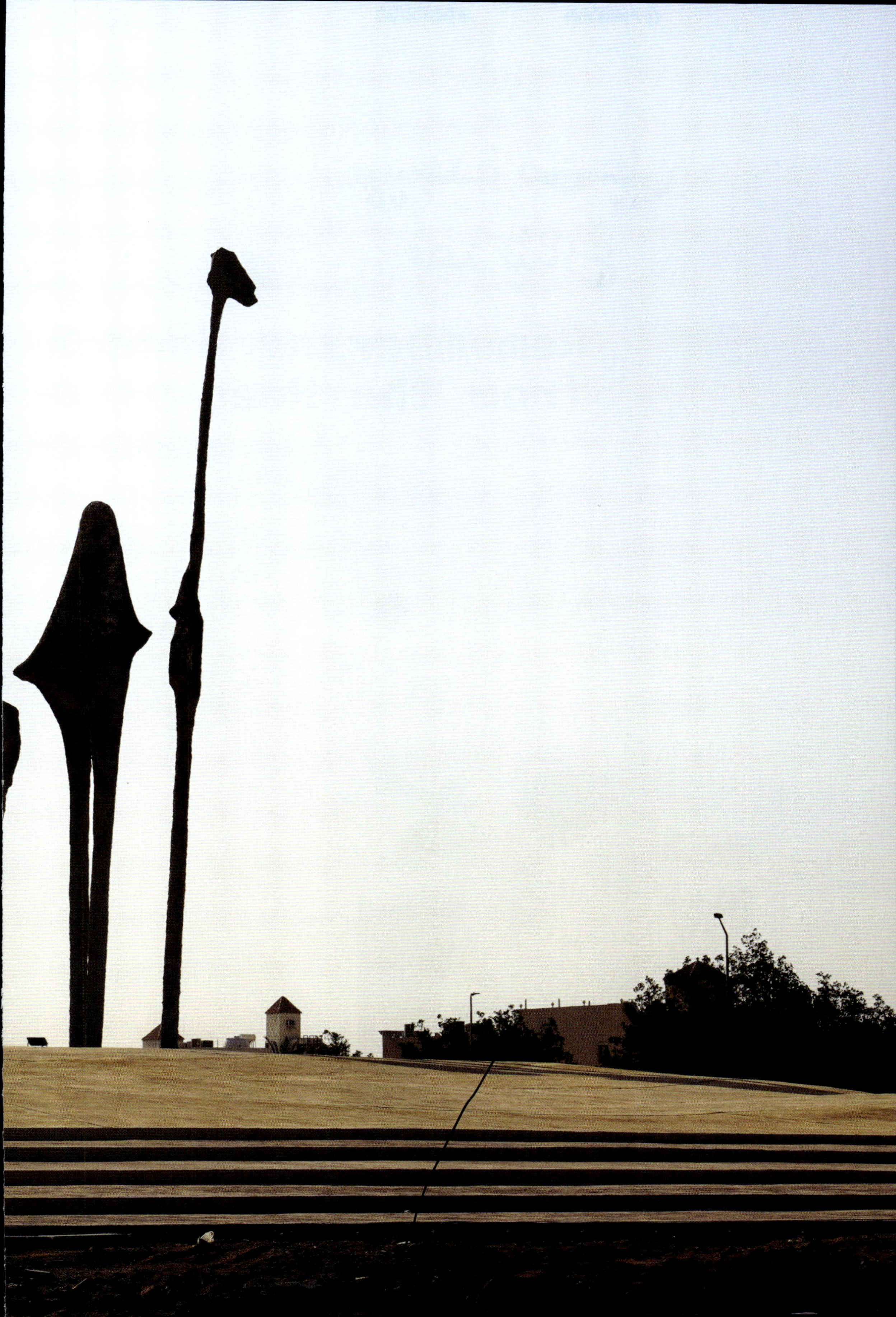

جدة من على
بُعد شارع

Remembering Jeddah from the Road

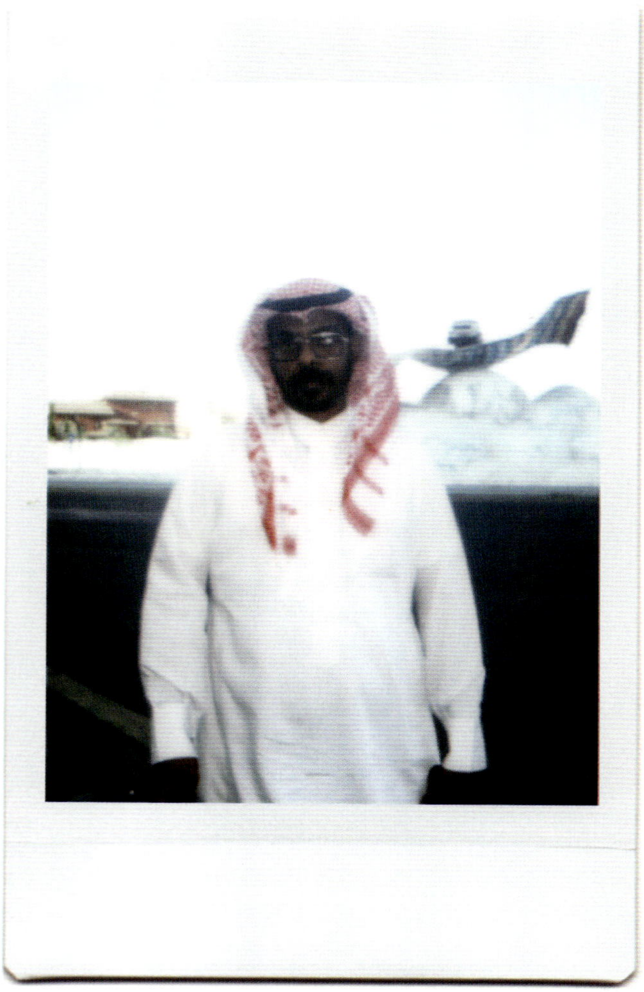

أبو سعيد

Abu Saeed

Nouf Al-Harthi **Thank you so much for your openness. I'd like to get to know you a little better. Could you tell me about yourself?**

Abu Saeed I've been driving as an informal driver for about five years. At first, I had an office job and offered informal rides on the side to help with expenses. Then, I ran into issues at the company and ended up resigning, so I devoted myself fully to driving. I now do airport pick-ups, sometimes go to Mecca, sometimes take trips within Jeddah, and occasionally to Medina. The income fluctuates, but it's still better than a fixed salary of 4,000 or 5,000 riyals[14]. Of course, violations are serious -they can wear you down- but we try to keep things smooth and work as legally as possible. I've been driving full-time this past year. It gives me structure and rhythm, even if it's exhausting at times. The goal now is to get a newer car, register officially, and do it properly.

Nouf **Speaking of the apps, are there specific requirements for the type of registered car?**

نوف الحارثي **شكرًا لك على رحابتك أبو سعيد، حابين نعرفك أكثر ونسمع عن تجربتك بالسواقة.**

أبو سعيد لي تقريبًا خمس سنوات أشتغل سواق غير رسمي. بالبداية كنت موظف مكتب، وأسوي مشاوير على جنب عشان أساعد نفسي بالمصاريف. بعدين صارت لي مشاكل في الشغل وقدمت استقالتي، فتفرغت للسواقة. الحين أسوي مشاوير مطار، أحيانًا مكة، أحيانًا داخل جدة، وأحيانًا المدينة. الدخل مو ثابت، بس أحسن من راتب ٤ أو ٥ آلاف[14]. طبعًا المخالفات متعبة وتستنزفك، بس نحاول نمشي أمورنا ونشتغل قد ما نقدر بطريقة نظامية. لي سنة تقريبًا متفرغ للسواقة. تعطيك نظام وإيقاع لليوم، حتى لو كانت متعبة. هدفي الآن أشتري سيارة أحدث، وأسجل رسميًا، وأشتغل صح.

نوف **وبخصوص التطبيقات، هل في شروط معينة للسيارة؟**

أبو سعيد إي نعم، الأنظمة واضحة، سواء أوبر أو بولت أو جيني[15]. شركات نظامية وآمنة، خصوصًا للي جايين من السفر وقلقانين ويفضلوا خدمة معتمدة. أهل جدة أهدأ، خصوصًا في المنطقة الغربية،

Abu Saeed Yes, the rules are clear, whether it's Uber, Bolt, or Jeeny[15]. These companies operate legally and are considered a safe option, especially for travelers arriving at the airport who tend to be anxious and prefer approved services. Locals are more relaxed, especially in the Western Region, many are used to informal rides as a cheaper option and as a way to support local drivers. Visitors from Riyadh and Qassim, when they come for Umrah[16], sometimes take informal rides with us as a friendly gesture. We make sure to give them a lower fare and usually don't add extra charges. A trip to Mecca is around 150 to 200 riyals[17], and sometimes families add a tip out of kindness.

Nouf **Have you always been based in Jeddah, or did life bring you here later?**

Abu Saeed I was born in Dhahran[18]. After my father retired, we moved to Jeddah and settled here. It's been about twenty-two years. The city has gone through many phases in that time, and I've witnessed a lot of the change firsthand.

Nouf **How would you describe what's changing?**

Abu Saeed I take most of my rides from the airport now.

أبو سعيد أكيد. الزحمة باتجاه الجنوب خفّت لأن الحياة تحولت للشمال. الجنوب أهدأ شوي، بس الإيجارات تغيرت[21]. من كيلو ١٠ إلى شارع فلسطين تشوفي فراغات، مستودعات وشركات أكثر من سكن. قدام محطة الحرمين في النسيم، كانت منطقة سكنية كاملة، نصفها انشال وصارت فاضية[22]. أتمنى يعيدوا تصميمها لسكن جديد أو وظائف أو فنادق، وتصير ضمن مشاريع أكبر زي مشروع وسط جدة.

نوف **كيف توصف الفرق بين شمال وجنوب جدة؟**

أبو سعيد الناس بعد الإزالة نقلت إلى الشمال بالتدريج. جنوب جدة كان فيه عائلات دخلها محدود، بعد الإزالات عوّضوا وانتقلوا لأحياء جديدة أو أبعد. حتى الشوارع تغيرت، جزء من حي العزيزية مثلاً انشال[23]. الناس تفرقت، الإيجارات ارتفعت، بس المجتمع بطبيعته قاعد يتكيّف.

نوف **مين أكثر فئة تركب معك من المطار؟**

أبو سعيد مهندسين، موظفي مطار، فنيين، دكاترة، طلاب. وأيام المباريات أغلب المشاوير للجوهرة[24]. الجمهور له إيقاع نعرفه ونتتبعه.

نوف **هل يخطر على بالك موقف مميز أو قصة مع هذا التنوع من الركاب؟**

Back in the day[19], the airport was considered far outside the city. Take Al-hamadaniyyah[20], for example: it used to be mostly empty plots with little appeal, far from the built-up areas. Today, after demolitions and development, it's one of the densest parts of the north. The new airport brought everything closer to central Jeddah and made access easier, so work opportunities became more plentiful and nearer.

Nouf **So, easier access is one big difference?**

Abu Saeed Yes. Traffic heading south eased up because so much of life shifted north. The south is a bit lighter now, but other things changed, like rents[21]. From Kilometer 10 up to Palestine Street, you now see gaps, more warehouses and companies than housing, and a drop in residents in some pockets. Opposite the Haramain train station in Al-Naseem, for example, it used to be a full residential area. With development, half of it was removed, and it's mostly empty now[22]. I hope they redesign it for new housing, open job opportunities, bring in companies or hotels, ideally, it becomes part of larger plans like Jeddah Central.

أبو سعيد متعودين على المشاوير غير الرسمية لأنها أوفر، وكمان دعم للسواقين. الزوار من الرياض أو القصيم، إذا جوا عمرة [16]، أحيانًا يركبوا معنا بنية طيبة. نخفّض لهم السعر وما نزيد. مشوار مكة تقريبًا من ١٥٠ إلى ٢٠٠ ريال[17]، وأحيانًا العائلة تزودك بقشيش من طيبها.

نوف **طول عمرك في جدة؟**

أبو سعيد لا، أنا مولود في الظهران[18]. بعد تقاعد الوالد نقلنا جدة واستقرينا فيها. صار لنا حوالي ٢٢ سنة. المدينة مرت بمراحل كثيرة وأنا شفت التغيير بعيني.

نوف **كيف توصف هذا التغيير في هاللحظة؟**

أبو سعيد أغلب شغلي الآن من المطار. مثلاً زمان كان المطار بعيد عن المدينة[19]. خذي الحمدانية[20] مثال: كانت أراضي فاضية وما فيها شي. اليوم بعد الإزالات والتطوير صارت من أكثر مناطق الشمال كثافة. المطار الجديد قرب كل شي لوسط جدة، وسهّل الوصول، فصارت الفرص أقرب وأكثر.

نوف **يعني سهولة الوصول فرق أساسي؟**

Nouf **Have you observed anything distinct between the northern and southern parts of the city during your rides?**

Abu Saeed The distribution has shifted; people have gradually moved north. South Jeddah had many low-income families; after the demolitions, some received compensation and moved to new or more distant neighborhoods. Even the streets changed; part of Al-Aziziyah, for example, was removed[23]. After the demolitions, people dispersed, some to the far south, others to areas they could afford. Communities adapt, but rents have risen.

Nouf **In your experience, have you noticed any patterns in the types of passengers you pick up from the airport?**

Abu Saeed Engineers, airport staff, technicians, doctors, and students. On match days, most trips head to Al-Jawhara Stadium[24]. Fans move in a rhythm we've come to expect.

Nouf **Do you have a story from these rides that stuck with you?**

Abu Saeed During the Barcelona - Real Madrid[25] match in Jeddah this year, some drivers raised prices.

أبو سعيد والله أهم قصة هي عن دوار الدراجة، اللي الناس تسميه "دراجة أبونا آدم"[27]. ودوار التصادم، هل تعرفي ان سيارّاته حقيقية؟ هذولي اللي عالقين في بالي وأحب أحكي عنهم دايمًا.

نوف **ولو تختار واحد مفضل؟**

أبو سعيد دوار السلام مول. أحب كيف الطريق حوله واسع ومفتوح، خصوصًا لو ما كان فيه زحمة. انحناءة الشارع مريحة، وتحس إنك تستمتع فعلاً بالسواقة.

نوف **بالحديث عن الزحمة، كيف تشوف زحمة جدة؟**

أبو سعيد الزحمة جزء من الحياة بجدة. تنتقل من مكان لمكان. ناس كثير ساكنين جنوب ويشتغلوا في الشمال، فالصباح كله رايح هناك وتكون أكثر الأوقات ازدحامًا. ويعني هي ما لها حل سحري، لكنها تعلّمك الصبر.

نوف **كدّاد ثاني قال لي بالضبط نفس الشي: «السواقة تعلّم الصبر»[28]**

أبو سعيد صحيح. تقابل ناس متوترين، غلطة بسيطة تعصبهم. لازم تستوعب وتعدّي بسلام. وكمان أحيانًا إحنا المستعجلين. المهم تراجع وتضبط نفسك.

Abu Saeed — I charged 50 riyals per person, or four for 100[26]. Another driver went higher, but a Pakistani driver stepped in and said, 'I'll take all four for 100,' and did. I believe our livelihood is ultimately in God's hands; you take opportunities, but reasonably. In the end, fair competition is what truly matters.

Nouf — **How do you imagine Jeddah's future?**

Abu Saeed — The waterfront, parks, and restaurants all point to a first-rate tourist city. I've visited Dubai a few times, and I feel we'll reach a similar level, maybe even surpass it in some ways, with the development happening now.

Nouf — **In everyday directions, do you use landmarks and roundabouts, or street names?**

Abu Saeed — Landmarks and roundabouts were our language. The White Horse Roundabout, the Fist Roundabout, the Airplane light by the old airport, the Kandarah light, the Screen Tower on King Road, we'd say, you'll hit a roundabout with such-and-such; after it, there's a building. That kind of description builds a map in your head. Even the story about the first plane gifted to King Abdulaziz

أبو سعيد — في مباراة برشلونة وريال مدريد في جدة[25]، بعض الكدادين استغلوا الموقف ورفعوا الأسعار. أنا قلت ٥٠ ريال للشخص أو أربعة بـ ١٠٠[26]. واحد ثاني زوّد، وثالث وهكذا. بعدين جا سواق باكستاني قال: أنا آخذ الأربعة بـ ١٠٠، وفعلاً أخذهم. الرزق من الله. الواحد يستغل الفرصة بعقل. والمنافسة العادلة هي الأهم.

نوف — **كيف تتخيل مستقبل جدة؟**

أبو سعيد — الواجهة البحرية، الحدائق، المطاعم، كلها تقول إننا رايحين لمدينة سياحية من الطراز الأول. زرت دبي كم مرة، وأحس بنوصل لنفس المستوى ويمكن نتعداه.

نوف — **في التوجيهات، تستخدم أسماء الشوارع ولا المعالم؟**

أبو سعيد — المعالم والدوارات كانت لغتنا. دوار الجواد الأبيض، دوار القبضة، إشارة الطيارة عند المطار القديم، إشارة الكندرة، برج الشاشة بطريق الملك. نقول: توصل دوار كذا وبعده المبنى. الوصف هذا يبني خريطة في بالك. حتى قصة أول طيارة أُهديت للملك عبدالعزيز كانوا الناس يحكوها هناك، وارتبطت بالدوار والمعلم.

نوف — **رائع، هذا يخليني أسألك عن قصصك مع الدوارات والمعالم؟**

has tales people share at that spot. That shorthand was used to guarantee people would arrive.

Nouf **Any particular roundabouts you're attached to?**

Abu Saeed The Bicycle Roundabout, people tell old stories about it, "Our father Adam's bicycle[27]." The Accident Roundabout, known as the Zahareen Roundabout, the cars in it are real. Those are the ones I remember now.

Nouf **If I asked you to pick a favorite roundabout?**

Abu Saeed Salam Mall Roundabout. The road is wide and open, especially when there's no traffic. It has a comfortable curve; you actually enjoy driving there, as you can breathe.

Nouf **How would you describe congestion in Jeddah?**

Abu Saeed Traffic is part of daily life. It shifts from place to place rather than disappearing. Many who used to live in the south now have work or schools in the north, so mornings push that way. There's no magic solution, but it teaches patience and toughens your nerves.

أبو سعيد بعدها قلت: الرياض طيارة أو نقل جماعي.

نوف **ذكرت النقل الجماعي، ممكن تحكيني أكثر كيف توصف هذي التجربة؟**

أبو سعيد النقل الجماعي مريح للمسافات الطويلة. في شركة يسموها "وست باص" جنب محطة الحرمين. يوصلوا مدن كثيرة، بـ ٤٩ راكب تقريبًا. أغلبهم كبار سن أو ما لقوا حجز طيران. المشوار أطول طبعًا بس مريح. وفي الرحلة يوقفوا كم مرة. (يشير للطريق) تذكرت "الحوت" اللي كان تمثال كبير هنا، مدري باقي ولا لا.

نوف **ايش شعورك لما تختفي المعالم المعروفة من المدينة؟**

أبو سعيد نحنا كنا نحدد بها مواقعنا. بس الحين بس تقول «أرسل الموقع». حتى لو قدامك معلم ضخم ومعروف ممكن ما تنتبه حتى، ولذلك تغيرت طريقة معرفتنا بالمدينة.

نوف **فيه كداد قال لي: حتى لو اختفى المعلم رح يضل يقول أنا «جنب المكان السابق» أو «اللي كان كذا»[31]. ذكر عزيز مول لو اختفى كمثال.**

أبو سعيد صحيح. بعض الأسماء محفورة بذاكرة جدة. عمري أربعين وأسوق من عشرين سنة. بس يعني الشباب اليوم كل اللي يقولوه أرسل اللوكيشن، وبس.

Nouf **Another driver told us, "Driving teaches you patience and deliberation."[28]**

Abu Saeed I agree. You run into tense people, maybe you didn't notice them, or a small mistake angered them. You need to absorb it and pass safely. Sometimes we're the ones in a rush. The point is to check yourself and slow down.

Nouf **Where do you usually commute from to come to work?**

Abu Saeed I don't have a strict "commute." I set my own schedule from Al-Khomrah[29] and take it as it comes.

Nouf **What does Al-Khomrah mean to you compared to moving around inside Jeddah?**

Abu Saeed Al-Khomrah is home, neighbors, and familiar faces. Like when we used to live on Baghdad Street[30]. The place changed, but the spirit stayed. When you move from one neighborhood to another, and the same faces move with you, you realize place is more than geography; it's the relationships that move with you.

Nouf **Did that move happen recently?**

نوف **وانت من وين تداوم بالعادة؟**

أبو سعيد ما أسميه دوام ثابت. لكن يبدأ مشواري من الخمرة.[29]

نوف **وش تمثل لك الخمرة؟**

أبو سعيد بيت وجيران ووجوه ومعارف. زي لما كنا كلنا عايشين في شارع بغداد بالجنوب[30]. انتقلنا والمكان تغير بس الروح تبقى. لما تنتقل ومعك نفس الناس تعرف إن المكان مو جغرافيا وبس، هو علاقات ومودة وتاريخ.

نوف **الانتقال لها كان قريب؟**

أبو سعيد قبل الإزالات بسنة تقريبًا، في ٢٠١٨ والإزالات بدأت ٢٠١٩.

نوف **كيف توصف الفرق بين الخمرة وبين تجربتك في جدة؟**

أبو سعيد بالبداية الخمرة كانت فاضية، بعد كورونا تحديدًا صارت مليانة حياة. قلنا: كنا مرتاحين وما درينا. بس الصدق، الجنة بدون ناس ما تنداس. الحياة بدأت في المنطقة، والفرص كثرت. الرجعة لجدة من الجسر ٨–١٠ دقايق. مو مرة زحمة زي الرياض. وأنا جربت الرياض ٢٠١٧ بسيارة قير عادي، مشوار ١٠ دقايق يأخذ ساعة.

Abu Saeed — About a year before the demolitions, around 2018. The demolitions started around 2019.

Nouf — **Is living in Al-Khomrah different from central Jeddah?**

Abu Saeed — At first, it felt a bit empty; the neighborhood was almost deserted. After COVID, it suddenly got crowded, no parking, and schools were full. We laughed at ourselves: "We were comfortable and didn't even realize." But honestly, as they say, a paradise without people isn't worth walking in. The neighborhood came to life with opportunities; if you've got a small business, you can open and succeed. Getting back to Jeddah via the overpass takes eight to ten minutes, a different kind of congestion from the city center, not like Riyadh. I tried Riyadh in 2017 in a manual-transmission car; a ten-minute trip took an hour each way. After that, I swore I'd only go to Riyadh by plane or by coach.

Nouf — **You mentioned coaches earlier. What has your experience with them been like in Saudi Arabia?**

Abu Saeed — Coaches are comfortable for long distances. You're free of the responsibility of driving,

أبو سعيد — نادر أشغل موسيقا. بس اسمع قناة لواحد يقال له أبو فهد، سوالف اجتماعية. وأحيانًا أشغّل إذاعة. أحب عبدالمجيد عبدالله بس القديم. اليوم كنت أسمع قصة عن "النظرة الشرعية" من حلو الكلام[32]. الحياة مفاجآت، وكل يوم تتعلم شي جديد.

Abu Saeed — and the fares are modest compared to flying. There's a company people call "West Bus," with offices near the Haramain station. They cover cities across the Kingdom with buses that seat around 49 passengers. Many travelers are older people or those who couldn't book flights. The trip is longer, but it's comfortable. They stop several times along the way, and time passes quietly (Abu Saeed briefly gestures to the road). Now, I just remembered "the Whale," a big fish sculpture we used to pass all the time. Not sure if it's still there.

Nouf — **When landmarks or roundabouts disappear, how does that affect you, since you used them as reference points?**

Abu Saeed — We used to give directions with them. Now it's "send the location." Even if there's a huge structure right in front of you, people might not notice. That's how pins work now. We used to memorize the city's features and navigate; now the map leads us. It's not necessarily bad, but it changes how we learn about the city.

Nouf — **Another driver told me that even if a landmark disappears, he'll say, "I'm by the former such-and-such."[31] He gave Aziz Mall as an example.**

نوف — **لو سألتك أبو سعيد وش إيجابيات وسلبيات التفرغ للسواقة تمامًا؟**

أبو سعيد — والله نقاط التفتيش تخليك دائمًا حذر وحاسب حسابك. ومن السلبيات بعض الركاب يحاولوا يتهربوا من الدفع، خصوصًا الصغار لذلك أتجنبهم. والإيجابيات فيه ناس كريمة تعطينا زيادة عن اللي نطلبه، وتفرجها علينا. والرزق على النية و«الإبل تمشي على نية راعيها».

نوف

نوف — **تحكي كثير عن تصميم الدوارات وخلاني أفكر أسألك لو تصمم منحوتة لدوار وش بتكون؟**

أبو سعيد — أدوات. مفكات، ونش، ترس. هذا أنا. افتحي الدرج، شوفي شهادتي. (درجة علمية في الهندسة).

نوف — **الله! بنغطي اسمك، بس هل نقدر نصور؟**

أبو سعيد — توكلي على الله، يمكن ألقى وظيفة عن طريقك (يضحك). ما توقعت الحوار يوصل كذا. فيه كثير كدادين عندهم قصص بس محد يسألهم.

نوف — **الله يعطيك العافية. أخيرًا، لو بنختم بأغنية تسمعها دائمًا بالطريق؟**

Abu Saeed True. Some landmarks are etched into Jeddah's memory. The name stays on people's tongues even if the structure is gone. I'm forty and have been driving since I was twenty; I've seen a lot and carry the roads in my mind. But young people today tell them a tower's name, and they won't know it. They'll just say, "Send me the location." Technology made things easier, but we lost some of the old wayfinding skills.

Nouf **Now that you're almost fully dedicated to driving, how do you see the pros and cons?**

Abu Saeed Because of the checkpoints and enforcement, I often have to make quick decisions depending on the passengers. Sometimes someone tries to trick you, you drop them off, they say 'I'll transfer it to you,' and then disappear, especially the younger ones, so I usually avoid them. But there are also generous people who tip extra, and that makes the day easier. It reminds you there's still good in the world. In this job, your income reflects your intentions. As they say, 'Camels walk according to their owners' intentions.' If you intend good, you'll find good along the road.

Nouf **If you could design a sculpture for a roundabout, what would it be?**

Abu Saeed Open the glove compartment, look at my certificates. I'm drawn to mechanics. The sculpture would be a set of tools: screwdrivers, a winch, and the gear of hard work. That's my honest self.

Nouf **We'll cover your name for privacy. Can we take a photo?**

Abu Saeed Go ahead, maybe I'll get a job through you (laughs). But really, I like the idea. I didn't expect the conversation to go this way. At first, I hesitated, then decided to help. What you're doing could become valuable material. It's the first time I've seen someone collecting this kind of story from drivers with such care. Drivers have stories that rarely get told, but when you ask, a lot comes out.

Nouf **Before we wrap up, if you had a favorite song to recommend for the ride, what would it be?**

Abu Saeed I rarely play music. I follow a YouTube channel called Abu Fahd, Sweet Talk[32]: daily social stories, twenty minutes to half an hour. I listen to it on the airport route. Sometimes I turn on FM or the news. I like old Abdul Majeed Abdullah songs, but my taste has changed. Today I was listening to a story about a "premarital meeting", a guy went with his friend to an arranged marriage, and fate wrote the match for the friend! Life's full of surprises. You learn something new every day.

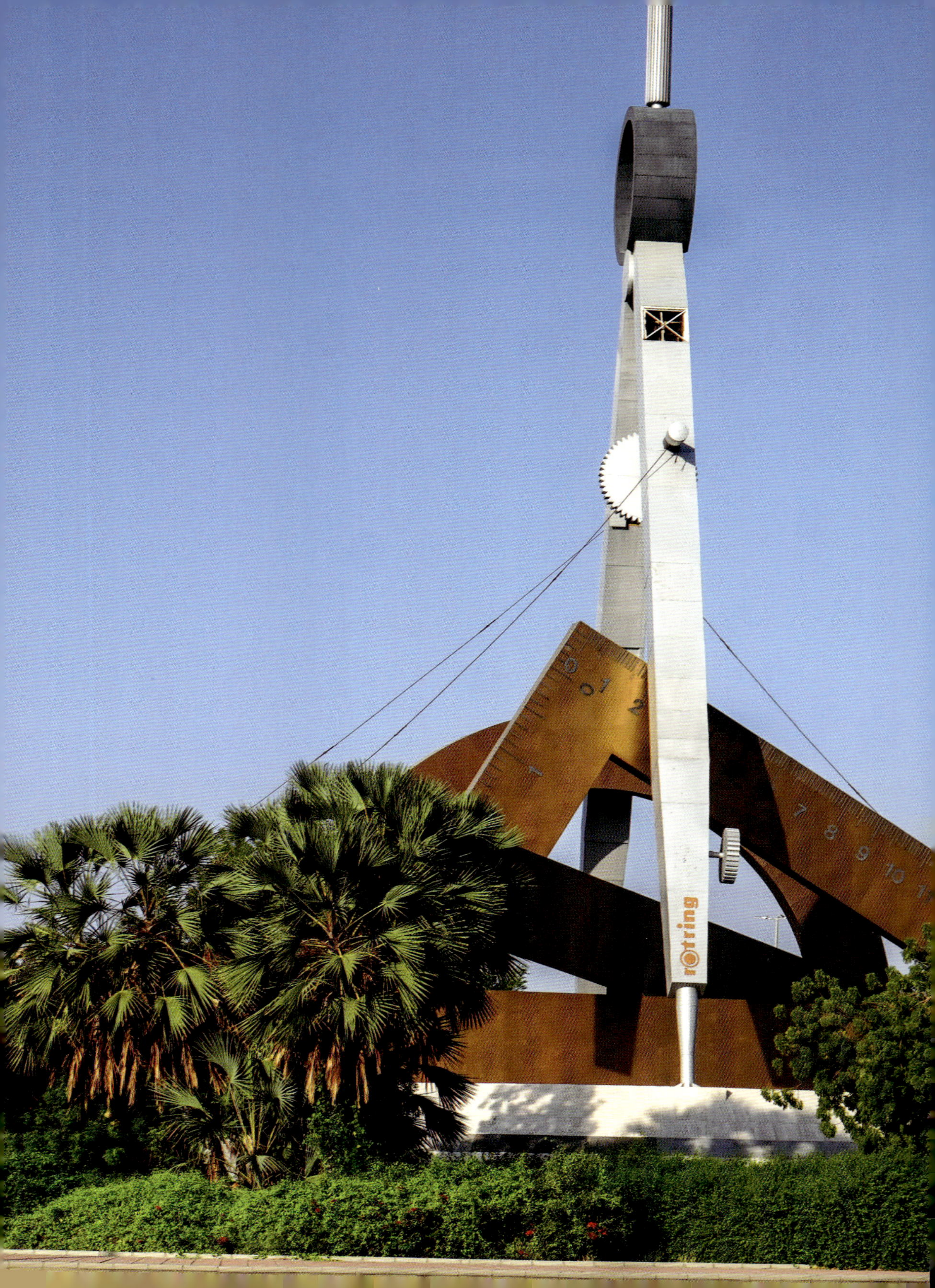
rotring

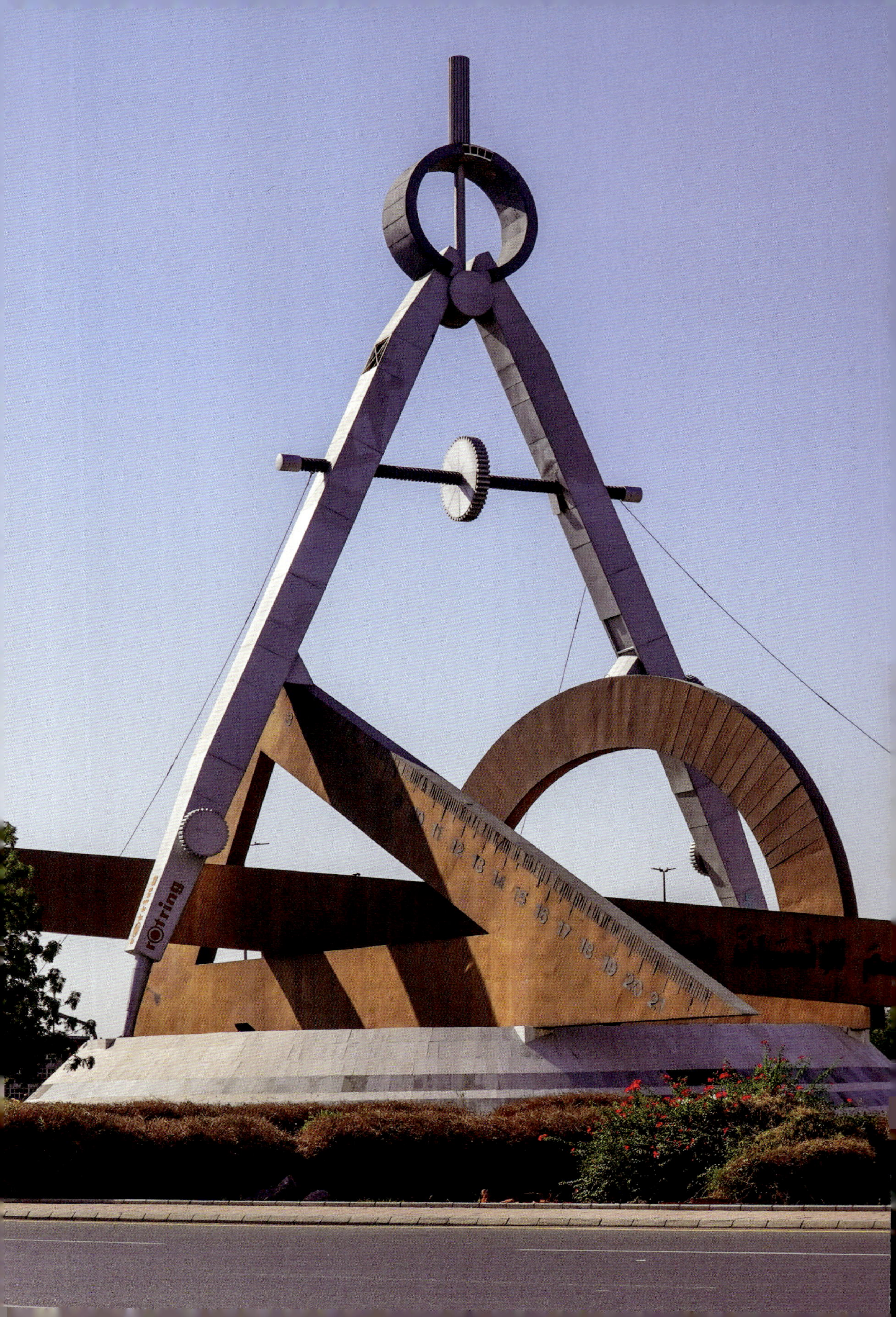
rotring
10 11 12 13 14 15 16 17 18 19 20 21

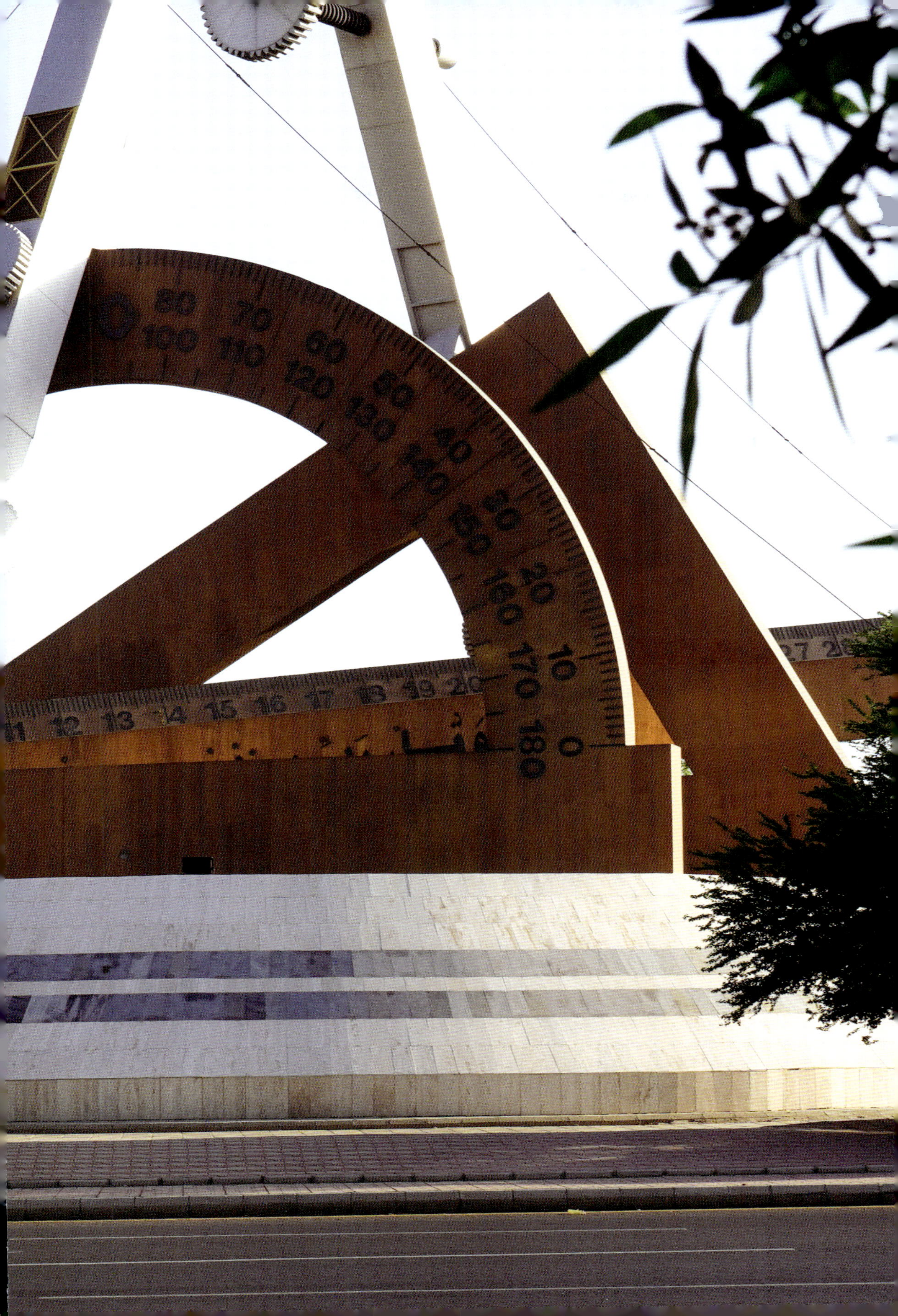

80 70 60 50 40 30 20 10 0
100 110 120 130 140 150 160 170 180
11 12 13 14 15 16 17 18 19 20

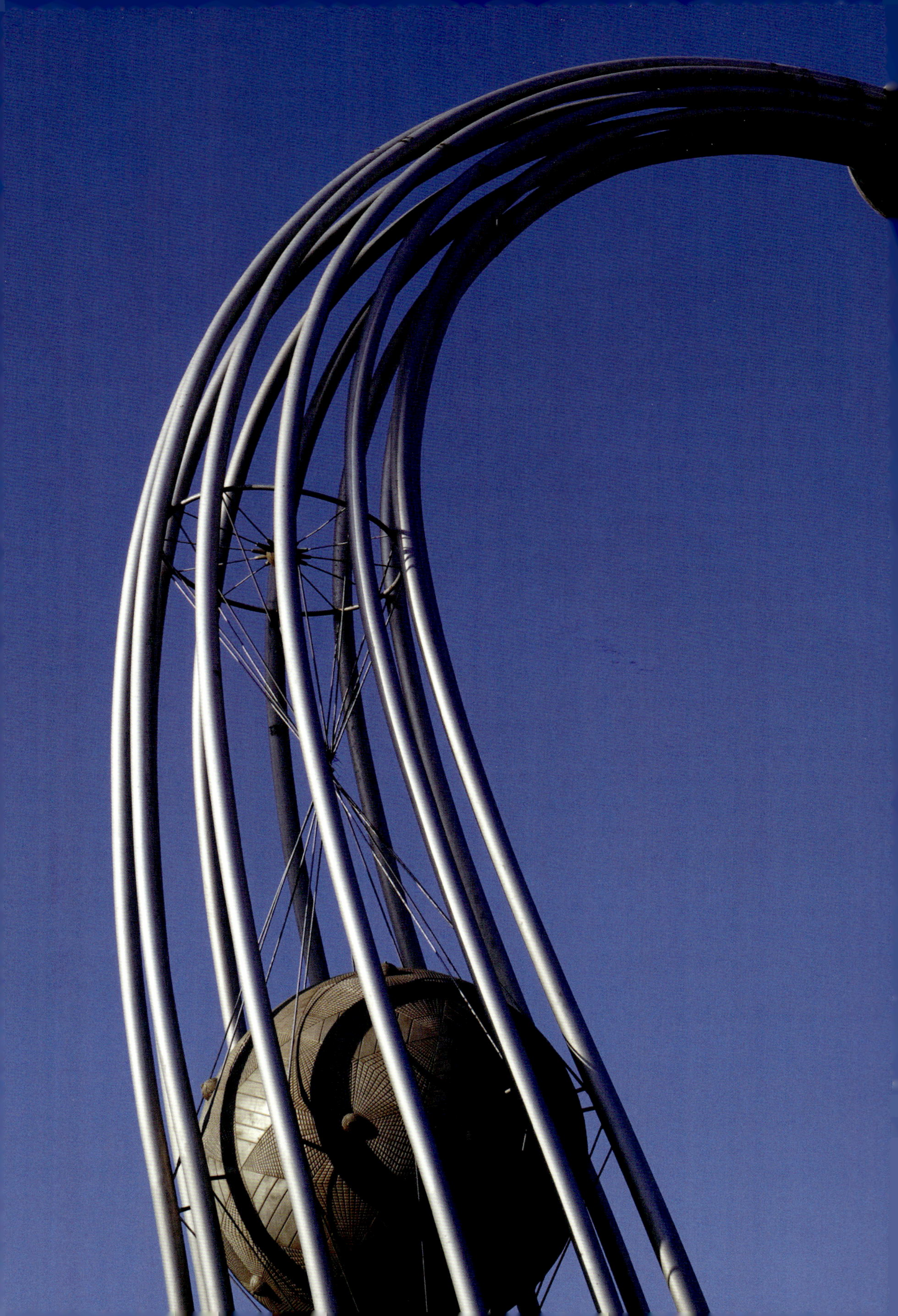

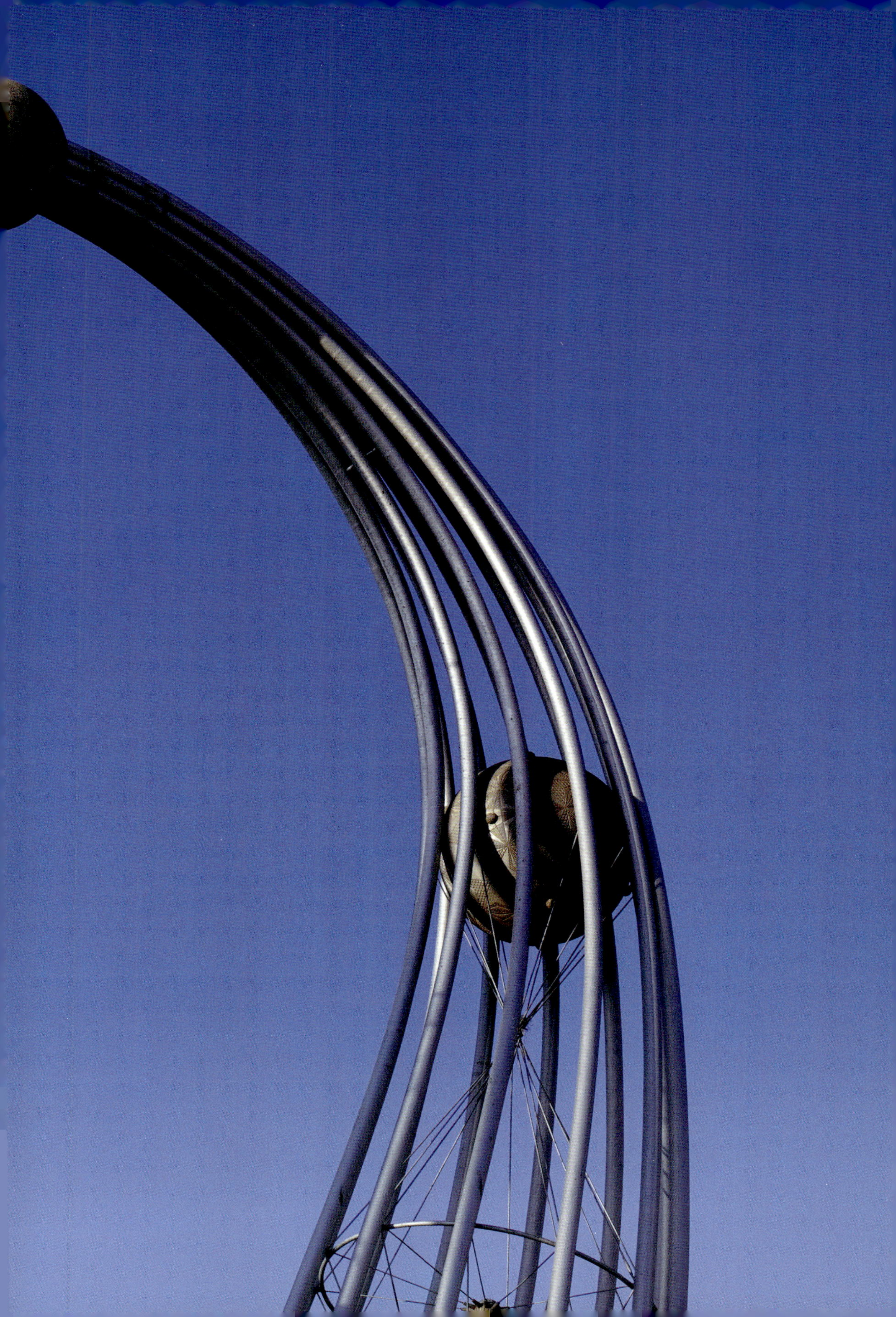

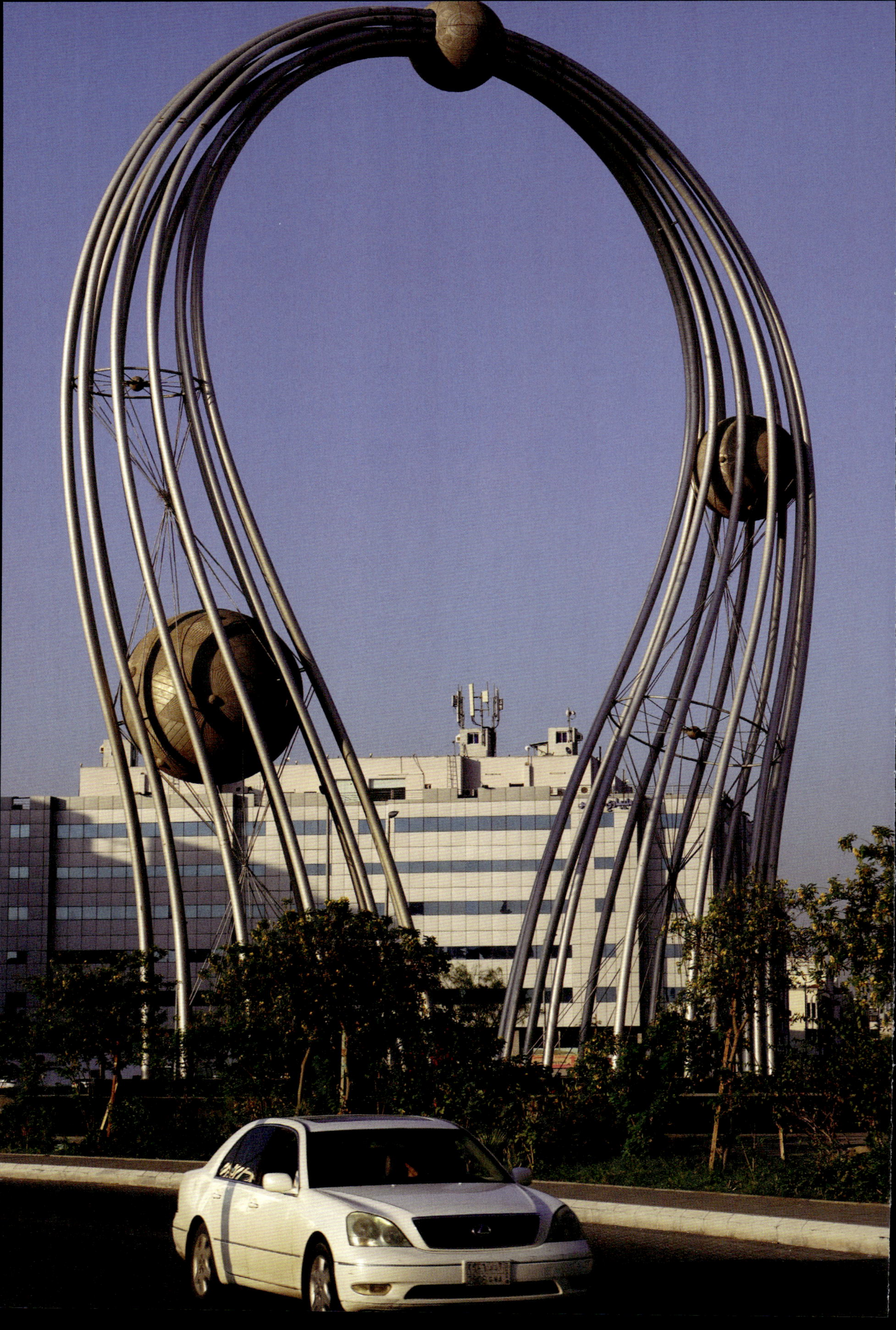

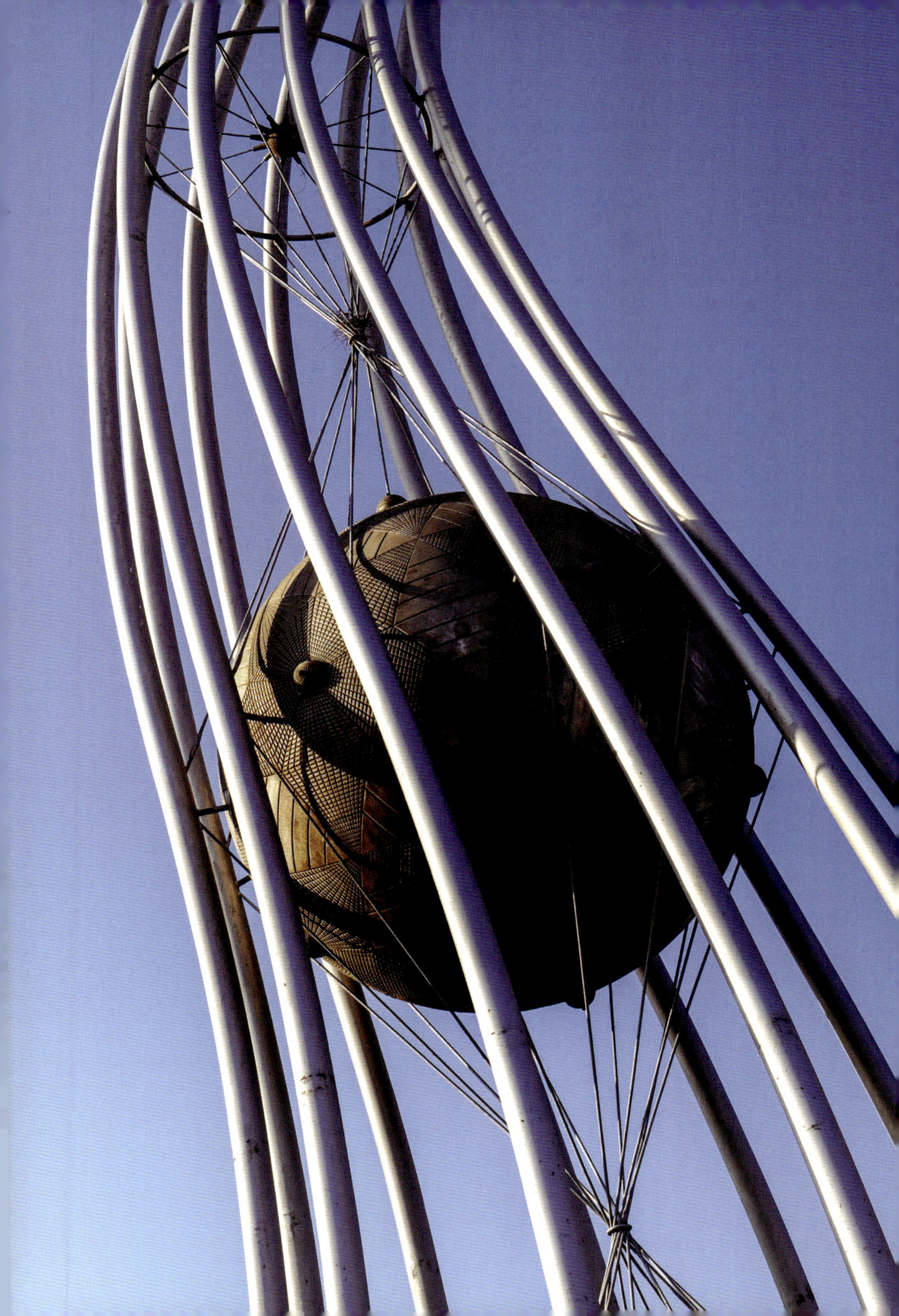

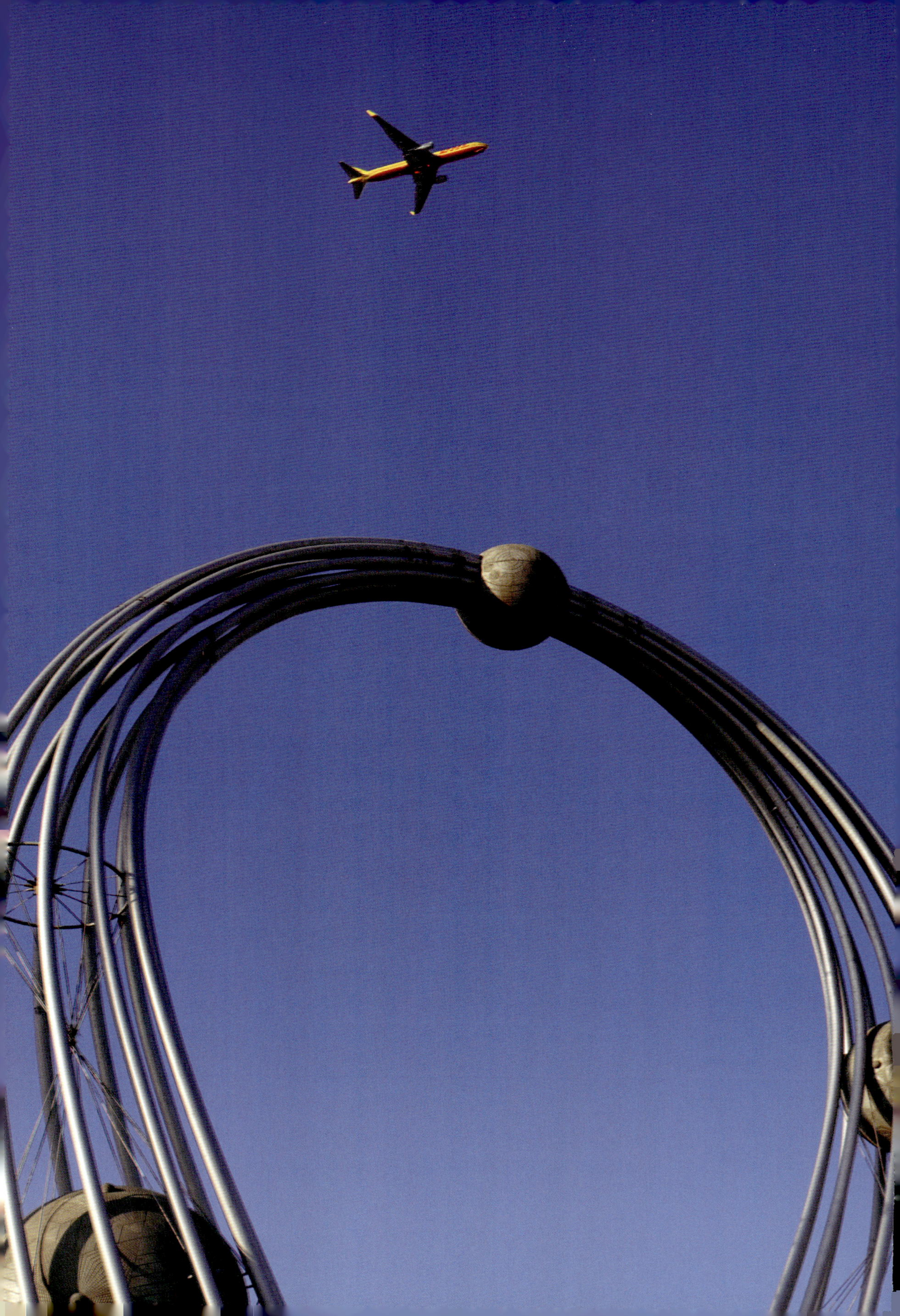

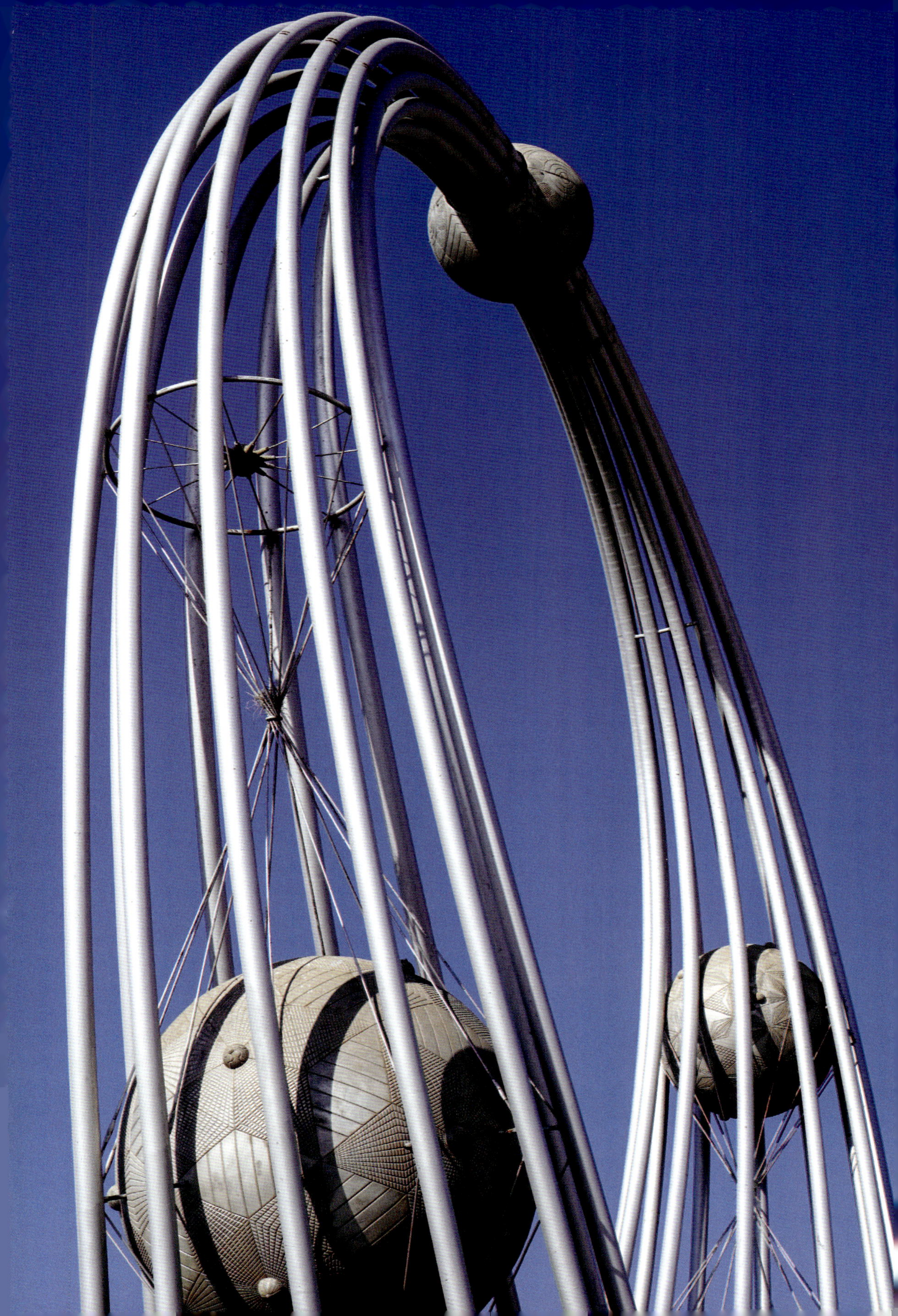

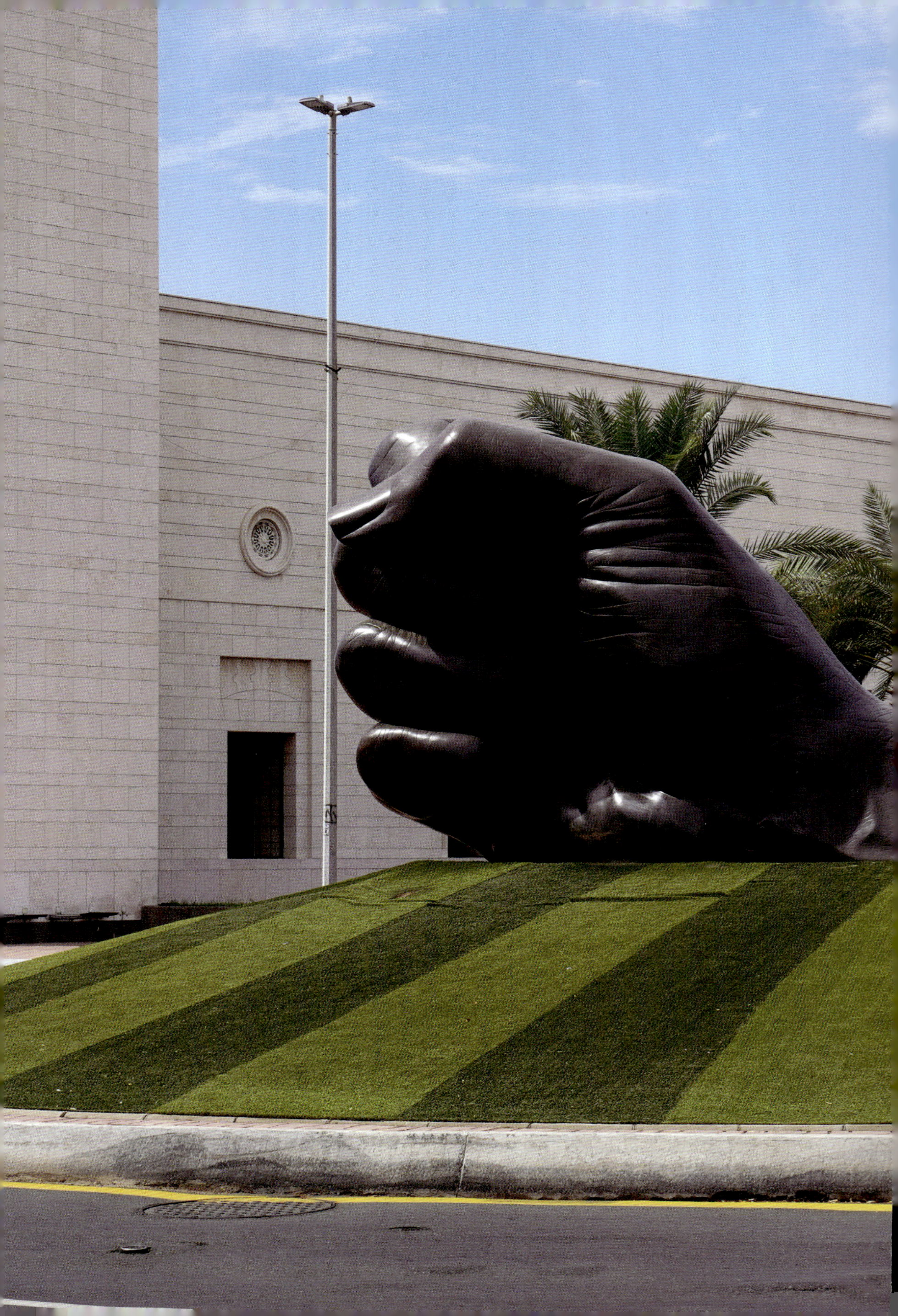

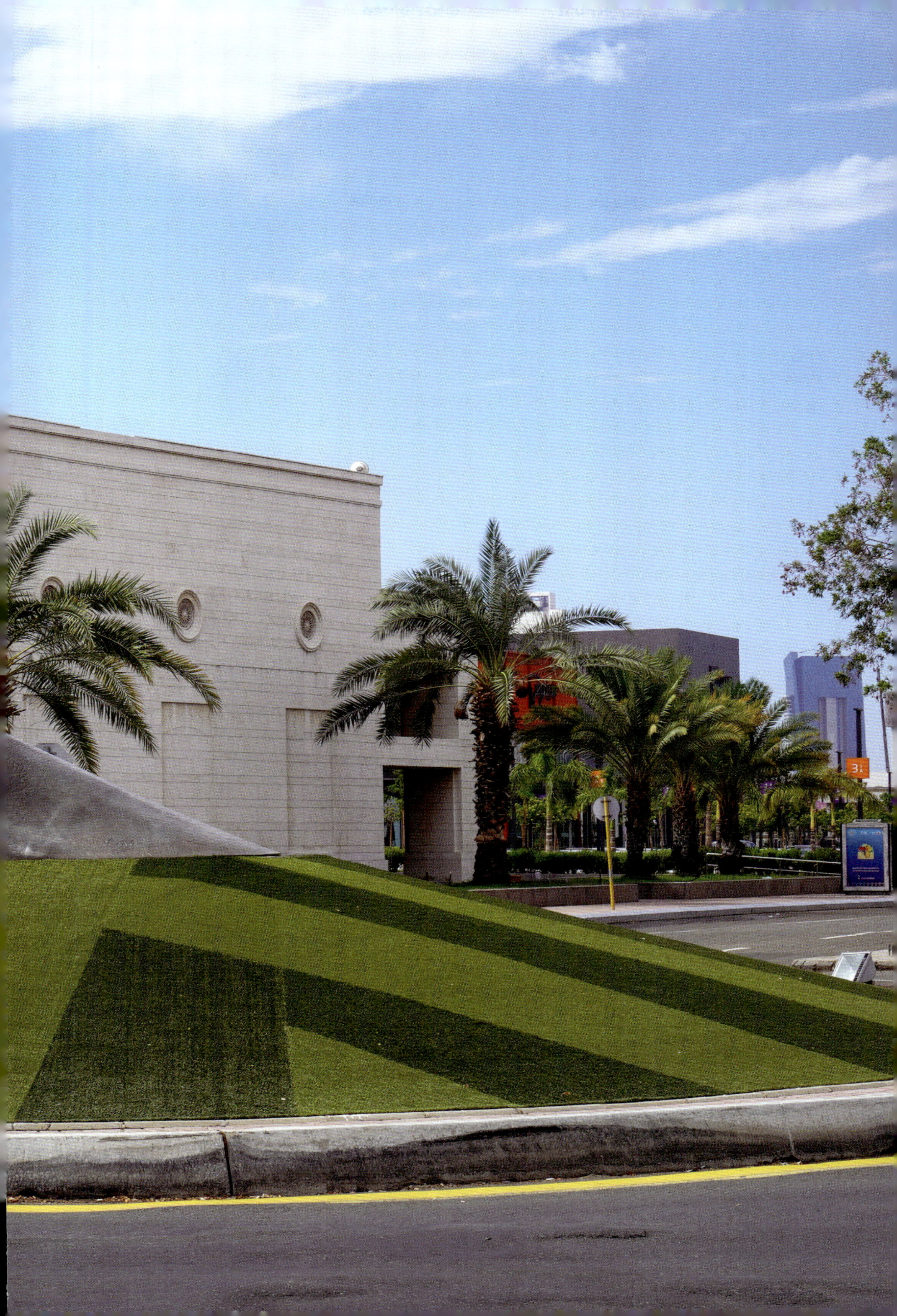

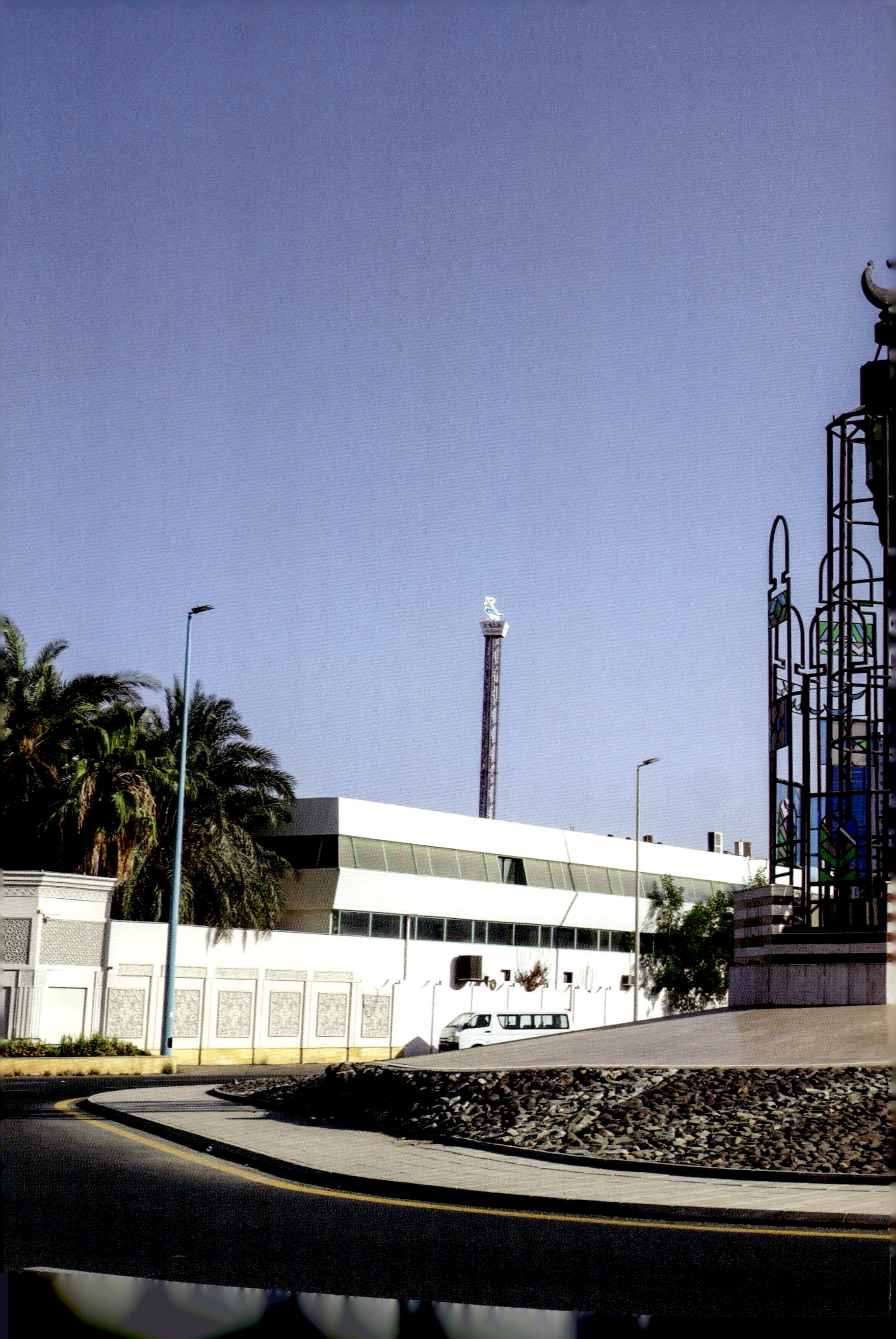

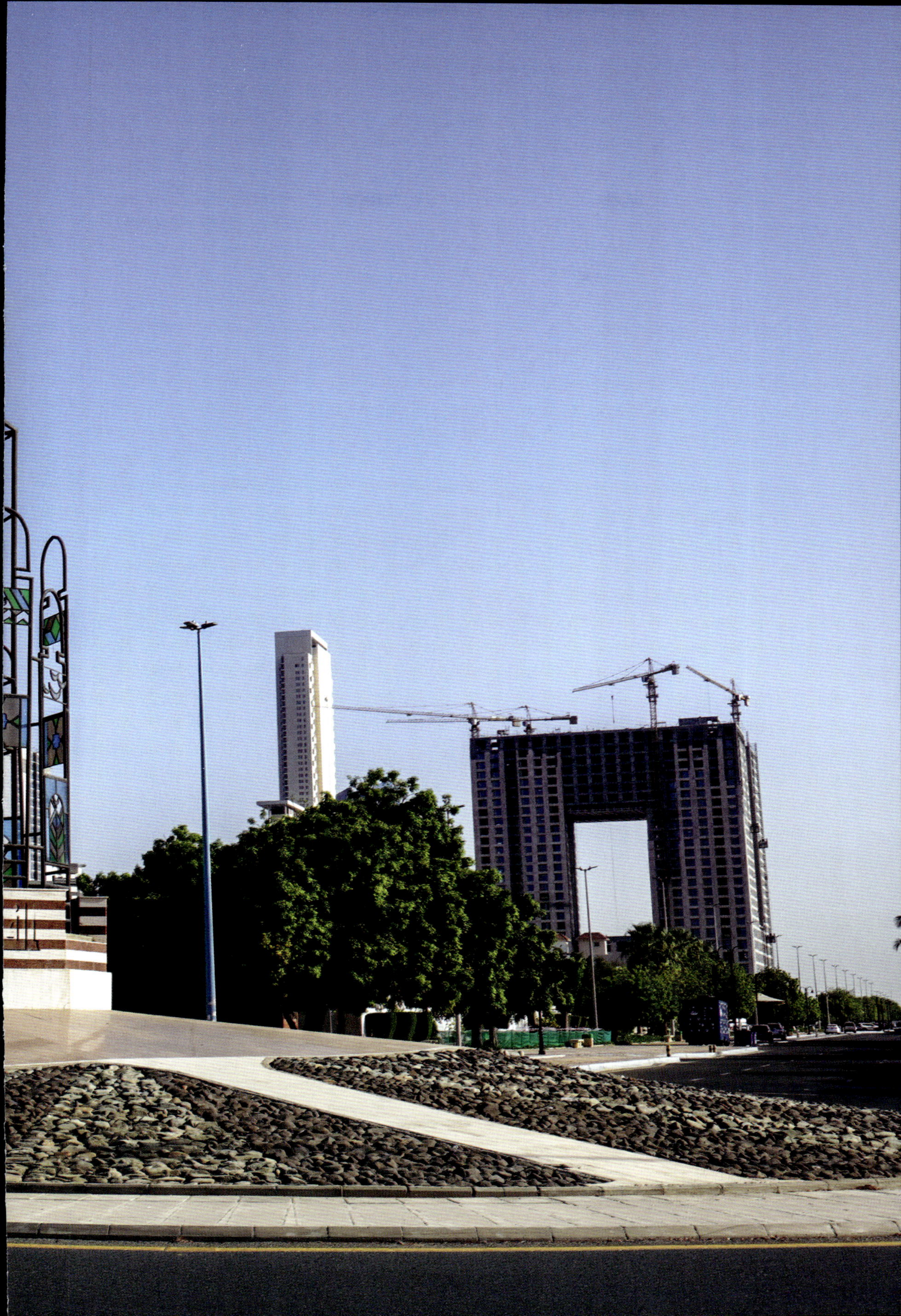

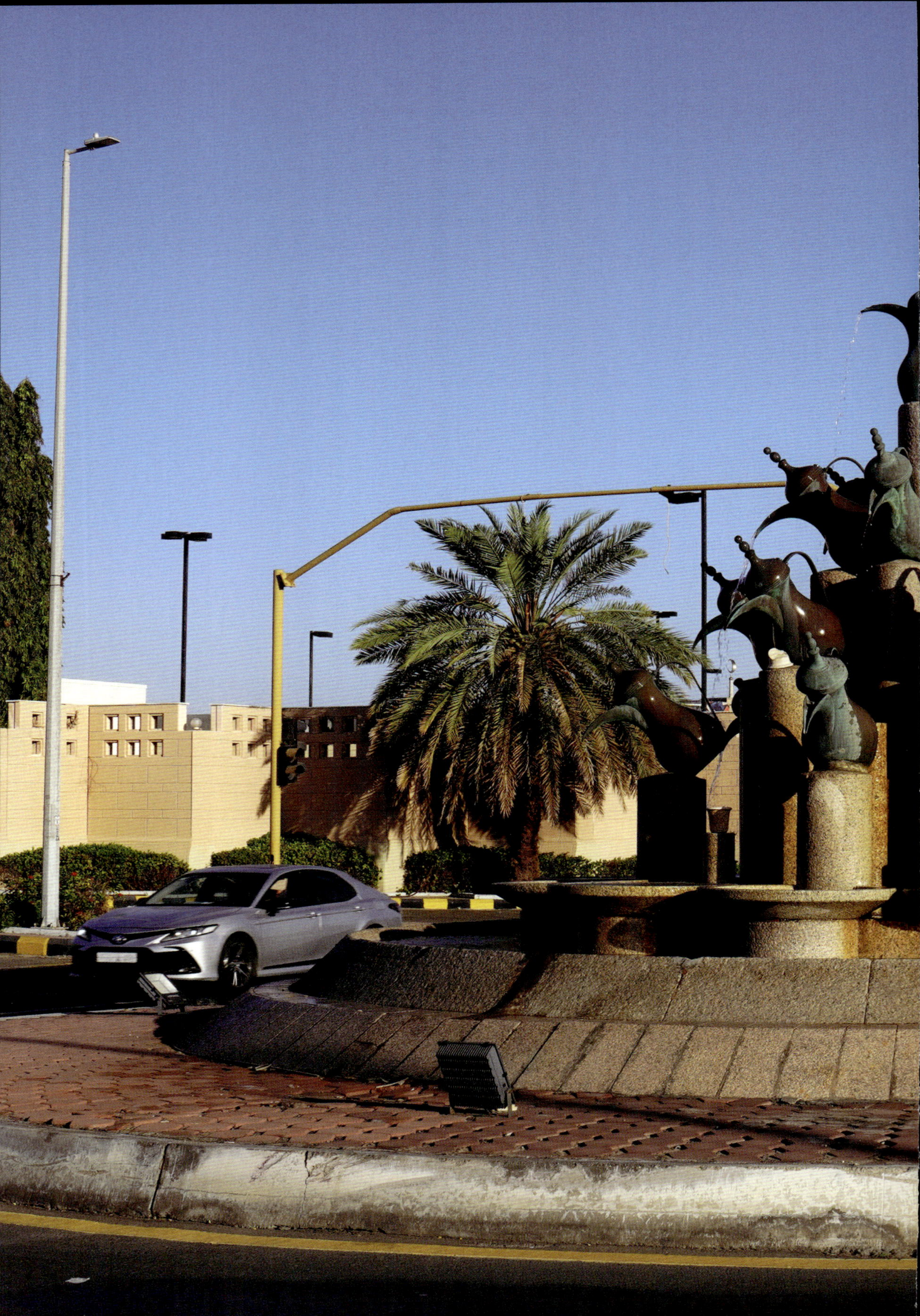

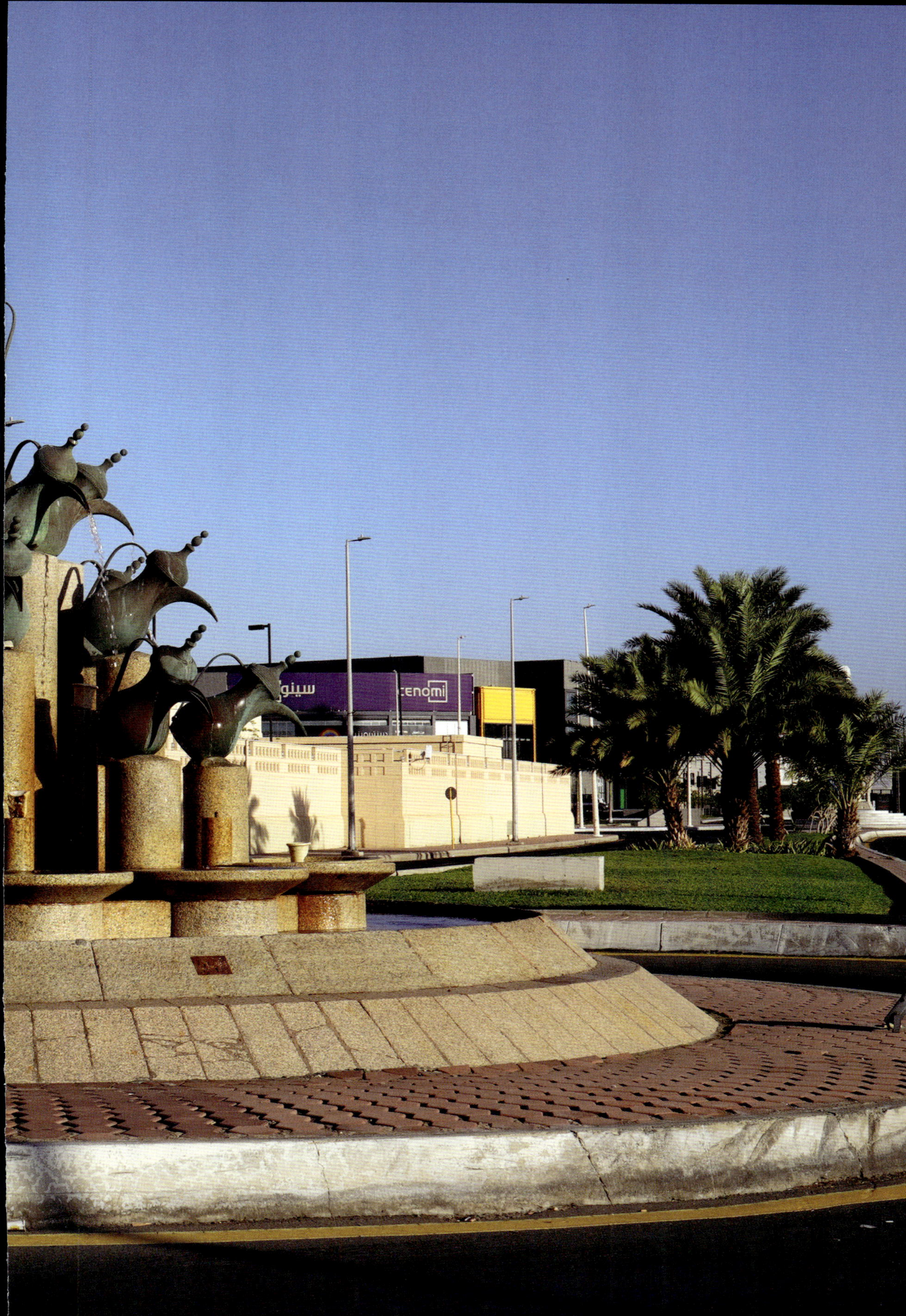
cenomi

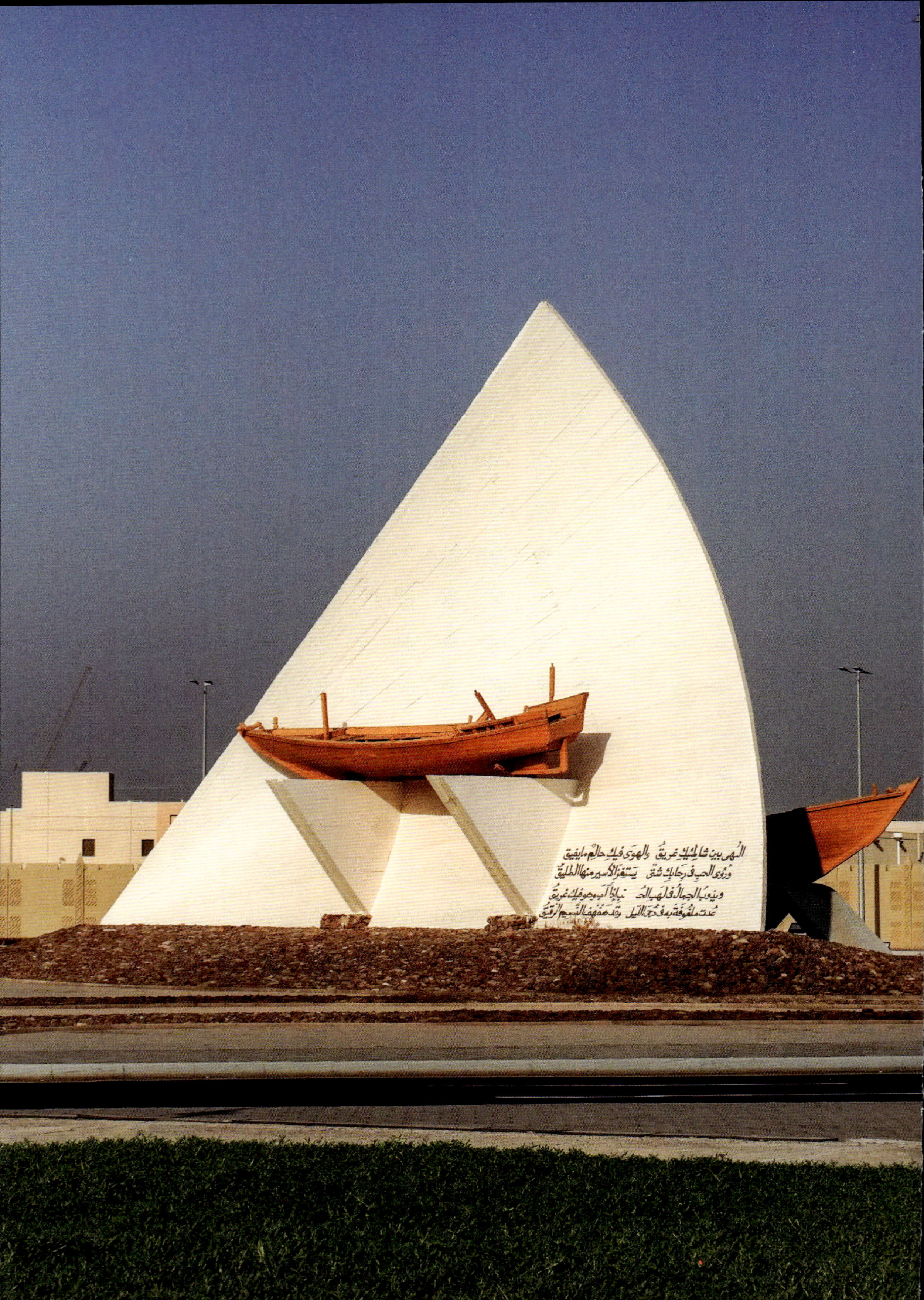
النهى بين شاطئيك غريق والهوى فيك حالم ما يفيق
ورؤى الحب في رحابك شتى يستفز الأسير منها الطليق
ويذوب الجمال في لهب الحـ ـب إذا آب وهو فيك غريق
غنت ملفوفة به في دجى الليل وقد هفهف النسيم الرقيق

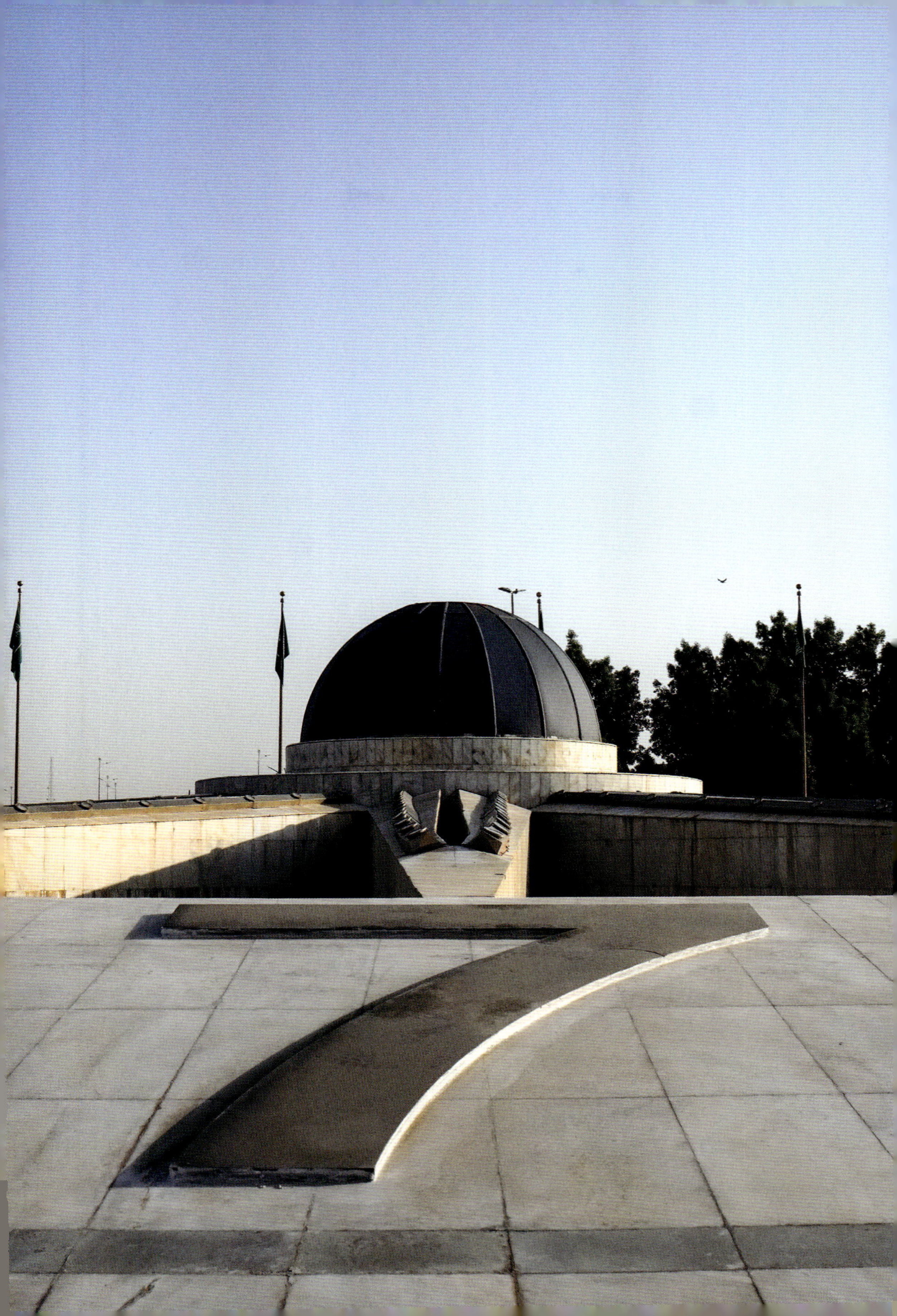

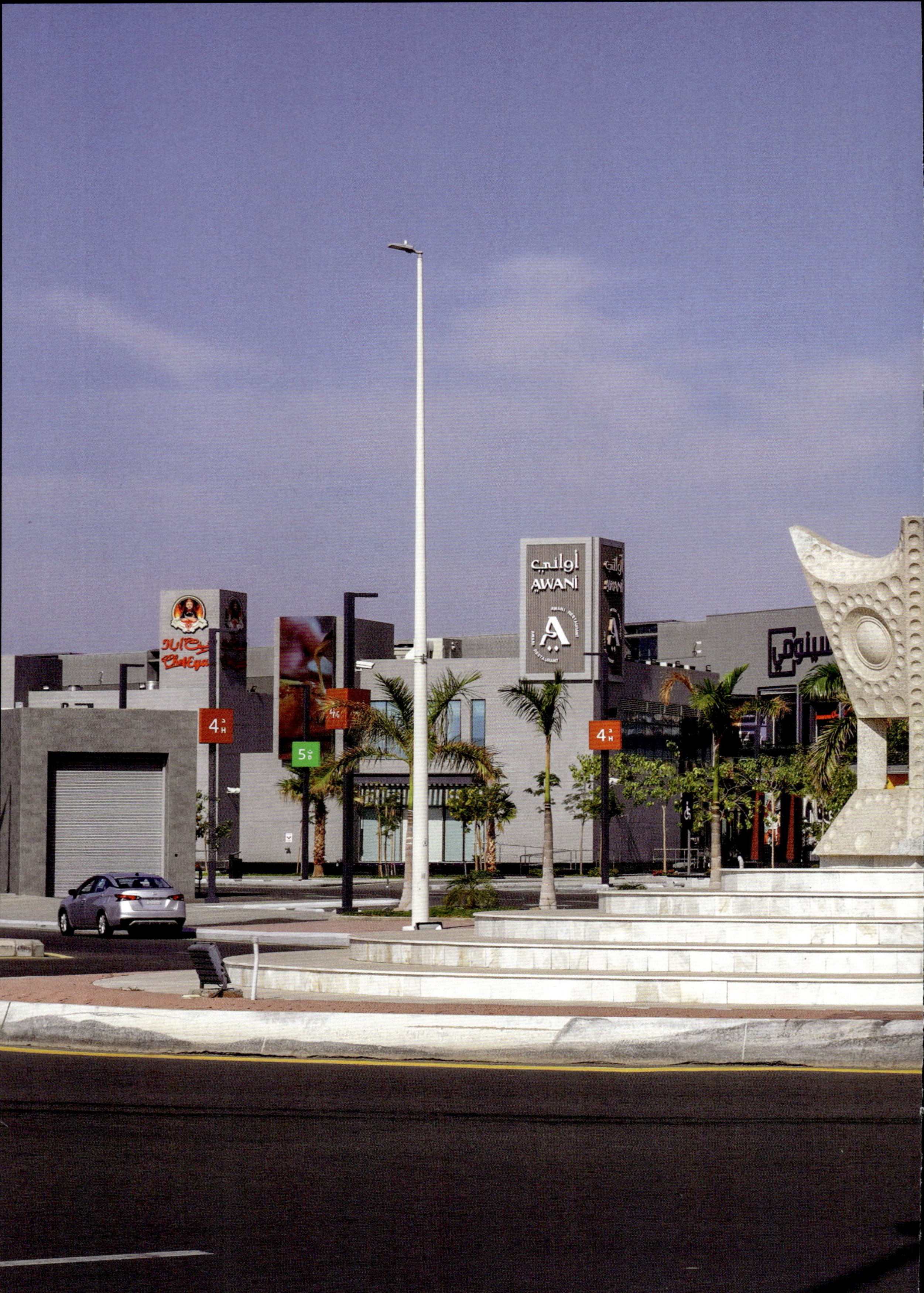
أواني
AWANI

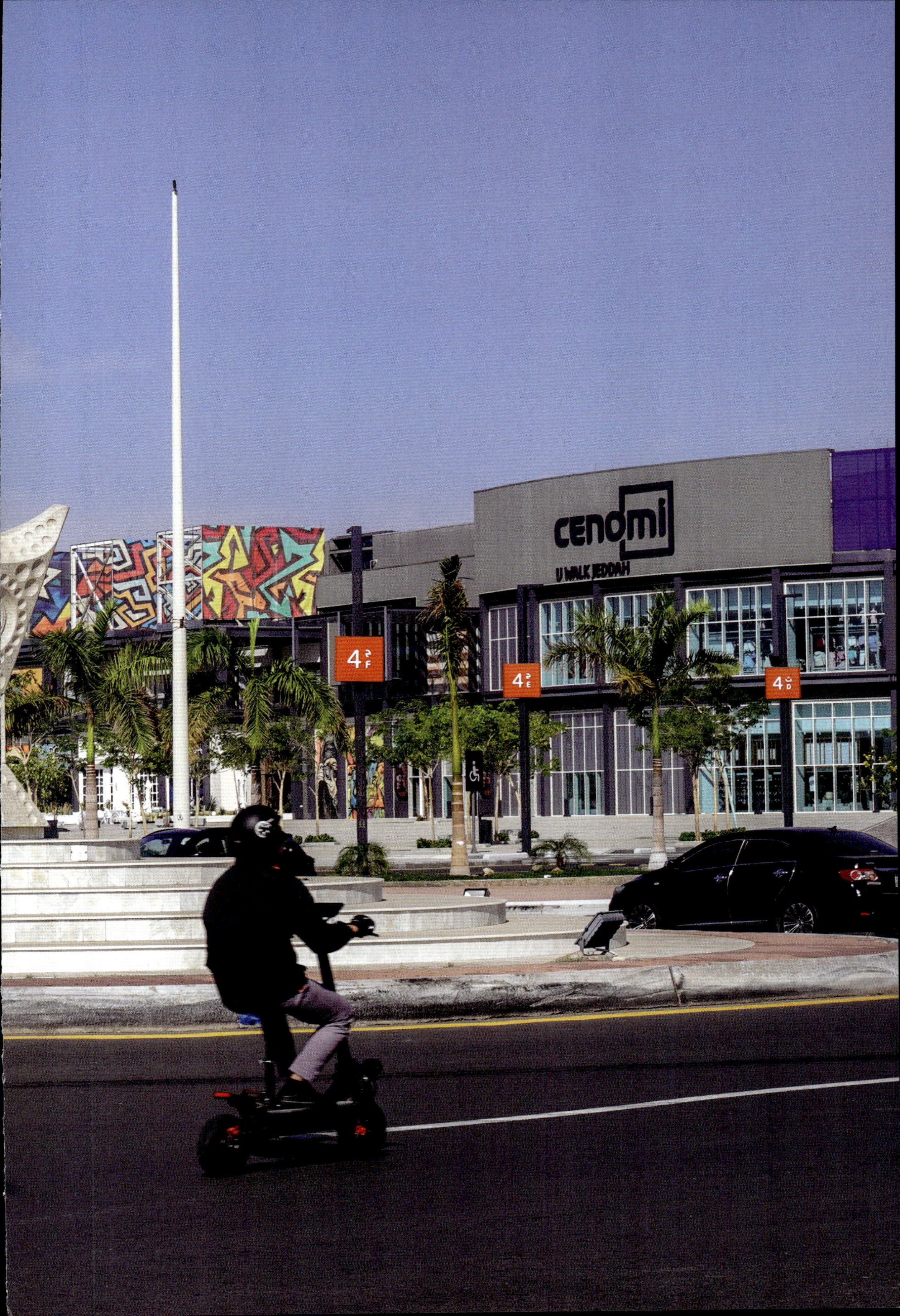
cenomi
U WALK JEDDAH

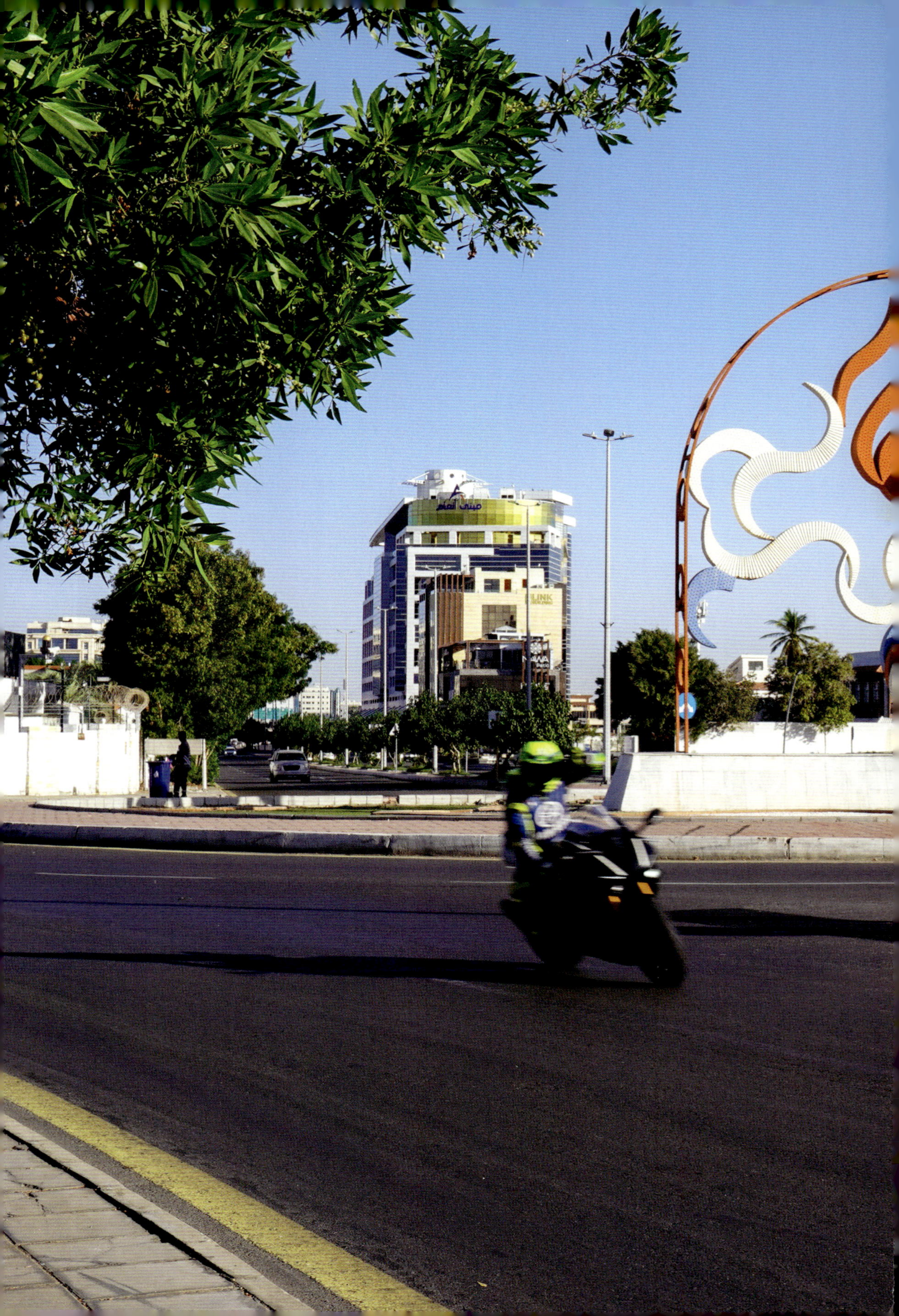
LINK
NAWA
Patio

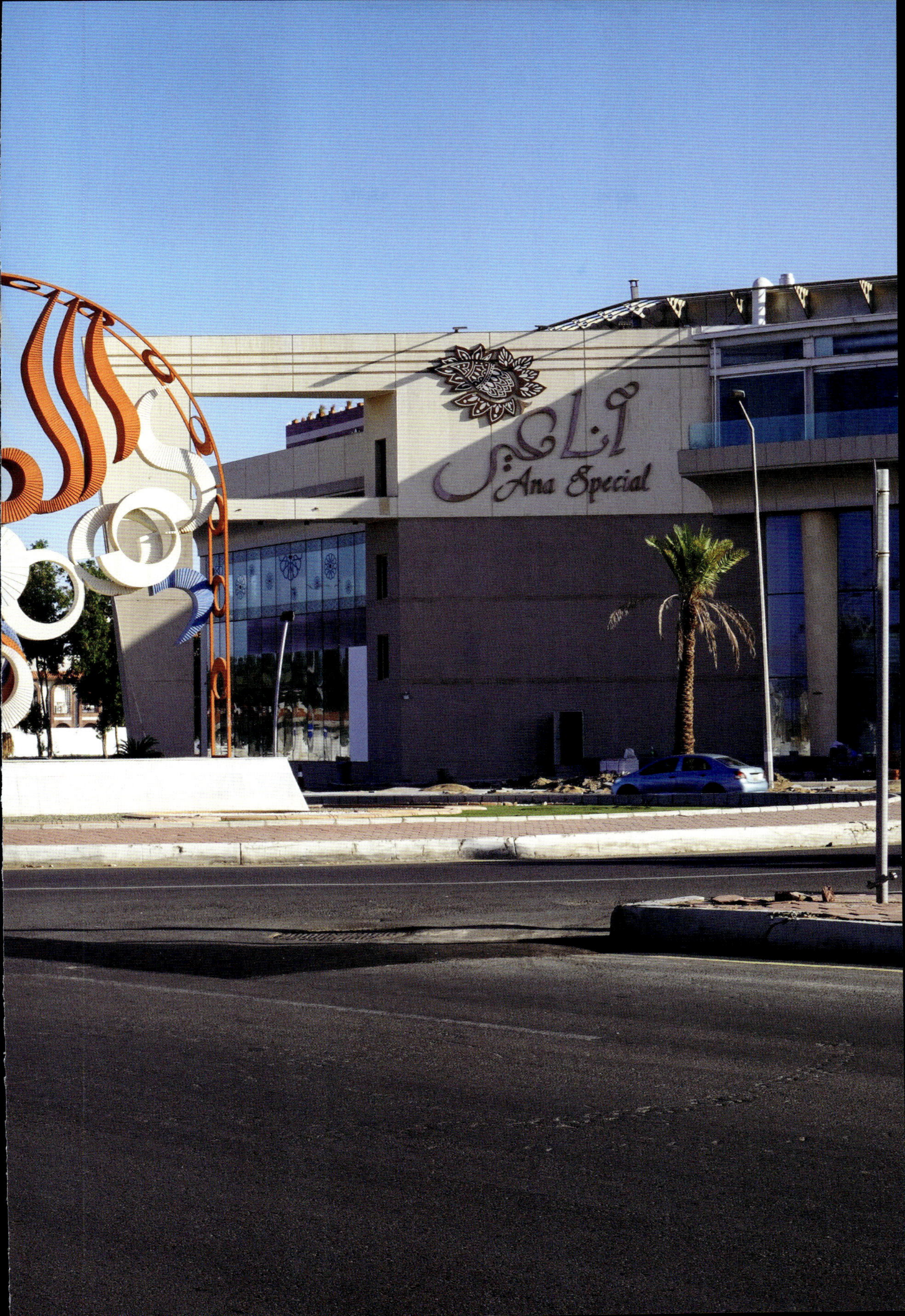
آنا غير
Ana Special

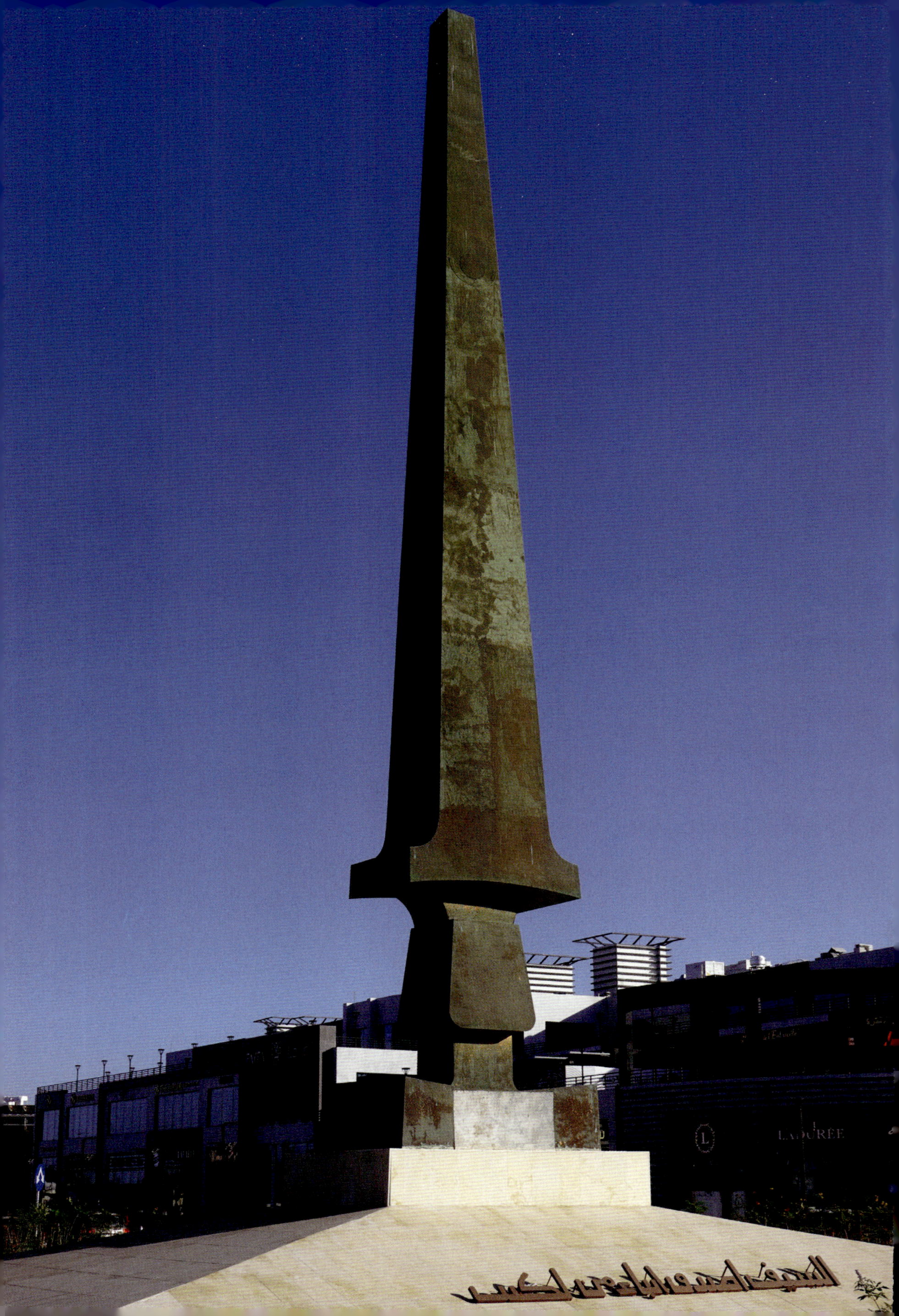
LADURÉE

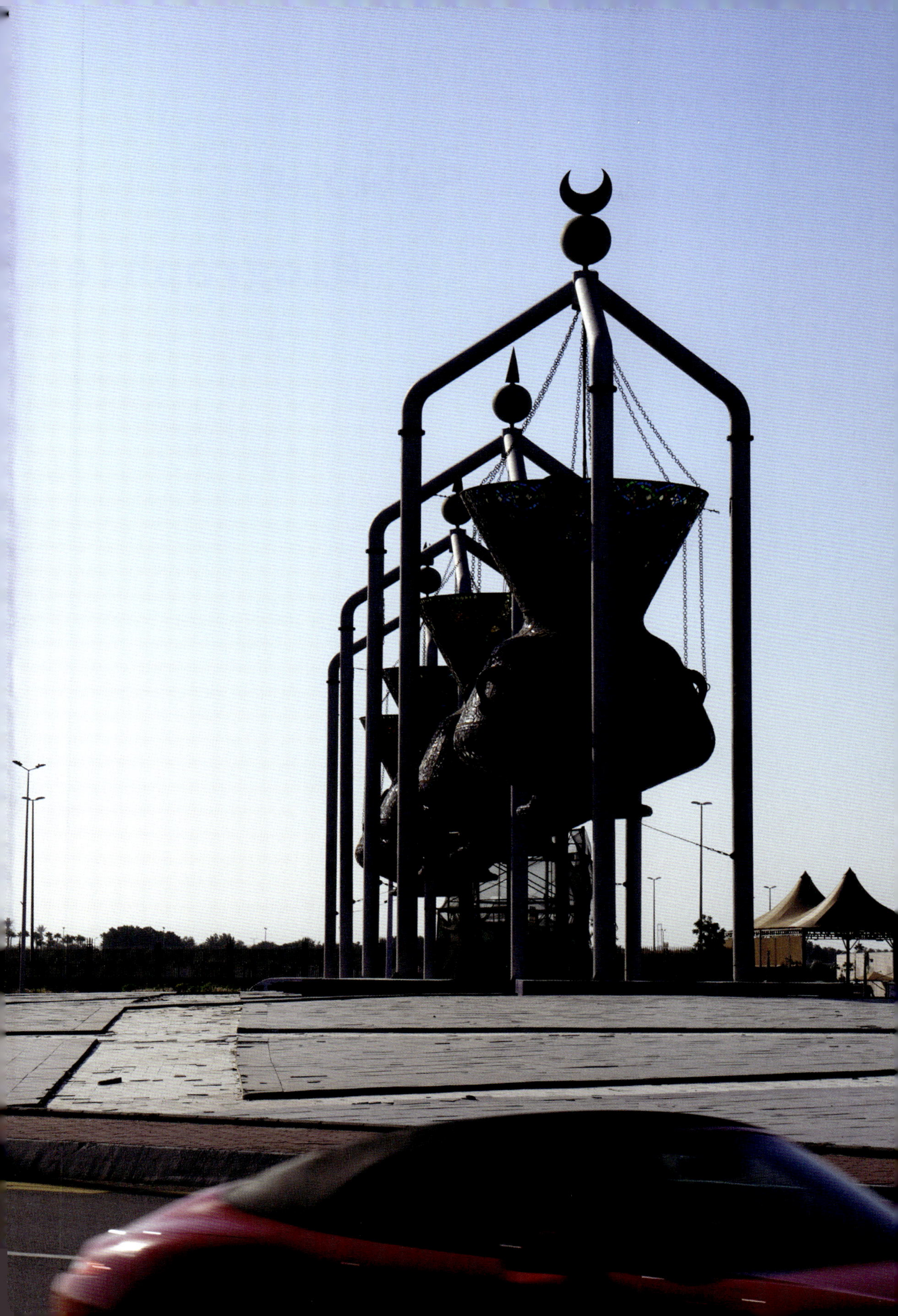

سِيَر ذاتية

Biographies

Turki Gazzaz

Turki Gazzaz, born in Jeddah, Saudi Arabia, in 1988, is an architect and researcher and the co-founder of Bricklab, a multidisciplinary design studio based in Jeddah operating at the intersection of architecture, material research, and cultural production. He holds a Master's degree in the History and Theory of Architecture from McGill University and, together with his brother Abdulrahman, leads the studio's work across architecture, urban research, exhibitions, and public-space interventions. Bricklab has realised projects for the Diriyah Biennale Foundation and the JAX Creative District in Riyadh, and designed the National Pavilion of Saudi Arabia for the 16th International Architecture Exhibition of La Biennale di Venezia. His studio's work has been exhibited internationally at institutions including MAAT Lisbon, the British Museum, and the Victoria and Albert Museum. Alongside his practice, he co-initiated Saudi Modern in 2021, a research platform examining post-oil architectural development in the region, and co-founded Raw Print, a publishing initiative supporting local and regional cultural production. In his essay for this project, the Jeddah-based architect traces a genealogy of the city's roundabouts, examining their conceptualisation and construction within broader projects of urban modernisation.

تركي قزاز

تركي قزاز، من مواليد جدة عام 1988، معماري وباحث. الشريك المؤسس لاستوديو «بريك لاب» (Bricklab)، استوديو تصميم متعدد التخصصات مقره جدة ويعمل عند تقاطع العمارة وأبحاث المواد والإنتاج الثقافي. يحمل درجة الماجستير في تاريخ ونظرية العمارة من جامعة ماكغيل، ويقود مع شقيقه عبدالرحمن أعمال الاستوديو عبر مجالات العمارة والبحث الحضري والمعارض وتدخلات الفضاء العام. أنجز «بريك لاب» مشاريع لصالح مؤسسة بينالي الدرعية وحي جاكس الإبداعي في الرياض، كما صمّم الجناح الوطني للمملكة العربية السعودية في الدورة السادسة عشرة للمعرض الدولي للعمارة في بينالي البندقية. عُرضت أعمال الاستوديو دوليًا في مؤسسات من بينها متحف MAAT في لشبونة، والمتحف البريطاني، ومتحف فيكتوريا وألبرت. وبالتوازي مع ممارسته المهنية، شارك في إطلاق منصة «سعودي مودرن» عام 2021، منصة بحثية تدرس تطور العمارة ما بعد النفط في المنطقة، كما شارك في تأسيس مبادرة النشر «مطبوعات الروضة» الداعمة للإنتاج الثقافي المحلي والإقليمي. في مقالته ضمن هذا الكتاب، يتتبع المعماري المقيم في جدة جينالوجيا دوارات المدينة، متناولاً تصوراتها وتنفيذها ضمن مشاريع أوسع للتحديث الحضري بالمدينة.

Nouf Al-Harthi

نوف الحارثي

Nouf Al-Harthi is a Saudi writer, researcher, and cultural practitioner with an MA in Social Anthropology from SOAS, University of London. Her work spans writing, sound, and memory, exploring how everyday narratives are shaped -and unsettled- through sonic and linguistic expression. Rooted in anthropology and curatorial practice, her research foregrounds listening, remembering, and storytelling as sites of cultural inquiry, engaging questions of place, voice, and shared experience. She has developed and presented projects at institutions including the Diriyah Contemporary Art Biennale in Diriyah, Hayy Jameel in Jeddah, IKLECTIK Art Lab in London, the Saudi Museum of Contemporary Art in Diriyah, and Fenaa Alawwal in Riyadh. For *Jeddah Roundabouts: Circling the City*, she undertook an extended field journey with photographer Hatun Al-Harthi, conducting in-car conversations with male and female informal taxi drivers. Circling the city's roundabouts, Nouf attends to the everyday narratives of those who traverse Jeddah, approaching dialogue and listening as ways of tracing how urban life is lived, navigated, and remembered.

نوف الحارثي كاتبة وباحثة وممارسة ثقافية، حاصلة على درجة الماجستير في الأنثروبولوجيا الاجتماعية من كلية الدراسات الشرقية والأفريقية (SOAS) بجامعة لندن. تتنقل اهتماماتها بين الكتابة والبحث في الصوت والذاكرة، مستكشفةً كيفية تشكّل السرديات اليومية واضطرابها عبر التعبيرات الصوتية واللغوية. تنطلق أبحاثها من الأنثروبولوجيا والممارسة القيّمية، مركّزةً على الإصغاء والتذكّر والسرد بوصفها مواقع للبحث الثقافي، ومتناولةً أسئلة المكان والصوت والتجربة المشتركة. طوّرت وقدّمت مشاريع في مؤسسات من بينها بينالي الدرعية للفن المعاصر، وحي جميل في جدة، ومختبر إيكليكتيك للفنون في لندن، والمتحف السعودي للفن المعاصر في الدرعية، وفناء الأول في الرياض. في مشروع «في العُمرانِ الدائر: جدّة ودواراتها»، خاضت نوف رحلة استقصاء ميدانية برفقة المصوّر هتون الحارثي، أجرت فيها حوارات مع سائقي سيارات الأجرة الخصوصية (الكدّادين)، رجالاً ونساءً، أثناء عملهم داخل سيّاراتهم. تتبع نوف في هذا المشروع السرديات اليوميّة لعابري المدينة من خلال دوّارات جدة، متخذةً من الحوار والإصغاء وسيلتين إلى قراءة الكيفية التي تُعاش بها الحياة الحضرية عبورًا يوميًا وذاكرةً ممتدة.

Art Jameel

فن جميل

Art Jameel is an independent arts organisation supporting artists and cultural practitioners through commissioning, research, and public engagement across the Middle East and internationally. In Jeddah, it operates Hayy Jameel, a multidisciplinary cultural complex that brings together exhibitions, studios, learning spaces, a library, and public programmes, situating artistic practice in close relation to its social and urban context.

«فن جميل» مؤسسة فنية مستقلة تدعم الفنانين والممارسين الثقافيين عبر التكليفات البحثية والإنتاجية وبرامج التفاعل العام في الشرق الأوسط وعلى الصعيد الدولي. وفي جدة، تدير «حي جميل» المجمّع الثقافي المتعدد التخصصات الذي يجمع بين المعارض والاستوديوهات ومساحات التعلّم والمكتبة وبرامج عامة، واضعًا الممارسة الفنية في علاقة وثيقة مع سياقها الاجتماعي والحضري.

Hatun Al-Harthi

هتون علي

Hatun Al-Harthi, born in 2003, is a Jeddah-based Saudi multidisciplinary creative director whose work is centered on photography, alongside design and filmmaking. Working primarily through image-making, she develops visual narratives that explore emotion, identity, and cultural experience. Through narrative-driven processes, her practice reflects on how images shape contemporary forms of storytelling and cultural representation. In the framework of this project, Hatun traversed the city from one end to the other with her camera, documenting and cataloguing Jeddah's most iconic roundabouts and capturing timeless portraits of their most faithful users: the city's taxi drivers.

هتون الحارثي، من مواليد 2003، مخرجة إبداعية سعودية متعددة التخصصات تقيم في جدة. تتمحور ممارستها حول التصوير الفوتوغرافي إلى جانب التصميم وصناعة الأفلام. تعمل أساسًا عبر إنتاج الصورة لتطوير سرديات بصرية تستكشف العاطفة والهوية والتجربة الثقافية. ومن خلال عمليات قائمة على السرد، تتأمل ممارستها في كيفية إسهام الصور في تشكيل أشكال معاصرة من الحكايا والتمثيل الثقافي. في إطار هذا المشروع، جابت هتون المدينة بعدستها، موثّقةً ومفهرسةً أشهر دوارات جدة، وملتَقطةً صور خالدة لأكثر مستخدميها وفاءً: سائقي الأجرة.

FLEE

فلي

Founded by Olivier Duport, Alan Marzo and Carl Åhnebrink, FLEE is an independent publisher, record label, and curatorial platform devoted to documenting and amplifying hybrid cultures. Operating at the intersection of print, sound, and exhibition-making, FLEE functions as a multidisciplinary engine producing books, records, and curated projects that trace the shifting contours of globalization. Through historically grounded research and contemporary artistic collaborations, FLEE brings overlooked cultural phenomena into dialogue with the present, reframing them as living, evolving narratives.

«فلي» ناشر مستقل وشركة تسجيل ومنصة قيّمية تُعنى بتوثيق الثقافات الهجينة وتعزيز حضورها. تعمل عند تقاطعات الطباعة والصوت وصناعة المعارض، بوصفها محرّكًا متعدد التخصصات ينتج كتبًا وإصدارات موسيقية ومشاريع قيّمة تتتبّع التحولات المتغيرة للعولمة. ومن خلال أبحاث متجذّرة تاريخيًا وتعاونات فنية معاصرة، تضع «فلي» الظواهر الثقافية المهمَلة في حوار مع الحاضر، معيدةً تأطيرها في سرديات حيّة ومتطوّرة.

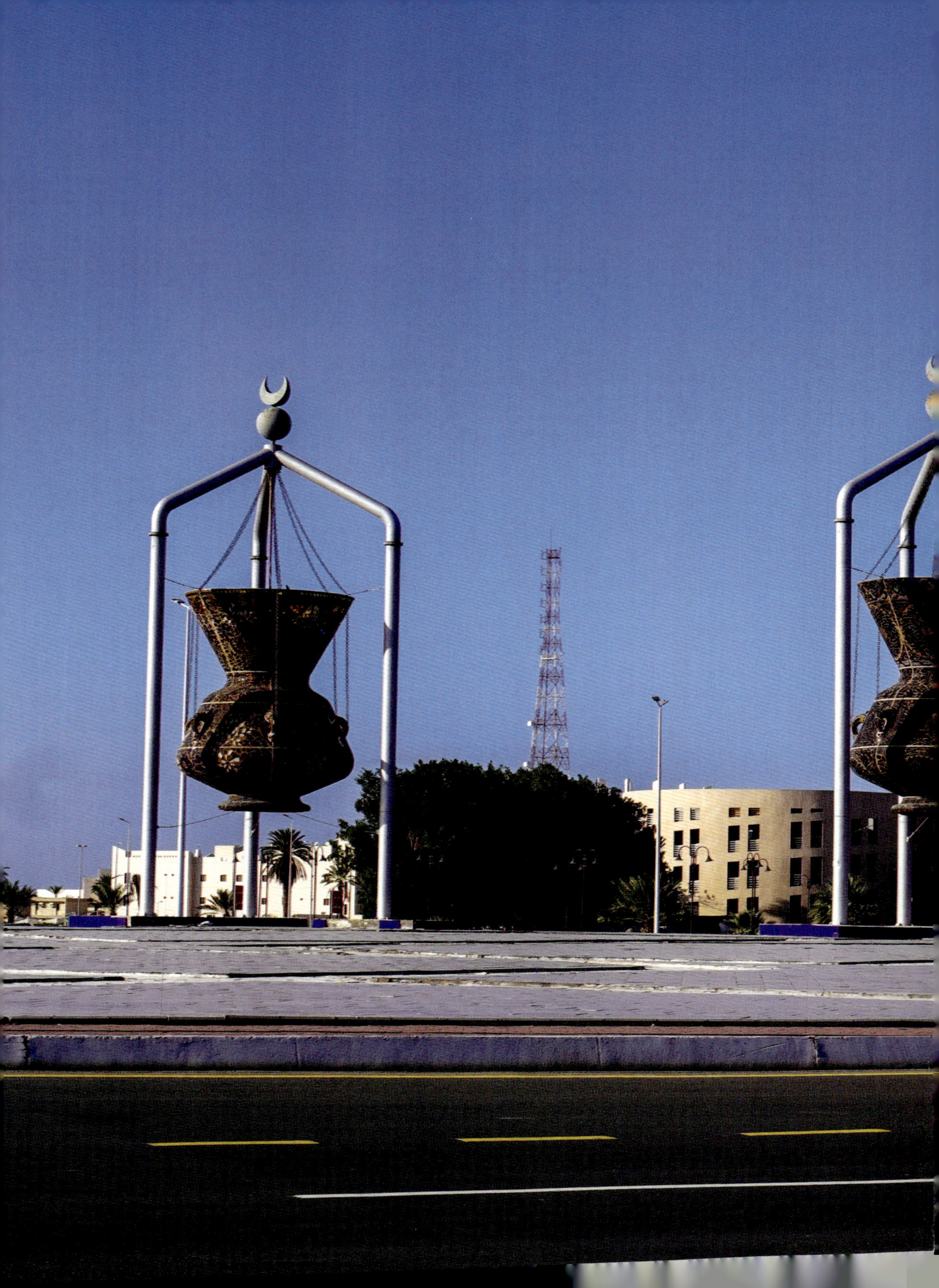

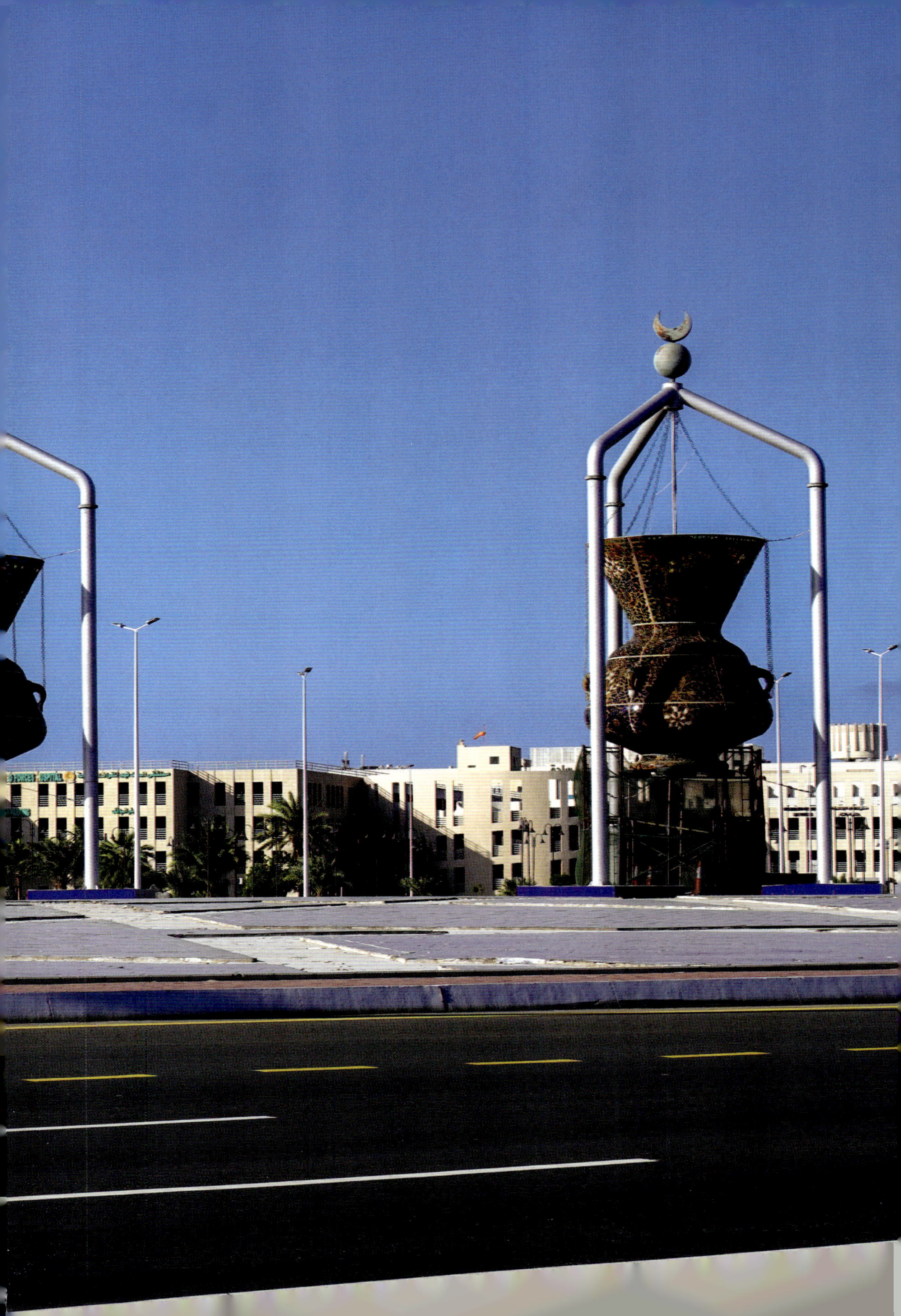
FORCES HOSPITAL

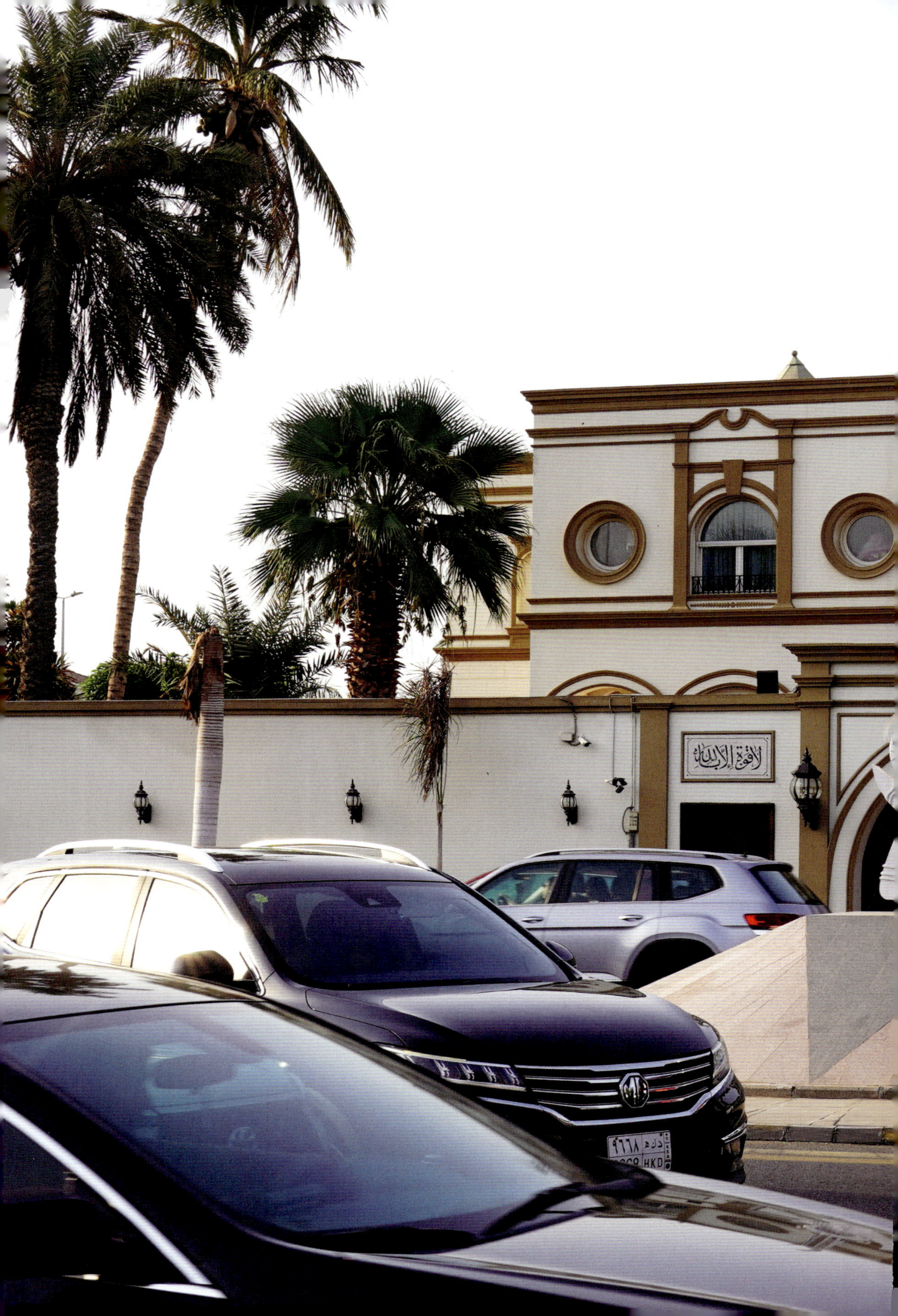
لا قوة إلا بالله

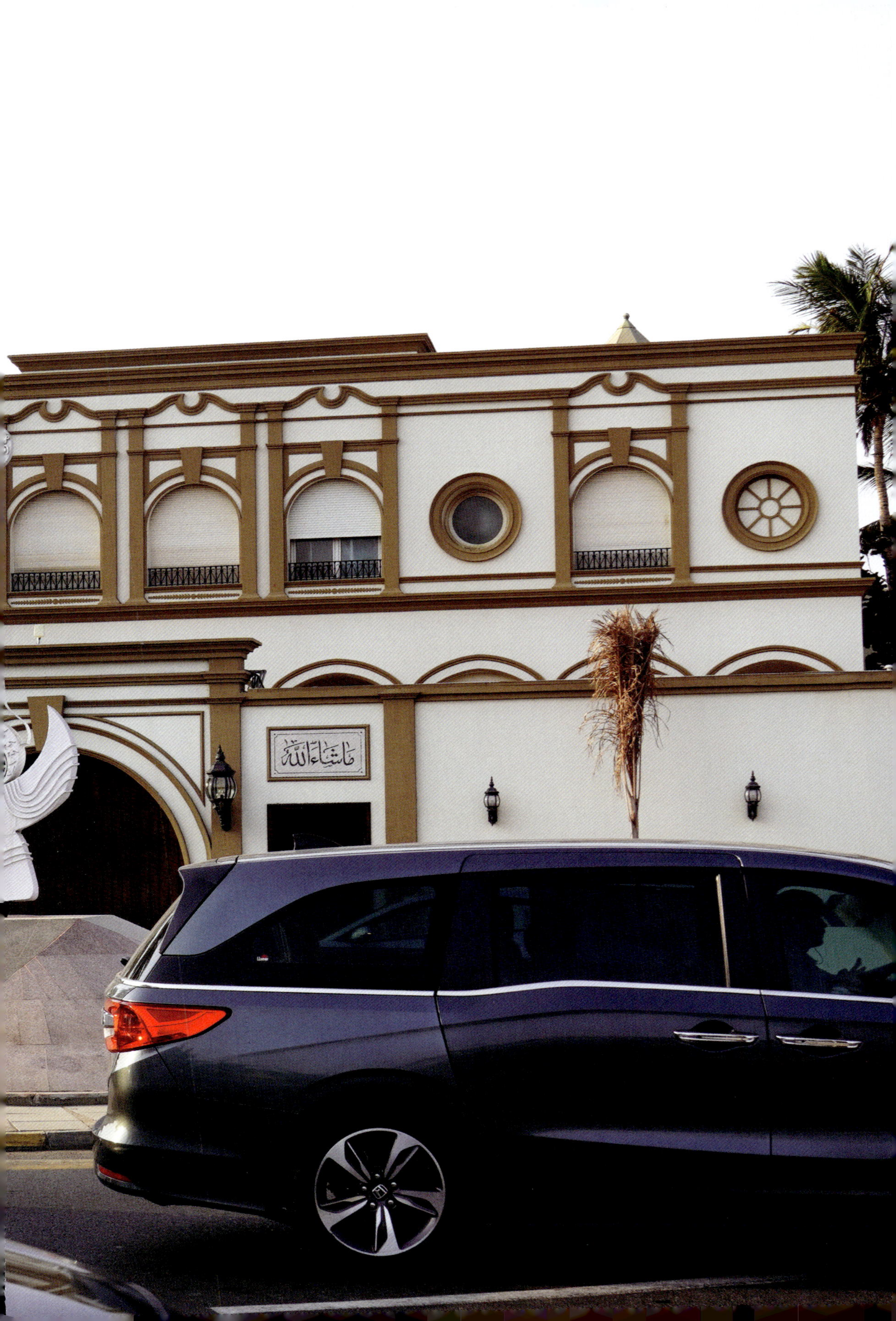
ماشاء الله

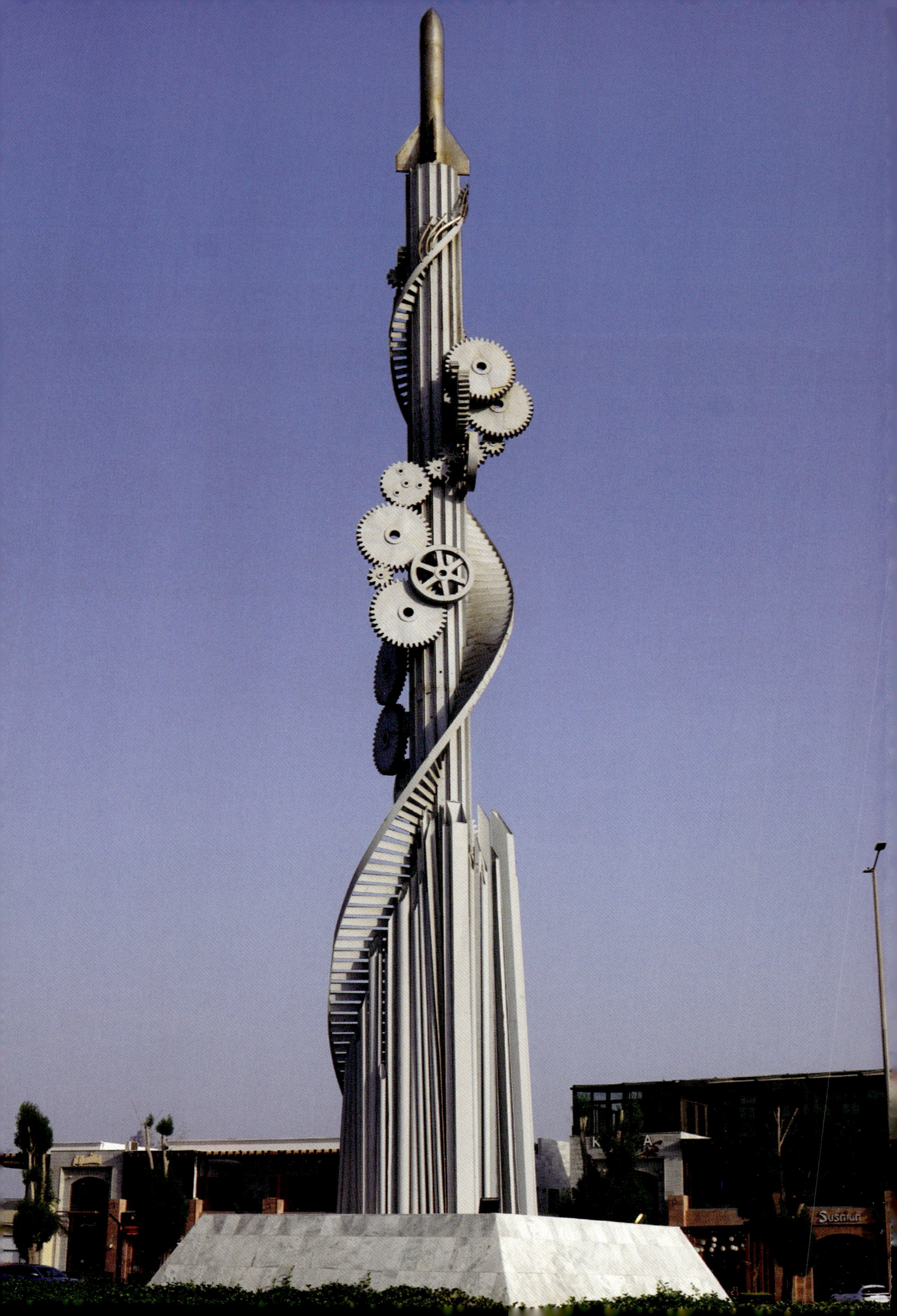

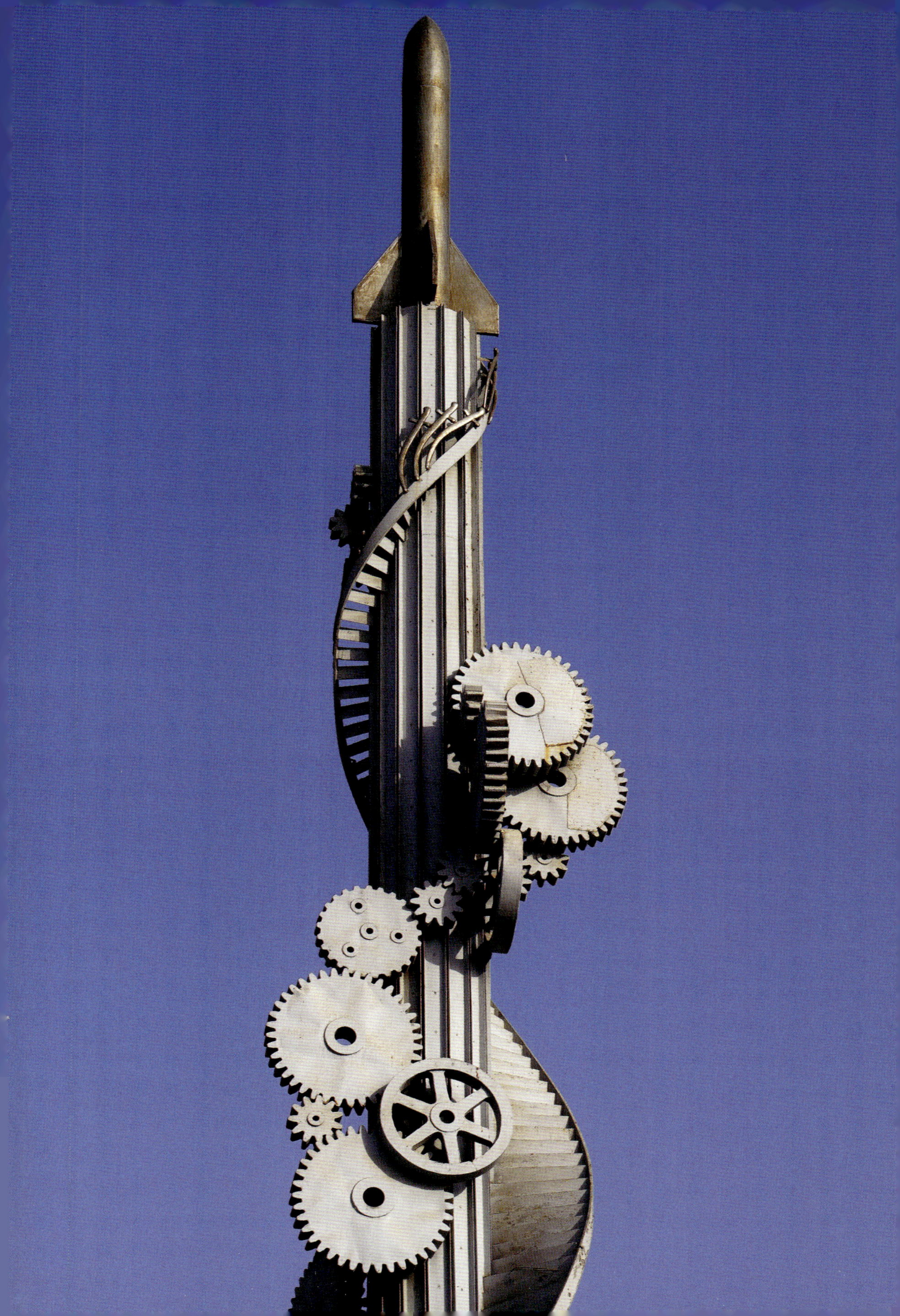

هوامش

Footnotes

1 Women in Saudi Arabia were officially allowed to drive beginning on June 24, 2018, following a royal decree issued by King Salman bin Abdulaziz Al Saud in September 2017 that lifted the long-standing ban.

بدأ سريان السماح للنساء بالقيادة في المملكة العربية السعودية رسميًا اعتبارًا من ٢٤ يونيو ٢٠١٨، وذلك تنفيذًا للأمر الملكي الصادر في سبتمبر ٢٠١٧ عن خادم الحرمين الشريفين الملك سلمان بن عبدالعزيز آل سعود، والذي نصّ على رفع الحظر القائم سابقًا على قيادة المرأة للمركبات.

2 According to the U.S. Commercial Service, there were approximately 2.5 million female drivers in Saudi Arabia as of 2021. See Saudi Arabia, Women Boost Automotive Industry, U.S. Department of Commerce, International Trade Administration, 2021.

وفقًا لخدمة التجارة الأمريكية، بلغ عدد السائقات في المملكة العربية السعودية نحو ٢,٥ مليون سائقة حتى عام ٢٠٢١. انظر: وزارة التجارة الأمريكية، إدارة التجارة الدولية. (٢٠٢١).

3 Al-Hamra, a historic coastal neighborhood in Jeddah, has long been associated with royal, diplomatic, and affluent residential life. Originally developed as a relatively secluded seafront area, it later evolved into one of the city's central urban and social hubs.

حي الحمراء في جدة هو حيّ ساحلي تاريخي راقٍ، ارتبط على مدى عقود بالسكن الملكي والدبلوماسي وشرائح اجتماعية ميسورة. بدأ تطوّره بوصفه منطقة ساحلية شبه معزولة، قبل أن يتحوّل لاحقًا إلى أحد المراكز الحضرية والاجتماعية البارزة في المدينة.

4 Each interview began at King Abdulaziz International Airport, where informal drivers typically congregate, and followed a consistent route extending from the north to the south of Jeddah.

استُهِلّت كل مقابلة في مطار الملك عبدالعزيز الدولي، كونه نقطة التقاء معتادة للسائقين غير المسجّلين رسميًا ضمن تطبيقات التوصيل، ثم اتّبعت مسارًا واحدًا ثابتًا يمتد عبر مدينة جدة من شمالها إلى جنوبها.

5 Lil Wayne - Mirror ft Bruno Mars, 2011

Mirror – ليل واين - مرآة (بمشاركة برونو مارس)، ٢٠١١

6 As part of its broader efforts to regulate the passenger-transport sector, the Ministry introduced measures aimed at preventing unauthorized transport activities, in what could be perceived as a protectionist attempt to curb increasing unemployment among young Saudi nationals. The authority emphasized that these measures seek to curb illegal practices, protect passengers, enhance service quality, and preserve the interests of licensed operators. Reference: Ministry of Human Resources and Social Development. (2020, April 1). Restricting the practice of transporting passengers 142257. Kingdom of Saudi Arabia.

في إطار جهوده تنظيم قطاع نقل الركاب، قامت وزارة الموارد البشرية بإقرار مجموعة من الإجراءات الهادفة إلى الحد من أنشطة النقل غير النظامية، وهو ما يمكن النظر إليه كمحاولة حمائية للحد من تزايد معدلات البطالة بين الشباب السعوديين. وأكدت الجهة المختصة أن هذه الإجراءات تهدف إلى كبح الممارسات غير القانونية، وحماية الركاب، وتحسين جودة الخدمات، والحفاظ على مصالح المشغلين المرخصين. المرجع: وزارة الموارد البشرية والتنمية الاجتماعية. (١ أبريل ٢٠٢٠). تقييد ممارسة نقل الركاب (١٤٢٢٥٧). المملكة العربية السعودية.

7 Al-Sabeen Street, better known in Jeddah as Prince Majed Road, is one of the city's main north-south routes. In 2015, it was upgraded with bridges and tunnels to ease traffic.

يُعد شارع السبعين، المعروف في جدة باسم طريق الأمير ماجد، أحد المحاور الرئيسية التي تربط شمال المدينة بجنوبها. في عام ٢٠١٥، خضع الطريق لأعمال تطوير شملت إنشاء جسور وأنفاق بهدف تحسين انسيابية الحركة المرورية.

https://www.arabcont.com/english/project-54

8 Private vehicles are not permitted to pick up passengers at the airport, and violations may result in fines.

لا يُسمح للمركبات الخاصة بنقل الركاب من المطار، ويترتب على مخالفة ذلك فرض غرامات مالية.

9 Locally known as the Baby Bottle Roundabout

يُعرف رسميًا باسم دوّار علوم البحار.

10 I was referring to the 2019 set of violent events and clashes in Sudan, including the mass protests that led to the removal of President Omar al-Bashir in April and the violent crackdown on protesters on 3 June. Source: United Nations OHCHR (2022). Sudan: UN experts urge authorities to ensure immediate accountability for past and recent violations.

كنتُ أشير إلى مجموعة الأحداث والاشتباكات العنيفة التي شهدها السودان في عام ٢٠١٩، بما في ذلك الاحتجاجات الجماهيرية التي أدّت إلى عزل الرئيس عمر البشير في شهر أبريل، إضافةً إلى القمع العنيف الذي تعرّض له المتظاهرون في ٣ يونيو. المصدر: مفوضية الأمم المتحدة السامية لحقوق الإنسان (٢٠٢٢). السودان: خبراء أمميون يحثّون السلطات على ضمان المساءلة الفورية عن الانتهاكات السابقة والحديثة.

https://www.ohchr.org/en/press-releases/2022/06/sudan-un-experts-urge-authorities-ensure-immediate-accountability-past-and

11 Demolitions in south Jeddah have been documented in public reports since October 2021 as part of the Jeddah Central Project, a large-scale urban redevelopment initiative aimed at modernizing the city and upgrading older neighborhoods. These descriptions in news and official project materials note that the redevelopment process has involved the relocation of residents and the clearance of unplanned areas.

وُثّقت أعمال الإزالة في جنوب جدة في تقارير عامة منذ أكتوبر ٢٠٢١، وذلك في إطار مشروع وسط جدة. مبادرة كبرى لإعادة التطوير الحضري تهدف إلى تحديث المدينة وتحسين الأحياء القديمة. وتشير هذه الأوصاف الواردة في التغطيات الإخبارية والمواد الرسمية للمشروع إلى أن عملية إعادة التطوير شملت نقل السكان وإزالة المناطق العشوائية من المدينة.

12 Many fans in Jeddah have been known to play Tamer Ashour's songs while driving along King Abdulaziz Road during evening cruises and traffic jams, creating an informal cultural link between the song and the road. Ashour himself acknowledged the phenomenon during a concert in Jeddah, where he performed Hijili Mawgou' one of his well known hits, while video clips of King Abdulaziz Road were displayed on the screens behind him.

يُلاحظ تداول غير رسمي بين بعض محبّي الفنان تامر عاشور في جدة يتمثّل في تشغيل أغانيه أثناء القيادة على طريق الملك عبد العزيز، ولا سيما خلال الجولات المسائية وفترات الازدحام المروري، ما أسهم في نشوء ارتباط ثقافي بين أغانيه والطريق. وقد أشار عاشور إلى هذه الرابطة خلال أحد حفلاته في جدة، حيث أدّى أشهر أغنياته «هيجيلي موجوع»، بينما عُرضت على الشاشات خلفه مقاطع مصوّرة لطريق الملك عبد العزيز.

13 Assiri, Khalid, Lil Eazy & Tahoun. FLO$ | خالد عسيري - ليل ايزي - طاحون: يبغالها فلوس. YouTube, uploaded by Khalid Assiri, 2025

عسيري، خالد؛ ليل إيزي؛ طاحون. FLO$ | يبغالها فلوس. يوتيوب، نُشر بواسطة خالد عسيري، 2025.

https://youtu.be/zba-D4JTv0Q

14 Between 1066 and 1333 USD.

بين ١٠٦٦ و١٣٣٣ دولارًا أمريكيًا

15 Jeeny is a Middle Eastern ride-hailing app offering on-demand transportation services. It primarily operates in Saudi Arabia and Jordan.

جيني هو تطبيق إقليمي لطلب سيارات الأجرة عند الطلب في الشرق الأوسط، يقدّم خدمات النقل الفوري. ويعمل بشكل أساسي في المملكة العربية السعودية والأردن.

16 Umrah is a non-mandatory Islamic pilgrimage involving specific rites of worship. It takes place in the holy city of Mecca, in Saudi Arabia. Most pilgrims enter Saudi Arabia through Jeddah, which is the main gateway to Mecca.

يدخل معظم المعتمرين إلى المملكة عبر مدينة جدة، التي تُعد البوابة الرئيسية المؤدية إلى مكة.

17 40 - 54 USD

≈ ٤٠–٥٤ دولارًا أمريكيًا.

18 Dhahran is a city in Saudi Arabia's Eastern Province, oriented toward the Arabian Gulf. It is known primarily as the headquarters of Saudi Aramco, one of the world's largest energy companies.

الظهران مدينة تقع في المنطقة الشرقية من المملكة العربية السعودية، وتطل على الخليج العربي. وتُعرف بشكل أساسي بأنها المقر الرئيسي لشركة أرامكو السعودية، إحدى أكبر شركات الطاقة في العالم.

19 When he says, "back in the day, the airport was considered outside the city," he is referring to the former Jeddah Airport -known as Kandara Airport, which was located much farther from the urban center at the time. It served as Jeddah's main airport until the 1980s, when King Abdulaziz International Airport opened. The area has since been completely redeveloped; the old airport site is now home to Al Andalus Mall, Salam Mall, and the surrounding residential neighborhoods.

عندما يقول: «زمان كان المطار بعيد عن المدينة»، فهو يشير إلى مطار جدة القديم المعروف باسم مطار الكندرة، والذي كان يقع آنذاك على مسافة أبعد بكثير من مركز المدينة. وقد شكّل المطار الرئيسي لمدينة جدة حتى ثمانينيات القرن العشرين، حين افتُتح مطار الملك عبدالعزيز الدولي. ومنذ ذلك الحين، أُعيد تطوير المنطقة بالكامل؛ إذ يضم موقع المطار السابق اليوم كلاً من مجمّع الأندلس مول والسلام مول، إلى جانب الأحياء السكنية المحيطة بهما.

20 Al-Hamadaniyyah's transformation was driven by state-led demolitions, rezoning, and northern urban expansion, alongside the redevelopment of King Abdulaziz International Airport, which reduced travel times to central Jeddah and integrated previously peripheral districts into the city's economic and residential core.

كان تحوّل حي الحمدانية نتاجًا لجملة من السياسات الحضرية التي قادتها الدولة، شملت أعمال الإزالة، وإعادة تصنيف استخدامات الأراضي، والتوسع العمراني شمالاً، إلى جانب إعادة تطوير مطار الملك عبدالعزيز الدولي. أسهمت هذه التحولات في تقليص أزمنة التنقّل إلى وسط مدينة جدة، ودمج المناطق التي كانت تُعدّ هامشية سابقًا ضمن القلب الاقتصادي والسكني للمدينة.

21 Following the demolitions in Jeddah, rents in the north of the city have reportedly risen by up to 20% due to increased demand from displaced residents.

عقب أعمال الإزالة في مدينة جدة، أفادت تقارير بارتفاع الإيجارات في شمال المدينة بنسبة تصل إلى ٢٠٪، وذلك نتيجة زيادة الطلب من السكان الذين جرى نقلهم من الأحياء المتأثرة. انظر

See: JLL. (2022). Jeddah's new look: The urban redevelopment. https://www.jll.com/en-ae/guides/jeddahs-new-look-the-urban-redevelopment

22 In December 2020, Jeddah Municipality, in coordination with the Civil Defense, removed unplanned buildings and informal yards on a 1,700-square-meter site in Al-Naseem neighborhood, west of the Haramain train station. The operation included demolishing four abandoned buildings and six unauthorized yards and clearing the area of harmful trees. See: Makkah Newspaper. (2020). إزالة مباني وأحواش عشوائية غرب محطة قطار الحرمين [Removal of unplanned buildings and informal yards west of Haramain train station] (Arabic).

في ديسمبر ٢٠٢٠، قامت أمانة محافظة جدة، بالتنسيق مع الدفاع المدني، بإزالة مبانٍ غير نظامية وأحواش عشوائية على مساحة تُقدَّر بنحو ١,٧٠٠ متر مربع في حي النسيم، غرب محطة قطار الحرمين. وشملت العملية هدم أربعة مبانٍ مهجورة وستة أحواش غير نظامية، إلى جانب إزالة الأشجار الضارّة من الموقع. انظر: صحيفة مكة. (٢٠٢٠). إزالة مباني وأحواش عشوائية غرب محطة قطار الحرمين.

https://makkahnewspaper.com/article/1527984/أخبار-للموقع/أمانة-جدة-إزالة-مباني-وأحواش-عشوائية-غرب-محطة-قطار-الحرمين

23 A part of Al-Aziziyah neighborhood in Jeddah was removed as part of a larger city-wide demolition campaign for redevelopment. This was part of a plan to demolish 32 slums and unplanned districts, with Al-Aziziyah being one of the eight neighborhoods located within the lands of the King Abdulaziz Endowment for Al-Ain Al-Aziziyah that were targeted. See: Saudi Gazette. (2022). Jeddah slums committee begins notifying Al-Montazahat residents in preparation to start the removal work.

أُزيل جزء من حي العزيزية في مدينة جدة ضمن حملة أوسع على مستوى المدينة لأعمال الإزالة وإعادة التطوير الحضري. وجاء ذلك في إطار خطة لهدم ٣٢ حيًا عشوائيًا ومنطقة غير مخططة، حيث كان حي العزيزية أحد الأحياء الثمانية الواقعة ضمن أراضي وقف الملك عبدالعزيز لعين العزيزية التي شملها الاستهداف. انظر:

https://www.saudigazette.com.sa/article/623234

24 King Abdullah International Stadium, located just 20 minutes from King Abdulaziz International Airport, is the largest stadium in Jeddah. Traffic congestion typically peaks during football matches.

يقع استاد الملك عبد الله الدولي (ملعب الجوهرة) على بُعد نحو ٢٠ دقيقة من مطار الملك عبد العزيز الدولي، ويُعدّ أكبر ملاعب مدينة جدة من حيث السعة، إذ يتسع لأكثر من ٦٢ ألف متفرّج. وتشهد شبكة الطرق المحيطة بالاستاد عادةً ازدحامًا مروريًا كثيفًا خلال مباريات كرة القدم الكبرى والفعاليات الجماهيرية.

25 Held in Jeddah as part of the 2025 Supercopa de España, which was hosted in Saudi Arabia under a multi-year agreement to stage the competition abroad.

أُقيمت المباراة في جدة ضمن منافسات كأس السوبر الإسباني ٢٠٢٥، التي استضافتها المملكة العربية السعودية بموجب اتفاقية متعددة السنوات لإقامة البطولة خارج إسبانيا. انظر: نادي برشلونة. معاينة السوبر:

FC Barcelona v Real Madrid, https://www.fcbarcelona.com/en/football/first-team/news/4432095/super-cup-preview-fc-barcelona-v-real-madrid

26 13 - 26 USD

≈ ١٣–٢٦ دولارًا أمريكيًا

27 The Bicycle is a 15-meter-tall sculpture created in 1982 by Julio Lafuente. Although a widely circulated myth refers to it as “Prophet Adam’s bicycle,” this attribution is understood locally as folklore or a tourist anecdote rather than a historical or religious belief. The narrative likely emerged due to the sculpture’s monumental scale and the Islamic tradition describing Prophet Adam as exceptionally tall. Local residents note that the story is shared playfully with visitors, particularly pilgrims. See Arab News. (2008). Myths abound on Jeddah’s monuments.

يُعدّ مجسّم الدراجة منحوتة يبلغ ارتفاعها نحو ١٥ مترًا، أنجزها الفنان خوليو لافوينتي عام ١٩٨٢. وتشيع رواية تُطلق عليه تسمية «دراجة النبي آدم»، إلا أن هذه التسمية تُعدّ من الموروث الشعبي أو الحكايات السياحية، ولا تستند إلى أساس تاريخي أو ديني موثّق. ويُرجَّح أن ظهور هذه الرواية يرتبط بضخامة المنحوتة، إلى جانب ما يرد في التراث الإسلامي من أوصاف لقامة النبي آدم عليه السلام بوصفها استثنائية. ويذكر بعض السكان المحليين أن هذه القصة تُروى غالبًا على سبيل الدعابة للزوار، ولا سيما الحجاج. انظر:

https://www.arabnews.com/node/307291

28 Interview with Mahmoud Najem.

مقابلة مع محمود نجم.

29 Al-Khomrah is a small town in Makkah Province in western Saudi Arabia. It lies just south of Jeddah, approximately 40 kilometers from central Jeddah.

الخُمرة بلدة صغيرة تقع في منطقة مكة المكرمة غرب المملكة العربية السعودية. وتقع جنوب مدينة جدة مباشرة، على بُعد نحو ٤٠ كيلومترًا من وسط مدينة جدة.

30 Located within the historic Al-Baghdadiyah district in central Jeddah, Saudi Arabia. The area forms part of the historic center, Al-Balad (the old town) which is a UNESCO World Heritage Site.

يقع شارع بغداد في حي البغدادية التاريخي بوسط مدينة جدة في المملكة العربية السعودية. وتُعدّ المنطقة جزءًا من المركز التاريخي للمدينة، المعروف باسم البلد (جدة التاريخية)، والمدرج ضمن قائمة مواقع التراث العالمي التابعة لليونسكو.

31 Interview with Mahmoud Najem.

مقابلة مع محمود نجم.

32 YouTube channel “Hilo Al-Kalam [Sweet Talk] Abu Fahad”

قناة يوتيوب "حلو الكلام - أبو فهد"، تاريخ الاطلاع: ٢٠ نوفمبر ٢٠٢٥.

https://www.youtube.com/@aaz

شكر وعرفان

Credits

Concept
Hatun Al-Harthi
Olivier Duport
Alan Marzo

المفهوم
أوليفييه دوبور
آلان مارزو
هتون الحارثي

Design
Mobius Design Studio

التصميم
استديو موبيوس للتصميم

Photography
Hatun Al-Harthi

التصوير الفوتوغرافي
هتون الحارثي

Photo Edition
Hatun Al-Harthi
Olivier Duport

تحرير الصور
أوليفييه دوبور

Contributors
Eiman Elnaiem
Hatun Al-Harthi
Nouf Al-Harthi
Sara Hammami
Turki Gazzaz

المساهمون
نوف الحارثي
هتون الحارثي
تركي قزاز
سارة حمامي
إيمان النعيم

Translation
Nouf Al-Harthi
Alan Marzo

الترجمة والمراجعة اللغوية
نوف الحارثي
آلان مارزو

Map
Muhammad Hussain Arafsha
(M.H.A Office)
Alhanouf M. Arafsha

الخريطة
مكتب محمد حسين عرفشه
للاستشارات الهندسية
الهنوف محمد عرفشه

Partners
Art Jameel

الشركاء
فن جميل

شكر خاص

سائقو سيارات الأجرة الخصوصية في جدة: نسرين، ومحمود نجم، وأبو سعيد؛ أنتونيا كارفِر؛ أنس قطان؛ بيشوي جرجس؛ دانيا جابر؛ دينا عزاب؛ ريم إبراهيم؛ روزا ليون؛ شهد السليمان؛ هانا عباس قزويني؛ هالة العاني؛ هشام حمامي؛ ماريا عالم؛ مها القريقري؛ منى الحارثي؛ راكان الحارثي؛ يوسف إدريس؛ عبدالحميد أبو حامد؛ عبدالعزيز الجهني؛ عبدالله الشيخ خليل؛ إيلين فاسكيز؛ د.أريج الغامدي؛ رغد العفيف؛ رؤى لمفون؛ رؤى سلطان؛ سحرش علي؛ سماح العرياني؛ شادن المطلق؛ شريفة الزياني؛ صفوان فلاتة؛ عبدالله فيصل؛ عبدالحميد نبيل؛ فايزة الرفاعي؛ خيرية رفعت؛ حسن حجيري؛ معاذ بن حافظ؛ المركز السعودي للموسيقى بجدة

Special Thanks

Jeddah taxi drivers: Nisreen, Mahmoud Najm, and Abu Saeed; Abdulaziz AlJohani; Abdulhameed Abu Hamed; Abdulhameed Nabeel; Abdulla Faisal; Abdullah Al Sheikh Khalil; Antonia Carver; Dr. Areej Alghamdi; Bishoy Girgis; Dania Jaber; Danah Garii; Dina Azzab; Eileen Vazquez; Fayza Alrifai; Hadeyeh Badri; Hala Al-Ani; Hannah Abbas Ghasvinie; Hasan Hujairi; Hisham Hammami; Saudi Music Hub - Jeddah; Khayria Refaat; Maha Alqureqrei; Maria Alem; Moath bin Hafez; Mona Al-Harthi; Rakan Al-Harthi; Raghad Alafif; Riem Ibrahim; Roaa Lamfon; Roaa Sultan; Rosa Lion; Safwan Fallatah; Sahrish Ali; Samah Alaryani; Shaden Almutlaq; Shahed Al-Suleiman; Shareefa Al Zayani; Uns Kattan; Yusuf Idres

ISBN

979-10-983080-2-4

فن جميل ART JAMEEL